M000316822

EFFECTIVE COMPETENCY MODELING & REPORTING

EFFECTIVE COMPETENCY MODELING & REPORTING

A STEP-BY-STEP GUIDE FOR IMPROVING
INDIVIDUAL & ORGANIZATIONAL PERFORMANCE

KENNETH CARLTON COOPER

AMACOM

American Management Association

New York · Atlanta · Boston · Chicago · Kansas City · San Francisco · Washington, D. C.
Brussels · Mexico City · Tokyo · Toronto

Special discounts on bulk quantities of AMACOM books are available to corporations, professional associations, and other organizations. For details, contact Special Sales Department, AMACOM, an imprint of AMA Publications, a division of American Management Association, 1601 Broadway, New York, NY 10019.
Tel.: 212-903-8316   Fax: 212-903-8083

This publication is designed to provide accurate and authoritative information in regard to the subject matter covered. It is sold with the understanding that the publisher is not engaged in rendering legal, accounting, or other professional service. If legal advice or other expert assistance is required, the services of a competent professional person should be sought.

Library of Congress Cataloging-in-Publication Data

Cooper, Ken
      Effective competency modeling & reporting : a step-by-step guide for improving individual & organizational performance / Kenneth Carlton Cooper.
            p.   cm.
      Includes bibliographical references and index.
      ISBN 0-8144-0548-7
      1. Organizational effectiveness.   2. Total quality management.   I. Cooper, Kenneth Carlton.
      HD58.9.C665   2000
      658.4'13—dc21   00-027350

© 2000 Kenneth Carlton Cooper, Ph.D.
All rights reserved.
Printed in the United States of America.

Competency Coach ® and Multi-Form ® are registered trademarks of CooperComm, Inc.

This publication may not be reproduced,
stored in a retrieval system,
or transmitted in whole or in part,
in any form or by any means, electronic,
mechanical, photocopying, recording, or otherwise,
without the prior written permission of AMACOM,
an imprint of AMA Publications, a division of
American Management Association,
1601 Broadway, New York, NY 10019.

Printing number

10   9   8   7   6   5   4   3   2   1

To **Sue,**
The most competent person I know.

Contents

List of Figures

List of Tables

Foreword

by Dave Vaughn, Board of Advisors, Corporate Universities International, Corporate University Xchange, Inc.

Over thirty years ago, most personnel development in the workplace was conducted on the job. There was a very clear understanding between the employees and supervisors as to what was expected, what was considered "standard," and what employees needed to be trained to do to meet the organization's job requirements. This worked very well. On-the-job training, or OJT, ruled when it came to helping people do their best. What happened before and after the training was actually more important to the success of the training than the training event itself.

Over time, though, as a gap grew between what an employee needed to know and actually did know, we began to see the evolution of the training profession. In the beginning this made sense, as it enabled the "art and science" of education and performance improvement to become a legitimate resource that frontline management could rely on to increase the level of individual performance in the workplace.

As company-training entities grew, so did the distance between employees, their training, frontline supervisors, and the organization. The end result is that we now have a training industry faced with the big challenge of bringing what we do—individual and organizational development and performance improvement—back in line with what the organization, and most importantly, frontline leadership, needs to accomplish for the organization to advance.

A second factor that has helped accelerate the disconnect of training from the organization has been the move from a "leadership of people and management of work" focus to "management of people only" focus. There continues to be more evidence that frontline supervisors have shifted their focus from the development and growing of people to just "getting the job done." The idea that their job as the "leader" is not only to provide competent clarity and direction but to take a genuine interest and active role in the development and growth of "their people" has been lost as we move through the maze of scientific management and reengineering. The resultant gap between the training function and frontline managers has widened to the point that we now see personnel development expressed as a cost to productivity rather than as an investment in performance improvement.

This text was written to bring performance improvement in the workplace back to the job. It is about changing the way we approach and deliver training. It is all about placing development activities within the context of work. It is based on the belief that for individual development to be effective, there must be an alignment with what employees need to know to successfully accomplish their assignments, to what we facilitate as learning organizations, and to what the person responsible for the effort needs to accomplish.

This book is not just a different twist on competency-based training but a proven approach to aligning what a person must know and experience (job standards) to what is taught and to what the frontline manager needs to accomplish.

The concept of competency modeling and reporting (CMAR) is based on the fundamental belief that every employee should be given the opportunity to do his or her best. CMAR provides both the structure and the discipline to help bring out the best effort in people. CMAR is based on the truth that given the opportunity to do their best, most people will exceed performance expectations and, in the end, produce the results needed to advance both themselves and the organization.

What "best effort" needs by way of support is very simple: clear standards and expectations; objective assessment of individual skills, knowledge, and experience to standard; personalized development or performance improvement plans; the opportunity to learn as an individual; and last, but most important, an engaging climate that provides support and encouragement to the person doing the work. This book provides human resource (HR) professionals with simple processes both to understand and to accomplish what they need to know to successfully improve individual performance on the job.

We are beginning to see the emergence of a new role for the HR professional. The downsizing of major corporations has forced a realization that the need for HR has shifted from one of "corporate staff" to one of "business partner." Gilley and Eggland, in their book, *Principles of Human Resource Development*, state, "The purpose of HRD is to bring about the performance improvements that will ultimately enhance the organization."[1] Nadler and Wiggs (1986) referred to this as "making a difference." In other words, learning is "transferred to on-the-job performance, reducing costs, improving quality, and increasing the competitiveness of the organization."[2]

The new reality is that the HR professional of the future will not be a member of corporate staff, in service to the executive suite, but a working member of a business team that is being held accountable for improving business results. The new role of HR team member is to facilitate the process that aligns business needs to performance needs to learning needs to individual skill and knowledge needs. The future of human resource development is based on the reality that our profession is not about the development and deployment of HR policy and procedure but about aligning what the individual person needs to know and do differently to advance both the employees' and the organization's future.

This text provides the HR development community a proven approach for integrating training into the workplace. The competency modeling and reporting process it details is the "best practice" that allows our industry to expand beyond the corporate office.

Notes

1. Jerry W. Gilley and Steven A. Eggland, *Principles of Human Resource Development*, (Reading, Ma.: Addison-Wesley Publishing Company, 1989), 13.
2. Leonard Nadler and Garland D. Wiggs, *Managing Human Resource Development*, (San Francisco: Jossey-Bass, 1986).

Preface

As a client recently explained, "Our company is changing from who you know to what you know." Organizations are no longer content to make their human resource decisions based on politics, time in grade, quick reviews, or half-hour interviews. Quality programs such as ISO 9000 and the Baldrige Award require employers to identify the standards for completing processes and to determine workers' qualifications to meet those standards. The result is the growth of competency-based HR applications throughout an organization.

In building these applications, power lies not with those who have all the answers, but with those who have all the questions. These include:

⋄ How can we measure employee competencies reliably and link them to the training and developmental resources we need to provide?

⋄ How do we ensure that our employees are receiving relevant training and are raising their competencies to required standards?

⋄ How can we use these measurements to coach and counsel employees to better performance?

⋄ Are we spending our human resource development dollars most effectively?

This book is designed to show managers and HR professionals how to answer those questions. It provides a step-by-step process that is based upon years of research and consulting experience in implementing competency-based applications. The focus is not on promoting a single design approach. Instead, the text explains the range of alternatives, provides an analysis of each, and helps a competency project team to understand the ramifications of design decisions and to avoid potential pitfalls.

Chapter 1 introduces the role of competency modeling and provides definitions of key terms. This is essential information if the project is to proceed smoothly, and it will eliminate later problems in defining competencies and in creating assessments.

Chapter 2 explains all the design decisions that are required of the competency team before beginning work. This avoids having to go back and redo previous steps due to unforeseen results or decisions inadvertently made by default.

Design teams often struggle with where to begin. Chapter 3 highlights all the sources of competency information available to an organization. Contrary to popular belief, there is no shortage of useful competency data in most organizations.

Chapters 4 through 6 detail the design alternatives and steps in building a competency modeling and assessment process that is valid, accurate, and reliable. Many examples are provided, and a working model is utilized throughout these chapters. Chapter 7 provides a brief discussion of how competency processes should be applied throughout the organization.

Chapters 8 and 9 provide complete design details, sample screens, and reports from a full-function stand-alone application and a Web-based competency application, respectively. These two systems illustrate the requirements of modeling applications and can be used as design templates for in-house development efforts.

Chapter 10 lists sources for a wide variety of competency-related information and products, including existing models, computing tools, and publications. This is not an exhaustive compilation of all available competency resources but highlights major sources of information. The goal is to help teams save research and development time by leveraging existing tools.

The CD-ROM accompanying this book contains reference files for the working model used throughout the book. Many of these files can be read and edited by readers and utilized in their own projects. The CD-ROM also contains a limited-save, full-function version of Competency Coach® for Windows, a competency modeling and reporting relational database program developed by the author. A working model is already loaded into the system and can be experimented with live in order to understand the functionality and operation of fully developed competency modeling application.

Reactions to the content in this book are usually twofold. New design teams discover that there is a starting point to this massive process and can begin defining terms and making initial decisions. Experienced design teams often have an "Aha!" experience as they realize where they went wrong. For either type of team, the journey is not one focusing on the starting point, only on the process of continuous improvement. That is the ultimate development competency for an organization.

Acknowledgments

No individual possesses all the competencies required to write a book about competencies. This text includes the results of many individuals' and organizations' efforts in developing competency-based human resource applications.

Thanks go to Adrian Ulsch at American Management Association for recommending this book project and to the publishing team at AMACOM for their guidance and support, including Adrienne Hickey and Shelly Wert. Literary agent Michael Snell also provided great advice and encouragement.

Special thanks go to those who helped develop CooperComm's Competency Coach® for Windows database system and its related processes. This includes Karen Gentles, Sue Cooper, John Bujnak, Pam Puricelli, Jan Fitzgerald, Henry Vanston, and Dave Telker. They handled back-to-back deadlines and piles of reports with aplomb.

We are especially grateful to the Field Sales competency project team at the Anheuser-Busch University. This included: Mark Danner, Dave Vaughn, Tom Nolan, Sue Landis, Bridget Price, Joe Pandolfo, Karlos Bledsoe, Lance McKinley, and Tom Shipley. For over two decades, these development professionals and others at the University have been a once-in-a-career client and business partner.

Finally, this text would have been impossible without the willingness of so many individuals and organizations to share their competency-based information. This includes Chuck Aranda at Librix Learning, Dan Shasserre at Business Training Library, Dave Vaughn at Anheuser-Busch, Katie Fisk at Connecticut Department of Education, Betty Laurie at American Competency Association, and the following organizations: AAIM, ANSI, Asymetrix, Crisp Publications, Department of Veteran's Affairs, EmCare, and Mallinckrodt.

EFFECTIVE COMPETENCY MODELING & REPORTING

Introduction to Competency-Based Human Resources Applications

Competence is one of the hot topics in the world of human resources. Top management is identifying corporate core competencies and working to establish them throughout the organization. Corporate universities support the learning organization in the development of competitive excellence. The human resources (HR) department builds competency-based models of performance measurement that drive business results. Enterprise resource planning (ERP) software vendors have integrated competencies into their human resource software modules. It is a regular extravaganza of jargon.

Commercially, there are lots of products and service offerings addressing competencies. Most include one or two components of competency-based solutions. Others provide little actual functionality while trying to capitalize on competencies as the latest fad.

Organizationally, everyone is talking about competencies. Some employers have truly worked the concept into several of their processes. But few enterprises have a fully implemented competency modeling and reporting system in place that addresses the development of people from process design through succession.

Several years ago at the user group meeting of a major training administration vendor, due to high interest in the topic, an optional 7:00 a.m. session on competency modeling was added to the agenda at the last minute. In an informal hands-up poll, only two of the approximately one hundred companies represented by the attendees had experience with any form of competency-based applications. Of these two, one was early in the design phase and the other appeared to have an initial process in place. There were two questions everyone in attendance was asking:

✧ What exactly is competency modeling?
✧ How do we measure up?

The user group attendees first wanted to understand exactly what competency modeling was. Everyone was talking about it, but no one could consistently define it. These training department and HR attendees also wanted to know what state-of-the-art was and how their organizations compared.

Since then, some large organizations have begun work on competency-based applications, particularly in training and development. But most organizations of all sizes are still struggling with defining, designing, and implementing competency-model projects. (For example, major ERP software vendors have competency capabilities built into their HR modules, yet customer implementations are currently almost nonexistent.)

This book is designed to provide a competency-based project blueprint. It provides definitions of the relevant terms, the lack of which is often a block to getting started. It defines the major process activities required, and it highlights specific decisions to be made at each step.

The process described is completely customizable. Individual competency design decisions are driven by a number of organizational factors, including management philosophy, customer requirements, business needs, and in-place processes. These factors are rarely consistent among different organizations, requiring a custom approach to competencies in the workplace. The result is that, although the book's content is the same for everyone, individual readers will end up with very different competency implementations depending upon their design decisions along the way. This customization is essential to the overall success of competency efforts, since every organization must integrate competency concepts into its own job design, recruitment, hiring, orientation, development, and succession processes.

Organizational Competencies vs. Individual Competencies

At this point, it is important to clarify the use of the word *competencies*. This term often refers to two related but separate concepts, *core competencies* and *workplace competencies*. Before proceeding, it must be absolutely clear which concept is being discussed here.

In their book, *Competing for the Future*, authors Gary Hamel and C. K. Prahalad wrote that "core competencies transcend any particular product or service, and indeed may transcend any single business unit within the organization."[1] The idea is that certain projects are so massive, so pervasive, that no individual can possess the competencies required to see them through to completion. Therefore, organizations have to identify, develop, and manage organizational core competencies that drive large, enterprise critical projects.

Examples of organizational core competencies include Anheuser-Busch's using attention-getting advertising and the brewing and delivery system to guarantee the freshest beer; IBM under Lou Gerstner adding the competencies of providing its leading edge business and Internet service to its manufacturing and sales orientation; and insurance companies building core competencies in banking. Core competencies can also be more generic, with leadership working to make everyone more creative, more quality oriented, or more financially astute with "open book management."

Table 1-1 summarizes the differences between these core and workplace competencies. Workplace competencies focus on individuals instead of the organization, and they vary by job position versus enterprise endeavors. The unit of measure is people rather than business unit. Although there may be core competencies that appear in every position's competency model, most workplace competencies are typically specific to the position. This means that it takes an enormous amount of work to set up organization-wide competency-based applications.

This book addresses workplace competencies. It details a customizable process to create complete competency-based HR applications addressing every position in the organization. It goes beyond core competencies to address the position competencies required to perform daily, tactical work tasks. To understand why this is such an important effort today, it is helpful to review the changing role of competency in modern organizations.

A Quick History of Competency

During the twentieth century, business has come full circle in its attitude toward workplace competencies. At the beginning of the century, workers brought complex skills to the job. Accountants knew how to post and balance ledgers. Cabinetmakers created marvelous individual pieces of furniture. The Wright brothers assembled bicycles and airplanes by hand. Horses were shod, houses were built, and engines were maintained by experts with skills developed throughout a lifetime.

Typical business processes of a hundred years ago required that people possess specific competencies for the task at hand. The necessary level of competency for many jobs was neither trivial nor easy to acquire. Few workers had a postsecondary education, and many had little education beyond grade school. Competencies could only be acquired through years of on-the-job

Table 1-1. Core competencies vs. workplace competencies.

	Core	Workplace
Scope	Organization	Individual
Purpose	Strategic	Tactical
Participant(s)	Business unit (and above)	Worker
Tasks	Processes	Activities
Competencies	Global	Position

learning and practice. But this soon changed. There were a number of significant influences that moved the focus away from competencies.

Frederick Taylor's "scientific management" and Henry Ford's use of the assembly line shifted competencies from workers to time-and-motion-study industrial engineers. The assumption was that minimizing the complexity of work would result in maximizing the efficiency of production. Any complex job could be broken down into a series of simple steps. With the workplace flooded by mass immigration from overseas and mass migration to the cities, this was a viable way to employ a largely unskilled and uneducated workforce.

With mass production, employee competency was defined as a physical factor. Simple work tasks could readily be mastered if the employee possessed sufficient dexterity, strength, and endurance. So the bicycle builder of 1900, working in a shop, became the tire mounter of 1930, working in the middle of an assembly line.

With this philosophy, and in a depression economy, employees had little value. They were considered more a consumable than a resource. Because process expertise resided at the management and engineering level, there was little training required. Costs of employee turnover were negligible. If workers could not handle the boredom or the physical strain, an unlimited number of applicants were available to fill openings.

World War II reinforced this management-centric view of work. Millions of men and women underwent the ultimate command-and-control experience—military service, where officers gave orders to subordinates who obeyed commands without question. Why? Because somebody had to run things and only those in command were assumed to have the information, perspective, and abilities to make decisions. Those who refused to follow orders risked loss of freedom or life.

Work in the military was highly segmented. Everyone had a specialization and a specific role, right down to the squad level. You were a mechanic or a pilot, but not both. People were trained to do a specific job, and then placed in the system.

At the end of the war, millions of veterans returned to the workplace. They had lived under a command-and-control hierarchy, fought under one, and naturally re-created it at work. Leaders led, and the front line charged up the next hill. People had specific roles and stuck to them. In civilian life after World War II, work was still divided into small tasks and handled by a series of specialists. At this point many jobs were not much fun, but the system was very efficient at turning out the mass quantities of goods Americans wanted after the war.

In the postwar decades of unparalleled demand and little competition, the focus was on getting the numbers out. Quality and service were secondary to meeting production quotas. Concerns about workers were more the result of pressure from organized labor than strategic thinking. This was the low point for the idea of competencies in the workplace.

The turnaround began with the work of David C. McClelland, a former

Harvard psychologist and founder of McBer, a consulting company that helps clients assess and train employees. In the early 1960s, McClelland wrote a landmark article in the *American Psychologist* asserting that I.Q. and personality tests then in common use were poor predictors of competency. He felt that companies should hire based upon competencies rather than test scores.[2]

A decade later, McClelland was asked by the U.S. Foreign Service to develop new methods that could predict human performance. The goal was to eliminate the potential biases of traditional intelligence and aptitude testing. This was the beginning of the field of competence measurement. The next step was for competency concepts to find their way into mainstream business practices.

Competencies and the Quality Movement

The quality movement began in 1950, but in Japan, not America. This is the year that Dr. W. Edwards Deming began teaching modern quality control methods to Japanese industries.[3] Deming emphasized that quality, not quantity, was the main goal. Quality processes, when combined with continuous quality improvement, would drive efficiency up and costs down. This, coupled with research into customer needs and expectations, would secure long-term success for an organization. Deming's approach was ultimately dubbed *total quality management* (TQM).

The Japanese were enormously successful in implementing TQM, rebuilding their economy and becoming strong competitors on the world market. All this was done using quality principles developed in the United States and taught by U.S. experts. Yet TQM was relatively unknown in the United States until the June 24, 1980, broadcast of a CBS documentary entitled, "If Japan Can . . . Why Can't We?" In the last portion of the program, Lloyd Dobyns interviewed Dr. Deming and the president of Nashua Corporation, who had saved millions of dollars as a client of Deming. The next day, both CBS and Dr. Deming were deluged with calls from managers seeking more information. Deming went on to become a leading spokesman and trainer for TQM.

Several principles of TQM are closely related to competencies. First, frontline employees are often far more knowledgeable than supervisors about the job and customer needs. Consequently, organizational authority to make important decisions should be placed further down the management chain. Empowering frontline workers to do planning, analysis, and decision-making tasks normally reserved for managers leads to quality improvements. (For the Japanese this involved the use of quality circles, a practice that met with mixed success in the United States.)

A second principle of TQM is that the best person to satisfy customers is usually the first employee contacted. When customer requests have to be passed up the line for management approval, customers begin to take emotional credit for demanding adequate service rather than being astounded and amazed by superior service.

Exceeding customer expectations and operating efficient processes require employees who are well trained and who are empowered to deal with situations on the spot. This mandates a very different set of employee competencies than the traditional "get the numbers out," command-and-control approach.

This is reflected in the various worldwide quality standards. For example, International Organization for Standardization (ISO) 9001, Section 4.18, states:

> The supplier shall establish and maintain documented procedures for identifying training needs and provide for the training of all personnel performing activities affecting quality. Personnel performing specific assigned tasks shall be qualified on the basis of appropriate education, training and/or experience, as required. Appropriate records of training shall be maintained.*

Organizations seeking ISO 9001 certification *must* develop a process to identify tasks that affect quality and to ensure that employees are qualified to correctly perform those tasks or are being developed to do so. Similarly, the Malcolm Baldrige National Quality Award Criteria for Performance Excellence states:

> 5. *Human Resource Development and Management*
>   Describe how the company's education and training address key company plans and needs, including building knowledge and capabilities, and contributing to improved employee performance and development.
>   *Notes N1.* Education and training address the knowledge and skills employees need to meet their overall work and developmental objectives.[4]

It is clear that enhancing individual workplace competencies is a required component in becoming a quality organization, and in achieving national and worldwide quality certifications. Organizations must be able to document job requirements, identify workers as certified to meet those requirements, and develop those who have gaps in knowledge or skills.

---

*International Organization for Standardization, *Quality Systems—Model for Quality Assurance in Design, Development, Production, Installation, and Servicing* (New York: American National Standards Institute, 1994), 10. Copyright International Organization for Standardization (ISO). This material is reproduced from ISO 9001:1994 with permission of the American National Standards Institute on behalf of ISO. No part of this material may be copied or reproduced in any form, electronic retrieval system or otherwise made available on the Internet, a public network, by satellite or otherwise without the prior written consent of the American National Standards Institute, 11 West 42nd Street, New York, NY 10036.

Reengineering and the "Case Worker"

In their landmark book, *Reengineering the Corporation*, Michael Hammer and James Champy discuss the difficulty in improving established workplace processes.[5] While TQM's continuous quality improvement (CQI) approach generates a nearly endless series of incremental process enhancements, it is not well suited to generating the fundamental, radical, and dramatic leaps that Hammer and Champy assert are required today.

Critical to the definition of reengineered processes is a reversal of the assembly-line approach. In the old system, processes were divided between many individuals and departments. The only individual common to the entire process was a higher-level manager who never talked to the customer or did any actual process work. With so many process participants, and with everyone responsible for the customer, no one was truly responsible.

The new worker in a reengineered process becomes what Hammer and Champy call a *case worker* (or part of a *case worker team*). Ideally, the case worker (or team) is responsible for a process from end to end. This provides a clear overall responsibility for process efficiency and for customer satisfaction.

Reengineered processes are no longer a series of predetermined decisions and steps. There is no single flowchart covering every possible situation. Because the case worker controls the process from end to end, procedures are much more flexible. Customers can now be handled on a case-by-case basis rather than as a group with an invariant process by class.

The potential improvements with reengineering can be startling. Technology becomes a key enabler and a strategic resource. Elapsed process time can be cut by 75 percent or more. Handoffs to other individuals or teams are eliminated. Customer issues are resolved immediately, by the first person the customer contacts. The organization is flattened and downsized. Multiple layers of management are no longer necessary since most of the work is delegated to frontline workers. The organizational pyramid truly is reversed, with process power and expertise residing at the base of the pyramid (frontline) rather than at the top.

The classic low-skilled, poorly educated worker doing simple tasks over and over under the guidance of managers and engineering "experts" has been replace by the educated, knowledgeable, and responsible case worker in control of an entire process without much management oversight. Instead of production volume, success is now measured on quality issues, such as cycle time, error rate, and internal and external customer satisfaction.

This completes the competency circle back to the early years of the twentieth century. Today's case workers not only require a new set of competencies but also demand much deeper competencies than ever before. Organizations that can identify competencies by position, measure the qualifications of workers to deliver those competencies, and develop those who fall short will succeed in the long term. Organizations that cannot adapt to this new competency-based approach will continue to have gaps between their goals and their actual business results.

Competency-Based Applications

Competency-based concepts apply to the full range of HR functions. Competency should play a role as the employee moves through the organization in cyclical fashion from position to position. These major HR functions are shown in Figure 1-1 and described below.

1. *Position Requirements*
    A. *Process design*. Everything starts with well-designed processes. The process determines what skills are required and what knowledge is needed. Desired business results form the basis of a measurement system for determining qualifications of workers in the process.
    B. *Job design*. Process tasks can then be assigned to individuals or teams. Job requirements are used to identify employee competency levels and qualifications.
2. *Position Fulfillment*
    A. *Recruitment*. Competencies are used to determine who should be interviewed and evaluated. This is a costly and time-consuming effort that can be reduced through proper understanding of what competencies a candidate brings to the job.
    B. *Qualification*. Competency evaluation is necessary to determine if a can-

Figure 1-1. Competency-based HR applications.

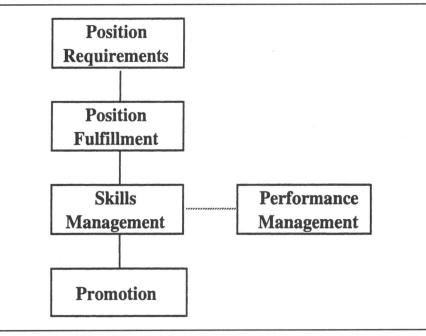

didate is qualified to perform the job or can master the requirements of the position.

C. *Selection*. Where more than one candidate appears qualified, competency assessments are used to determine the best person to fill the position.

D. *Orientation*. This refers to developing the general competencies required of an employee by the organization.

E. *Training*. This refers to developing the specific competencies required to meet performance standards for a position being filled. Of particular interest will be the discussion in Chapter 2 concerning whether candidates should possess required competencies before being selected or whether they are expected to obtain them after being put in the position.

3. *Skills Management*

A. *Measurement*. This is the classic competency-based application. The measurement of workplace competencies is essential in modern organizations, where people drive processes rather than the reverse.

B. *Development*. This differs from training, which is received before and immediately after obtaining a new position. Whereas training focuses on developing required competencies and is intended to meet a minimum absolute standard, development activities are relative in that they are designed to support the continuous improvement of workplace competencies while on the job.

4. *Promotion*

A. *Training*. This is similar to the training that takes place in the Position Fulfillment function. Again, the idea is to prepare individuals for new positions before placing them there. The goal is to be immediately productive. Competencies help determine when a candidate is ready to move up.

B. *Succession*. This function provides a stronger personal link between incoming and departing employees. The added requirement here is for continuity of effort, meaning that incoming workers need more than baseline competencies; they must be able to take over current projects without disrupting the processes involved. The goal is to cause as little disruption as possible with the personnel change.

Note that performance management was not part of the flow described above. This is a point that will continue to be made strongly throughout this discussion of competency-based applications. Performance management measures both results and what is required to improve those results. While competencies are assumed to drive performance, they are not an equivalent or substitute for performance. These are two separate issues.

Most organizations implement competency-based applications from the middle of the flow outward, starting with Skills Management then working backward toward Recruiting and forward toward Promotion. This is because competency concepts have typically taken root in the training group, which uses competency information to design course materials and learning exercises. This practice has been reinforced by the ready availability of training administration software and ERP mainframe computer systems, which have facilitated the record keeping of course attendance and certification status.

It makes the most sense to integrate competencies into the HR flow as early as possible. Competency issues should be considered in the design of all processes and positions. Then the remaining applications proceed naturally from the competency model created along with a specific position. For existing positions in current processes, the immediate benefits accrue from identifying competency gaps and eliminating them. This means focusing first on Skills Management.

A small percentage of organizations have begun integrating competency concepts into their HR processes. Early indications are that these efforts can deliver some immediate benefits, but that the real payoff may be longer term.

Experiences of Early Adopters

There is some initial data on the experience of early adopters of competency-based HR applications. In 1996, the American Compensation Association (ACA) mailed questionnaires to HR professionals in 19,106 North American companies.[6] Two percent (426) were returned. From these, a total of 1,257 competency-based applications were identified, 70 percent of which were under development. The response pool was eventually consolidated down to 217 companies with 247 competency-based applications in place or under development.

The generally low response rate and the small percentage of in-place applications are an indication of how early in the adoption cycle Competency Modeling and Reporting (CMAR) was in 1996. Table 1-2 shows how long four types of competency-based applications had been installed. The bulk of applications were in place for less than two years.

While organizations have made some progress with competency-based HR applications in the years since this study, these figures are still indicative.

Table 1-2. Durations of competency-based HR applications.

Application	In Development	< 1 yr.	1–2 yrs.	3–5 yrs.	> 5 yrs.
Staffing	29%	26%	29%	12%	3%
Performance Management	33%	25%	28%	11%	3%
Training and Development	44%	14%	25%	10%	7%
Compensation	52%	17%	21%	7%	2%

Adapted from "The Role of Competencies in an Integrated HR Strategy" by ACA's Competencies Research Team. Reprinted from *ACA Journal*, Summer 1996, Vol. 5, No. 2, with permission from the American Compensation Association (ACA) 14040 N. Northsight Blvd., Scottsdale, Az. U.S.A. 85260, telephone (480) 951-9191; fax (480) 483-8352; aca@acaonline.org; /www.acaonline.org. © ACA.

The 2 percent who responded in 1996 were early adopters. The bulk of nonrespondents were likely to be late adopters or nonadopters. And current project development has slowed while many organizations pause to determine how to utilize new technologies such as Intranets and ERP software to perform some of the project administration.

These early adopters were implementing competency-based HR applications for a number of potential benefits. Table 1-3 shows how respondents thought competency-based HR applications would help their organizations focus behavior.

The ACA data provides further insights into the effectiveness of competency-based applications. Feedback on 148 models that were in place for more than a year showed mostly positive experiences, but with a different applicability from that shown in Table 1-3.

In Table 1-4, the close alignment of competency applications with customer-centered behaviors is apparent, and is seen as an immediate result by respondents. They also report a positive effect on competitiveness. But the impact on actual reduction of employee skill gaps, the rise in overall employee competency levels, and the support for superior performance of key individuals and departments was less clear.

The findings may have something to do with the overall newness of the competency applications, but they may also reflect problems with implementation. The applications evidently got everyone thinking in the right direction, but not necessarily performing at a higher level. Focus and emphasis were increased, yet improvements in competency, skills, and performance were still

Table 1-3. How competency-based HR applications focus behavior.

Factor	Percent of Respondents Selecting*
Communicate valued behaviors	48%
"Raise the bar" of the competency level of all employees	45%
Emphasize people (vs. job) capabilities enabling the organization to gain competitive advantage	42%
Encourage cross-functional/team behaviors critical to business success	34%
Reinforce new values while continuing to support achievement of business objectives	27%
Close skill gaps	26%
Support superior performance in roles/units that have a critical impact on organizational success	22%
Focus people on total quality/customer-centered behaviors	22%
Provide an integrating vehicle for human resources	20%
Ease the flow of people across business and global boundaries	8%

*Up to three responses permitted

Adapted from "The Role of Competencies in an Integrated HR Strategy" by ACA's Competencies Research Team. Reprinted from *ACA Journal*, Summer 1996, Vol. 5, No. 2, with permission from the American Compensation Association (ACA) 14040 N. Northsight Blvd., Scottsdale, Az. U.S.A. 85260, telephone (480) 951-9191; fax (480) 483-8352, aca@acaonline.org; /www.acaonline.org. © ACA.

Table 1-4. Effectiveness of competency-based HR programs.

Factor	Positive Effect	Don't Know/ Too Early to Tell	No Effect	Negative Effect
Focus people on total quality/customer-centered behaviors	80%	20%	0%	0%
Emphasize people (vs. job) capabilities enabling the organization to gain competitive advantage	69%	23%	4%	4%
"Raise the bar" of the competency level of all employees	59%	41%	0%	0%
Close skill gaps	50%	50%	0%	0%
Support superior performance in roles/ units that have a critical impact on organizational success	30%	70%	0%	0%

Adapted from "The Role of Competencies in an Integrated HR Strategy" by ACA's Competencies Research Team. Reprinted from *ACA Journal,* Summer 1996, Vol. 5, No. 2, with permission from the American Compensation Association (ACA) 14040 N. Northsight Blvd., Scottsdale, Az. U.S.A. 85260, telephone (480) 951-9191; fax (480) 483-8352, aca@acaonline.org; /www.acaonline.org. © ACA.

too early to tell for many respondents. The focus must be on developing competency-based processes that drive improvements.

Defining Competence

In migrating to a competency-based approach, there is often much confusion about exactly what a competency is. It is not unusual to encounter an organization that is deep into the application development process and still struggling because there is no explicit agreement on what this critical term means. Here are two basic definitions:

> *Competent:* Qualified to perform to standards the processes of a job.
> *Competence:* The condition or state of being competent.

Employees are competent if they can correctly perform the processes required in their job. Using the three standard TQM measures, this means that the process can be done (1) within the specified cycle time, (2) without defects, and (3) to customers' satisfaction expectations. When workers can accomplish this, they indicate competence in that process. This is what competence is. It is equally important to understand what competence is not.

Competence Is Not Performance

The most common error in beginning a competency-based project is to confuse competence with performance. Competence is a state of being, a qualification to perform.

Competence, in relation to performance, is what mathematicians call "a necessary, but not sufficient, condition." Workers can't perform to standards without competencies. But competencies cannot guarantee that workers will perform adequately. Everyone has seen extremely competent workers fail on the job due to a variety of personal or outside factors. And workers lacking complete job competencies can make up for a lot of shortcomings with exceptionally hard work. Competence has to be there, but it cannot guarantee results, nor can its absence always predict failure.

As shown in Figure 1-1, it is *critical* to keep a CMAR system completely separate from a performance planning and appraisal system. Otherwise, it is all too easy to confuse competency measurement with performance measurement. Competencies are all about being qualified to do a position's work. Performance is all about results of the actual work.

Organizations that blend these two activities are primed for disaster. They end up doing a poor job of both competency assessment and performance management, to the detriment of the entire organization.

Competence Is Not Process Input

A standard concept in continuous quality improvement is the SIPOC process description. SIPOC stands for Suppliers of Inputs to a Process generating Outputs to Customers. Inputs are typically defined with the classic TQM four M's: manpower, materials, methods, and machinery.

The four M's, as shown in Figure 1-2, have nothing to do with a worker's qualifications to do a job. They are resources used to complete the process. In the context of a SIPOC process definition, manpower is used to denote the number of people required to perform the process, not their capabilities. Mate-

Figure 1-2. SIPOC process definition.

Suppliers   Inputs   Process   Outputs   Customers

Manpower   Materials   Methods   Machinery

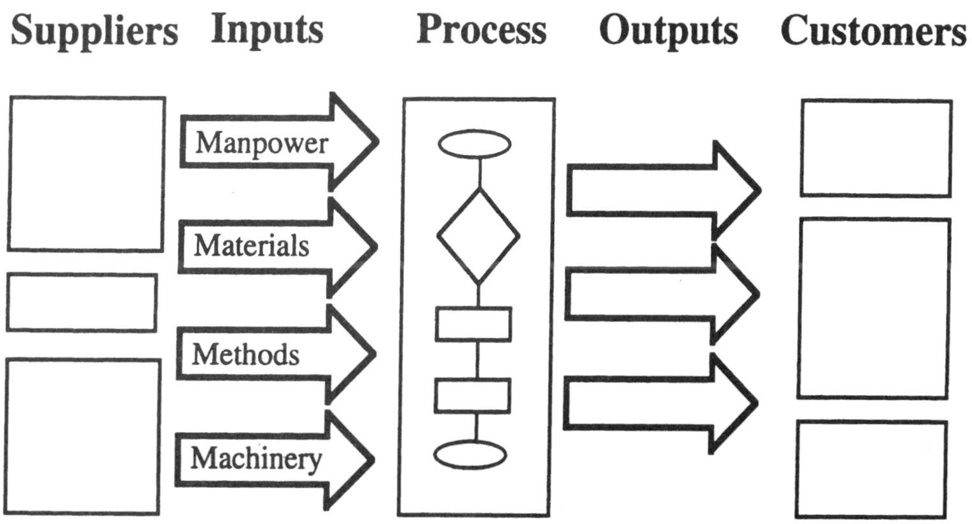

rials, methods, and machinery are part of the process as designed. In essence, they are the resources used by people completing the process.

For example, a major ERP software product is designed to include machinery in the list of position competencies. This is incorrect and leads to later problems in measuring competencies and developing skills. A machine either performs to specifications or it does not. Machinery is not a learning entity. Despite recent efforts in fuzzy logic, technology is not quite to the point where equipment can be trained and will develop skills as a human does. Machinery is a tool, not a competency.

Competence Is Not Process Output

Confusing outputs with competence is another common mistake. Outputs are defined as the business results of a process. They are the productive outcome of competent workers. Results are not competencies. Process results are just one of many measures of competence.

For example, "making sales quota" is not a competency. It is a measure of the output of a sales process. A "zero-defect production run" is not a competency; it is a result of the manufacturing process. An "overhauled transmission" is not a competency. It is an output of the repair process.

It is easy to mistake outputs for competence because competence is closely related to output. Sales competencies are required to make quota. Operations expertise is needed to turn out zero-defect products. Mechanical skills and automotive knowledge are necessary to overhaul and reassemble a complex automatic transmission. But these are cause and effect relationships, not equivalencies.

Competence Is Not a Trait

A trait is a distinguishing characteristic of personality. The classic Scout Pledge is a perfect example of a traits list—courteous, kind, obedient, cheerful, thrifty, brave, clean, and reverent. In the work world, there are a number of common traits that creep into competency model lists:

Confidence	Problem orientation
Loyalty	Openness
Honesty	Change orientation
Innovation	Commitment
Valuing people	Team orientation
Influence	Flexibility
Results orientation	

Personality traits are formed at an early age, and some researchers believe that certain elements of personality may have a genetic factor. Personality is hard to change, even with the help of a trained therapist. So traits end up being what someone brings to the job. Once people are on the job, typical development activities have little chance of changing personality.

An old saying in the personnel department is, "Hire for traits, train for skills." Competency projects deal with performance issues only. Consequently, traits have no place in a competency model.

Competence Is Not Capability or Ability

Here are two very similar words that create significant confusion at the start of competency projects. These terms must be defined and understood before continuing.

A good definition of *capability* is a "workplace capacity." Capability connotes potential future performance. For example, employers hire college graduates, not for what they know and can do, but for what a college education indicates. The college education itself may have little bearing on the position being filled. However, it is assumed that college graduates are capable of learning in a competitive environment, of self-discipline in studying, of working with others in teams, of finding and utilizing appropriate information resources, and of achieving to specified standards.

As another example, early in their careers, Mark McGwire and Sammy Sosa showed the capability of hitting many home runs. They possessed the physical size, strength, coordination, mental approach, and swing. Baseball scouts might say they "had the tools."

A 140-pound second baseman may have the same coordination, mental approach, and home-run swing. Yet without sufficient physical size and strength, he lacks the capability to hit fifty or more home runs in a season. No amount of training and practice will turn him into a home-run powerhouse, because he can't develop capability.

Ability is a closely related issue. In a competency context, ability is a reflection of talent, of being able to perform. Continuing the baseball example, strength and size do not necessarily guarantee success in hitting home runs. A mere quarter-inch variance in where a baseball is struck can be the difference between a home run and a long fly ball. The successful home-run hitter must possess superb eye-hand coordination, quick reactions for adjustments at the last instant, and a patient approach to wait for the right pitch. As the scouts might say, McGwire and Sosa also "had the gifts."

Neither capability nor ability guarantees performance. Many professional ballplayers have had the tools and gifts of McGwire and Sosa yet never broke the fifty home-run level. Similarly, having the "gift of gab" doesn't guarantee success as a salesperson. Having the ability to concentrate for extended periods does not ensure developing a high-performance claims adjuster. Graduating with a perfect 4.00 college grade-point average doesn't mean that any process can be learned and performed correctly.

It is an early warning sign when "capable of . . . ," "able to . . . ," and ". . . ability" creep in to competency names. Samples of what to avoid are:

Sales ability
Administrative ability
Leadership ability
Capable of taking independent action
Capable of resolving problem on his/her own
Able to identify solutions to customer problems
Ability to learn new skills

The competency process should consider, not what workers could potentially do or what talents they could have if they chose to use them, but what workers actually need to be qualified to do. This means that capabilities and abilities are not part of the model.

Competence Is Not a Motivational Attitude

The final mistake often made in defining competence is to include motivational elements. The reason these should be excluded from a discussion of competence is similar to that for traits. Motivational attitudes are integral to the personality of a worker. These attitudes include items such as:

Motivation
Aggression
Self-confidence
Assertion
Ambition
Dedication
Decisiveness
Commitment
(Any word)-focus

Attitudes can work their way into a discussion of competence because of the way leaders are trained to evaluate employee problems. A popular performance analysis tool that allows this approach is the Can Do/Will Do chart. "Can Do" refers to the employee's qualification to do the job. "Will Do" refers to the employee's motivation to perform. This results in four possible alternatives as shown in Figure 1-3:

✧ *Can Do/Will Do.* This is the ideal situation. The employee is fully qualified and is doing the job as designed. The supervisory response is to provide appropriate rewards.

✧ *Can't Do/Will Do.* Here the employee is putting out the effort, but is not getting the results (a skill problem.) For example, a salesperson might be making the proper amount of calls but not generating expected sales. This suggests a competency gap that should be resolved with relevant sales training.

Figure 1-3. Can Do/Will Do evaluation chart.

	Can't Do	Can Do	
	Train	**Motivate**	Will Do
	Job in Jeopardy	**Counsel**	Won't Do

- ✧ *Can Do/Won't Do.* Here the employee possesses the competencies to do the work but is not completing work processes as designed (a motivation problem). This might be an experienced salesperson who has a successful track record and who knows how to sell but who is just not making the calls. This suggests a motivational gap that must be resolved with formal workplace counseling.
- ✧ *Can't Do/Won't Do.* This employee has deficiencies in both skills and motivation. A decision has to be made as to the development/counseling resources required versus the expected success of the effort. The result may well be a job-in-jeopardy situation.

This model is a common way of looking at improving employee performance. In a competency project, the problem occurs in thinking about both dimensions when defining competence. The Can Do-Can't Do dimension of this model is certainly within the purview of a competence effort. But the Will Do-Won't Do dimension is not competency based. It is a matter of motivational attitude. Attitudes cannot be developed, only counseled. Therefore, they cannot be part of a definition of competence.

This section has provided a solid definition of competence that will survive the trials of a competency-based application development project. Once everyone in a project understands and agrees upon what competence is and is not, the team can move on to the next definition.

Defining Individual Competencies

With a clear idea of what competence means in HR applications, the next step is to define individual competencies, as used in the context of building a competency model for a job position. In a June 1998 issue of *Training* magazine, author Scott Parry suggested a very useful four-part definition of a competency: (1) A cluster of related knowledge, attitudes, and skills that affects a major part of one's job; (2) that correlates with performance on the job; (3) that can be measured against well-accepted standards; (4) and that can be improved via training and development.[7]

Discussing competencies also requires that we look at processes. Figure 1-4 shows the two primary shapes in a process flow chart that relate to competencies. The diamond represents a decision. Making proper decisions requires *knowledge* in the form of facts, figures, procedures, guidelines, rules, judgments, ramifications, and experiences. The rectangle represents a process activity. Performing activities requires task *skills* to move a process forward. Table 1-5 shows examples of how these relate to each other.

Figure 1-4. Competency-related process flowchart symbols.

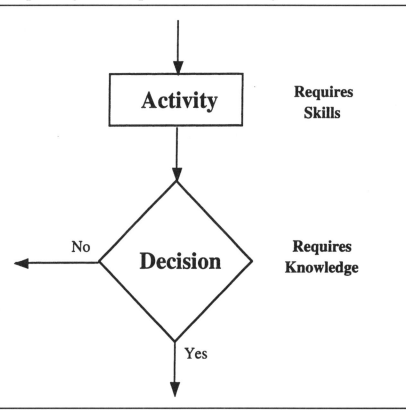

Table 1-5. Sample competency requirements for processes.

Knowledge (Decision)	*Skill (Activity)*
When to close a sales prospect	Mastery of ten different closing strategies
When to choose to give a refund	Compute lifetime customer value
When to assign work to best team member	Accurately appraise subordinates
When to approve a loan	Use the loan scoring software
When to reject a part	Operate test equipment

Parry extends this decide/do definition to include *attitudes* in a manner very different from motivational attitudes. He suggests that beliefs and formal and informal organizational culture are also part of the competency definition. For example, salesperson performance in closing a sale varies widely based upon mindsets, such as "Close early and often" versus "Only twisted minds twist arms." Customer service competency will be very different using "Whatever it takes to make customers happy" rather than "Customers are always trying to cheat us."

The second part of Parry's competency definition requires relevance. The competency must have a positive correlation with job performance. Keeping a neat, well-organized workspace may not be a valid competency for most employees but could be critical for a person in a job-sharing position. Having a pleasant telephone voice is critical in telemarketing but a nonissue for the general rank and file worker or manager.

Relevance can be verified by examining a position's processes. Every competency should apply to at least one diamond or rectangle. The more applicability, the higher the criticality of the step and the more important the competency is.

The third part of Parry's competency definition addresses the issue of *objectivity* in two ways: it must be measurable, and there must be standards. For example, "eagerness" is not a competency because it can't be measured. It is a trait. The proof is in trying to define it. Does "eagerness" mean panting and drooling, jumping up and down with excitement, bothering everyone in the office, raising an arm up in office meetings and shouting, "Ooh, ooh . . . me, me," or being willing to say "yes" to each request? The old bromide, "If you can't measure it, you can't manage it," applies here.

Another problem that crops up with items mislabeled as competencies is the lack of an acceptable standard for performance. Consider "works hard" as a competency. Does this mean putting in the full forty hours per week without any personal time off? Taking few breaks? No personal phone calls? Hustling all day? Volume of output? Attention to detail and accuracy under deadline pressures? Not conversing with coworkers? Eating lunch at the desk while working? It may be possible to measure hard work, but what is the standard? One person's eager employee is another person's sluggard. To paraphrase the previously mentioned old bromide, "So you can measure it, does it make sense to manage it?"

The fourth and final part of Parry's competency definition links to realistic potential for improvement. If there is no possible way to teach and develop a factor, then there is no reason to include it in a competency model. Basketball coaches observe, "You can't teach height." While it is certainly a characteristic successful teams need, it is not something you train for and develop. You recruit and select for height; you train and develop shooting skills. The former is a trait, the latter is a competency. Here is proof that Shooting is a competency for a basketball player, using the four definitions of a competency:

1. The object of basketball is to score points by shooting baskets.
2. The related skills in knowing when to shoot, where to shoot, and how to shoot are critical to success in scoring.
3. Shooting has well-accepted standards of success. The goal is to make at least 50 percent of field goals, 80 percent of free throws, and 35 percent of three-point attempts.
4. Shooting skills can be improved by developing better technique, by shooting drills simulating game conditions, and by extensive practice and play.

Therefore, Shooting is a valid competency for a basketball player.

This basketball example may be somewhat trivial, but the exercise is critical. Before any item can be accepted for discussion as a competency, it should be measured against the four-part definition. Here is a workplace example that is somewhat more difficult to determine: Conflict Management as a competency for an office administrator:

1. *Conflict Management does require a cluster of knowledge, attitudes, and skills.* It is not something that people do naturally. (In fact, it is quite the opposite.) It is also a complex task requiring the integration of various ideas and techniques.

2. *Conflict Management correlates with interpersonal office interactions.* Certainly, everyone can benefit from conflict management skills. The question arises whether this skill is needed to perform a "major part of one's job." In a cubicle environment where there is little interaction between workers, conflict management may not be deemed important enough to be singled out, measured, and managed separately. It may be enough to have it included with Communications Skills or some other competency. On the other hand, if the department is team oriented in its work and decision processes, then Conflict Management is a critical competency requiring formal modeling and management.

3. *Standards for Conflict Management need to be well accepted.* It can be difficult establishing standards for interpersonal skills such as conflict management. Most workers handle conflict situations based upon their personality, their individual style, their relationship with the other person, and the business situation. Customers are handled differently from coworkers or bosses. Strangers receive a different response than do acquaintances or friends. So should Conflict Management be removed from a competency list?

The answer is often found in the training materials and processes of an organization. With this type of soft-skills competency, it will be very difficult to pass the third part of the definition test without documentation. For example, there may be a four-step difficult-customer process taught in a service course, which becomes the well-accepted standard for Conflict Management for office workers. Where no such material exists, either the standards must be developed or Conflict Management must be removed from the competency model.

4. *Conflict Management can be improved via training and development.* Conflict management is a skill that can be improved. There are numerous publications and a myriad of training materials addressing various techniques for dealing with and resolving interpersonal conflict. Skill in understanding a conflict management process and in using the techniques can be tested for and observed during training case studies and in the workplace. Mastery of the basic skills can be measured, and improvements can be verified.

So Conflict Management can be a valid competency depending upon various workplace factors that vary from position to position. Although it is a generally useful skill, it may not be significant enough to include in all position competency models. The four-part definition helps to determine when to include it.

Figure 1-5 shows a worksheet that can be used to evaluate quickly whether a competency fits the definition. List the candidate competency, describe the competency so that everyone will be in agreement as to exactly which competency is being considered, and then evaluate how the competency fits within the four-part definition framework. The analysis should resemble the one just used for Conflict Management. Reject any competency that does not fit all four parts of the definition.

This worksheet is also useful in showing why the traits and capabilities discussed in this chapter's "Defining Competence" section are not proper competencies. Typically, they fall short of the third and fourth parts of the definition. There is no way to measure items such as leadership ability, motivation, or customer focus. Therefore, there are no well-accepted standards, and valid development activities cannot be established.

This section completes the definition of competence, competent, and competencies. Without proper definitions, a shared understanding, and consistent application of these terms, the competency-based application development process will be flawed. The proper use of these concepts will ensure that applications will include proper competency elements, and that the resulting HR process will lead to improved business results.

A Competency Modeling Vocabulary

There are a number of related terms that will be used throughout the book. These must be defined and agreed upon by the implementation team in order to ensure consistent meanings and accurate communications:

- ✧ *360-degree feedback.* A measurement or feedback approach where a worker's managers, subordinates, and coworkers provide a performance evaluation. The participants may also include nonemployees such as suppliers or customers.
- ✧ *Ability.* Being able to perform. While it may be possible to develop abili-

Figure 1-5. Competency definition worksheet.

Definition of an individual "competency" as used in building a competency model: (1) Cluster of related knowledge, attitudes, and skills that affects a major part of one's job. (2) Correlates with performance on the job. (3) Can be measured against well-accepted standards. (4) Can be improved via training and development.		
Competency	*Description*	*Definition*
		1 ☐ 2 ☐ 3 ☐ 4 ☐
		1 ☐ 2 ☐ 3 ☐ 4 ☐
		1 ☐ 2 ☐ 3 ☐ 4 ☐
		1 ☐ 2 ☐ 3 ☐ 4 ☐
		1 ☐ 2 ☐ 3 ☐ 4 ☐
		1 ☐ 2 ☐ 3 ☐ 4 ☐

ties, they cannot be created. They are the result of natural talents, not training.

✧ *Appraisal.* A formal evaluation of performance compared to established standards. Appraisals should be kept separate from the measurement of competencies. (See *Assessment.*)

✧ *Assessment.* A formal evaluation of competencies relative to a specific position's competency model. Assessments should be kept completely separate from the measurement of performance. (See *Appraisal.*)

✧ *Attitude.* A mindset that affects the way a person feels, thinks, and acts.

✧ *Behavior.* The way a person feels, thinks, and acts. In a competency context, behavior is the observable set of actions that demonstrate a competency.

✧ *Belief.* Opinions or judgments about the workplace, work, and people involved that affect a person's behavior. Beliefs may be the result of logical analysis or be based on personal convictions.

✧ *Business result.* A consequence of work processes that is linked to an organization's strategic and tactical goals.

✧ *Capability.* A workplace capacity, typically indicating a competency that that can be further utilized or developed.

✧ *Case worker.* An individual worker who is responsible for a reengineered process from end to end. The case worker has a wide ranging knowledge of the process and can handle most situations without assistance. The small number of process exceptions that cannot be handled by a case worker are passed on to a process specialist. (See *Expert.*)

✧ *Case worker team.* A group of individuals acting as the equivalent of a case worker. While each member of the team may have a specialty, members are cross-trained so that they can handle the most common situations without assistance. Any process exceptions are forwarded to the team member specializing in that area.

✧ *CMAR.* Competency modeling and reporting process. The fundamental competency-based application that includes identifying competencies, creating position models, assessing employees, reporting results, and creating input to development planning. The models can then be expanded into recruitment, hiring, orientation, employee development, and succession planning processes.

✧ *Competency.* A cluster of knowledge, skills, and attitudes that affects a major part of one's job. Must meet the four-part definition in the "Defining Individual Competencies" section in this chapter.

✧ *Competency model.* Collection of competencies and standards of performance establishing qualifications for a specific job position.

✧ *Core competency.* A competency that applies to the entire organization. It is typically seen as a strategic factor in the overall success of the organization.

✧ *Curriculum.* A series of established development activities that, upon successful completion, qualifies an employee as being competent for a specific job position.

✧ *Culture.* Accepted ways of behaving within the organization. This typically includes attitudes, communications, and actions.

✧ *Customer.* The recipient of product and service outputs of a process.

✧ *Expert.* A process specialist who handles special situations that are exceptions to the processes handled by case workers or case worker teams.

✧ *Focus groups.* A team of subject matter experts assembled when it is not possible to perform a thorough individual survey of a population. The team environment is assumed to generate proportionally better input due to the synergy among attendees.

✧ *Input.* The manpower, materials, methods, and machinery that are resources used to complete a process. Inputs can optionally be expanded to include funds and information.

✧ *Job analysis.* The process of gathering position information needed to build a competency model.

✧ *Knowledge.* The intellectual and information capital of an organization. This includes facts, data, procedures, and experiences of the collective organization.

✧ *Measurement instrument.* A measurement tool used to assess the qualifications of an individual relative to established competency standards for a specific position.

✧ *Output.* The productive outcome of processes in terms of products and services.

✧ *Performance.* The act of executing a specified task within a work process.

✧ *Process.* A series of activities that results in an output that adds value to customers.

✧ *Position.* Work done by a single person. Used interchangeably with *Title* and *Job*.

✧ *Proficiency.* Demonstrated competency to exceed the required performance standards of a process activity. (See *Expert.*)

✧ *Skill.* Demonstrated competency to meet the required performance standards of a process activity.

✧ *Standard.* An objective measure used as a basis of comparison for measuring competency to perform a process activity. Specifically, a standard is the minimum acceptable level of performance.

✧ *Subject matter expert.* An individual who possesses a great degree of knowledge about workplace processes. Subject matter experts are useful in developing competency models.

✧ *Supplier.* An entity that provides inputs to a process.

✧ *Temperament.* A typical frame of mind. This refers to a person's natural disposition.

✧ *Trait.* A distinguishing characteristic of personality. This can refer to a physical quality or a behavioral style or tendency.

✧ *Values.* Socially accepted organizational principles concerning how individuals and the organization should behave. These include issues such as organizational ethics, treatment of individuals, leadership practices, personal behavior, and so on.

These definitions are not unchangeable. They are versions that have been proven useful in past projects. The important point is to make certain everyone on the project team has a common language before beginning to work. This will prevent later conceptual problems and difficulties in communicating.

Using the Definitions

Some of these definitions can be very helpful. Of particular value are the definitions for skill and proficiency. The dictionary definition of skill has a connotation of being superior at some activity. This seems to overlap with proficiency. Some dictionaries even use proficiency to define skill. But there is no word other than *skill* that is adequate to describe meeting minimum required standards for an activity.

Discussions of competency levels are simplified by agreeing to let skill stand for baseline performance and have proficiency stand for superior performance. "They have the skills" then means that employees can do the job. "They are proficient" then means that employees exceed standards for the job.

These word meanings also support the definition of competence. Without a clear understanding of competence, project teams inadvertently insert factors such as traits, attitudes, capabilities, or abilities into competency models. The damage isn't immediately apparent. It shows up later in trying to create a competency assessment instrument and related development resources. The team then finds itself deep into the project design, yet having to rework models nearly from the start.

Semantics are important, especially with a project as new and different as competency modeling. By first agreeing to a common vocabulary, competency-based application development participants will avoid many problems and will create better competency models.

Competency Coach Definitions

There are additional terms that have special meanings within the Competency Coach software provided with this book. These words appear in program menus, dialog box titles, and data entry screens:

- ✧ *Category.* A group of related competencies, used to simplify the design and data entry process. Each position competency model can have multiple categories with multiple individual competencies included. Example categories in the working model include: Management/Leadership, Sales/Marketing, Technical, Administration, Personal Computing, Personal, and Quality.
- ✧ *Person.* Individual employee to be included in the competency modeling and reporting process.
- ✧ *Resource.* Any development resource that can be used by a person to address shortfalls in measured competence versus competency standards. (See *Type.*)
- ✧ *Response.* A number that represents an employee's measured competency level for a single competency compared against an objective stan-

dard. Response, when used in a menu, refers to the entire set of competency measurements for a single person, title, or assessment.

✧ *Title*. A job in the organization that requires competencies. A specific competency model must be created for each title.

✧ *Type*. A group of related development resources. Types are user defined and can include items such as courses, multimedia training, videos, audio tapes, on-the-job learning, mentoring, or self-study.

✧ *Workgroup*. A group of people related by some common organizational factor such as geography, department, region, division, or team.

The above terms will be capitalized and combined with a descriptor when referencing Competency Coach. Examples of these terms in use are: Response screen, Category window, and List/Person menu sequence.

At this point, the conceptual tools are in place. There is a clear understanding of the role of competency-based HR applications in the organization, there is agreement as to what competence is, and there is a common vocabulary of related terms. The next step is to examine the key decisions that must be made before beginning application development.

Learning Points

1. Competency-based HR applications must focus on job position competencies, not organizational core competencies.
2. Quality standards mandate that organizations document the qualifications of their employees to perform to standard and have processes in place to eliminate competency gaps.
3. Today's competitive environment requires frontline workers who are qualified to perform complex processes end-to-end in order to maximize efficiencies and customer satisfaction.
4. Competency-based applications apply to the entire spectrum of HR functions but are easiest to initiate in the Skills Management step.
5. Most organizations are still no further than the early adoption cycle and have yet to see strong benefits from the application of competency principles.
6. Competence is the qualification to correctly perform processes of a job position. It is not performance or an input, output, trait, capability, ability, or attitude. Letting these be considered competencies will destroy subsequent efforts to build valid models and assessment instruments.
7. Key factors in the definition of competence are: (1) significance to the job, (2) correlated with performance, (3) measurable to standards, and (4) can be improved.
8. Develop and agree on a vocabulary before initiating any other tasks, or

risk having difficulty throughout the entire life of competency-based HR application development.

Notes

1. Gary Hamel and C.K. Prahalad, *Competing for the Future* (Boston: Harvard Business School, 1994), 201.
2. David C. McClelland, "Testing for Competence Rather Than Intelligence," *American Psychologist*, January 1973, 1–14.
3. Mary Walton, *The Deming Management Method* (New York: Perigee Books, 1986), 8–21.
4. National Institute of Standard and Technology, *1997 Criteria for Performance Excellence: Malcolm Baldrige National Quality Award* (Gaithersburg, Md.: U.S. Department of Commerce, 1997), 12–13.
5. Michael Hammer and James Champy, *Reengineering the Corporation* (New York: Harper Business, 1993), 52.
6. Michael A. Thompson, et al., "The Role of Competencies in an Integrated HR Strategy," *ACA Journal* 5 (summer 1996): 6–20.
7. Scott B. Parry, "Just What Is a Competency? (And Why Should You Care?)," *Training*, June 1998, 58–64.

Initial Design Decisions

There's an old saying, "Power lies not with those who have all the answers, but with those who have the questions." In building competency-based HR applications, where so many tasks are either new or are being accomplished in a very different fashion, there are a host of questions that occur. The problem is that there may not be specific right or wrong answers to the questions. Instead, there are alternatives in designing the applications. The best that a competency expert can do is bring up the issues, the alternatives, the pros and cons, the resources required, and past results. Valid competency implementations have varied from a simple flat-file database designed in a morning on a PC to complex HR modules in an ERP system requiring millions of dollars and several years to install—and everything in between.

It is the answers to the design questions in this chapter that determine the scope and complexity of an application, and also its ultimate effectiveness. Addressing these issues now will eliminate many problems later on in the project. And it all starts with a very basic question.

Does the Organization Really Mean It?

Anything less than total commitment will doom a competency project. Sometimes "meaning it" is as simple as top management's stating that the organization is seeking ISO 9000 certification, or a national or state quality award. Because employee qualification processes are a standard quality requirement, competency-based HR applications are a mandate driven by audit standards. If workers understand that an ISO certification may be necessary to keep certain customers, and that a quality award helps in marketing the organization's products and services, then there is buy-in from top to bottom.

It is far more difficult in most cases. Competence is seen as a potential tool, but no one is clamoring for another HR program. Why? Because all too often they have been just programs, rather than strategic initiatives that drive business results. For example, the vice president of strategic planning for a large oil company was concerned about misguided HR projects. His biggest fear was that a new competency project would be one of those activities that sound like a good idea to somebody at the top but then become a total time-waster.

Some projects develop a life of their own. They put an organization into what Jerry B. Harvey calls "The Abilene Paradox."[1] This is a situation where group agreement is mismanaged and organizations find themselves "on the road to Abilene." On this path, individuals take actions that are different than what they want to do and thereby defeat the purpose they are trying to achieve. Everyone may agree that a project is a waste of time, but no one will make the group deal with it. It is no wonder that workers and leadership alike are initially skeptical of new concepts such as competency-based applications.

The oil company vice president's latest albatross was a bottom-up, formalized strategic planning process requiring mandatory participation by everyone in the organization. Frontline teams met to determine their strategies. They then appointed representatives to meet and develop workgroup strategies, and so on. The result was a gigantic process generating lots of meetings, pages and pages of minutes, hundreds of sets of completed planning forms, and a steady income stream to the consulting group that had sold the project to top management.

The workplace is littered with the wreckage of organizational fads. A perfect example is the quality circles movement. In its eagerness to catch up with the Japanese, American management tried to implement quality improvement teams without the corresponding quality focus, training, and group consensus culture of the Japanese. The results in many companies were meetings where everyone sat around saying nothing. This early failure with quality circles made it much harder in many organizations for its relative, TQM, to succeed years later.

Organizations also have a collection of worthwhile projects that were killed by the "shark pool" of managers and supervisors who were required to execute them, or by the frontline employees who supposedly benefit. Without their buy-in, top management can make all the decisions it wants, but the project will fail.

The result of such false starts is a near-permanent cynicism about the usefulness of new projects. Employee reluctance becomes a self-fulfilling prophesy of project failure that dooms further efforts to get it right. Both management and workers are forever wary of resurrecting what *Dilbert* cartoonist Scott Adams dubbed "a dead woodchuck." All this can happen to a competency-based project without the proper organizational buy-in.

Some of the best competency-based decisions are those that were not made. There are a myriad of conditions that can derail a project. If the organization does not have total commitment top to bottom, if it cannot see the benefits and does not have the culture to support a competency philosophy, then the process should be halted. For competency-based HR applications, it is better to have never started than to begin and fail.

It can also be difficult to play at competencies. Competency-based HR applications address core organizational processes, such as hiring, development planning, and promotion of employees. With today's mobile workforce and changing job assignments, it is nearly impossible to isolate a single department or workgroup. An organization puts itself at legal risk when its methods for making personnel decisions vary from department to department. The standardization normally found in performance management must be duplicated in the area of competency assessment. Competency-based applications must be universal within the organization.

At the very least, top management has to really mean it. Leadership has to have the vision to drive the process and the stamina to complete it. Benefits have to be so clear that managers and supervisors willingly perform the extra work to be trained on the process and administer it. And frontline workers have to believe that the application will support them in their jobs by helping them:

1. Get the development that they need to succeed.
2. Skip being trained on what they already know.
3. Verify what they can do.
4. Become qualified for the next promotion.

Without this support at all levels, the development project is seriously compromised. Many experienced HR consultants will bypass business opportunities where top management is not fully supportive of competency applications.

Recommendations

To be effective, executive leadership must project an assumptive attitude about competency-based projects. There is no "if," just "how." Putting competencies into HR processes cannot be a tryout effort. Competence must be at the same strategic level as quality or service. These are not items for discussion. They are no longer competitive advantages. They are required to stay in the game. Every vendor must bring them to the table.

It is the same situation with workforce competence. The organization must go into the project with an attitude of "whatever it takes" to make competency-based applications work. Competence then becomes a condition of employment issue for managers and supervisors. They *will* complete competence-related leadership activities with subordinates. HR *will* utilize competency concepts in its training and development processes. Information Technology (IT) *will* build competence data into its knowledge management data architecture. Frontline workers *will* be responsible for completing assessments in an accurate and timely fashion. There is no alternative.

Is the Goal Quality or Excellence?

This is a question that often is not asked until late in the development cycle, when people start to wonder about what to assess and how it should be measured. The solution is driven by a question that should have been asked at the start of the project. What is the organization trying to accomplish? While the concept of improving individuals' performance is implicit in competency-based HR applications, it is not enough to proceed. If they are to design useful position competency models and assess qualifications accurately, organizations must understand whether they are striving for quality, for excellence, or for both. The first step is to differentiate these two terms.

Quality is often confused with excellence. Historically, quality has referred to expensive goods and services. A Cadillac was assumed to have more quality than a Chevrolet due to its higher price and luxury features.

Quality has a very different meaning in a TQM context. Quality expert Philip Crosby defines quality as "conformance to requirements."[2] Crosby's quality is an *absolute* state. A product, service, or activity either meets standards or it does not. Crosby admonishes organizations to do things according to standards, or else change the standards. With this definition, a Chevrolet may represent as much quality as a Cadillac. It depends on how the two models were made in conformance to General Motors' specifications.

Excellence is a *relative* term. Excellent products or services excel or surpass others. Excellence is the state of being better than something else. It requires a comparison, not to a standard, but to similar items in a category.

One way to think of these terms is that quality is built in—excellence is designed in. Considering durability, the taxicab that is designed to last hundreds of thousands of miles is excellent compared with the household car. Considering comfort and features, the personal auto is excellent compared with the taxi. Yet both may be constructed with equal quality. Quality is determined by how each conforms to its requirements.

What is the goal for competencies, quality or excellence? It is the difference between "good enough" and "how good." As a surgery patient once asked, "I wonder if my doctors were A students, or whether they crammed for exams and sneaked by with Cs?" The patient was far more concerned with excellence than minimum standards.

Will the competency application be designed for quality? This means that individuals will be assessed on whether they meet preestablished standards in a pass/fail approach. The result is the number of workers meeting and not meeting position standards. In the TQM world, this is called *counted* data, or pass/fail data.

Certification through training is one type of counted competency approach. Schoolteachers are certified when they have satisfactorily completed a specified number of continuing education courses per year. Medical personnel are required to complete a continuing course sequence, or may be required to attend an annual refresher course on CPR. Once the course has been passed, each individual is assumed to possess the minimum competencies, and there is no further competency differentiation between individuals.

Or will the competency application be designed for excellence? This means that individuals will be assessed on their competence levels based on some sort of continuous scale. In TQM terminology, this is called *measured* data. The goal is to be able to compare the relative competence between two employees in addition to measuring their competence against a standard scale.

School grading systems are examples of the measurement approach. Competency is measured by academic achievement. Other measurement systems include competitive sports, sales quotas, factory piecework incentives, and see–do–master–teach competency continuums.

Setting up applications that assess to standards is much easier than building a competency measurement system. The reason many organizations have set up curriculum-based competency applications is that they require little more than an upgrade to the course attendance administration database.

Competency-level measurement systems are much more difficult to build. They require a thorough understanding of organizational processes and position needs, and they necessitate complex and time-consuming assessment methods.

Some systems are hybrids. Schools issue grades that are measurements (excellence) and give diplomas to students who are have met the graduation standards (quality.) A driver's license exam is given a grade, and then the license is awarded for achieving a minimum passing score.

Recommendations

Competency-based HR application designers must decide what they want to track—data on meeting minimum standards or measures of individual competency levels. The highest value comes from hybrid systems, measuring the competency levels of individuals, much like the driver's license test. There are minimum standards required, but there is also an assessment of levels of competence.

Ultimately, the capability to perform multilevel assessments, while making the development of an assessment system far more difficult, will provide important benefits later. Then an individual competency can map to various positions while requiring different standards for each. This will facilitate the assessment process, allow a single instrument to cover multiple jobs, and also make it possible to map employees to potential promotion positions.

Is the Development Effort Periodic or Continuous?

In a stable environment, perhaps in service industries such as hospitality, worker competencies have been little changed over the years. In these situations, it is possible to design competency models and to administer them over a long period of time. Updates can be completed as needed on a special project basis. HR department and organizational development resources are therefore required only periodically.

In most organizations, work activities, job responsibilities, and personnel assignments are in a constant state of flux. Each change that generates new job titles and/or process activities requires a corresponding adjustment in position competency models. Here is where problems can begin if competency requirements are not planned for.

Where continuous modeling is required, there are two possible outcomes. The first is that change is slowed down to the capacity of HR to keep models up to date. HR competency modeling becomes the final activity of every change project affecting personnel. If HR does not have sufficient resources, overall organizational performance can be hurt. Project cycle time is increased and responsiveness is reduced.

A second possibility is more likely. Change is driven by customer demands and competitive pressures. It has its own pace because it is out of the control of the organization. If HR cannot keep up, the outcome is that competency models will lag behind the real world by an ever-increasing margin. When this occurs, competency-related applications are in real danger of becoming dead woodchucks.

For example, one client implemented a thorough competency modeling application for its headquarters workforce. A model was created for all positions, and an assessment was created and used annually for individual development planning and for organizational training planning. The problem was that the model was not changed over a four-year period, yet the positions were redefined twice during that time. Minor adjustments were made to the competency standards and titling, but the model competencies and assessment questionnaire remained unchanged. At this point, the entire application was only moderately effective and had lost significant credibility with employees and their managers.

Recommendations

This is when HR finds out whether or not management "really means it" concerning competencies. Management must be willing to provide sufficient development resources periodically and then to fund HR permanently for maintenance of the models and assessment instruments. Competency-based applications become part of the HR installed base, similar to IT mainframe computer programs that must be administered, maintained, and updated. An organization can no more use an unchanging competency model for its personnel assessment than it can use the same balanced scorecard over time for its overall performance measurement.

This continuing resource requirement, if needed, is best discussed with management at the start and linked to any changes planned or anticipated in the near future. Agreement should be obtained up front as to the resources required to implement and support a continuing competency-based effort.

Is Assessment a Rolling Process or a Batch One?

The assessment process requires a scheduling decision similar to development. Should it be periodic, or is it possible to allow assessments to be completed on demand? These are issues of both preference and technology.

An important preference indicator is how the organization handles an annual appraisal system. Are appraisals done for everyone at the same time? Or are appraisals completed on employees' hiring anniversary date? Similarly, should assessments be completed annually, or would the organization prefer to have them completed in a rolling process?

The determining factor is likely to be how development resources are scheduled. For example, if an annual learning plan is published for the entire year, then a batch assessment process must be completed in order to create this plan. If development resource needs are continuously monitored and scheduled, then it may be possible to create a rolling assessment application.

Assessment administration is also a major factor. With manual or stand-alone relational database competency applications, it is customary to do the assessments and reporting for an entire workgroup at once. Forms are distributed and returned, responses are batched and entered, reports are generated and distributed, counseling sessions are mass scheduled, and all development resource planning is completed for the period. This is a classic centralized-control approach driven by HR.

Intranet technology is now enabling candidate- or employee-driven HR systems. Competency assessment and reporting can be completed over the organization's Intranet at any time for any position. Organizational resource needs are then continuously updated with the results of each individual assessment.

The technology decision depends upon several factors. First, are computing resources and expertise available to the application designers? Second, will the assessment process be voluntary or mandatory? And third, what is the maturity of the competency application?

The batch approach is useful when starting up. Simple stand-alone systems can be created using text files or e-mail for assessments, spreadsheets as input, and a simple relational database program for comparing and reporting. Every individual is assessed at once. Group results are immediately available so that assessment project design decisions can be validated. A picture of an overall workgroup is developed. And the larger number of responses provides a more statistically valid sample for study.

Interactive assessment on the organization's Intranet requires a significant commitment in customized interactive site programming, which is a scarce resource in many organizations. The programming must integrate the assessment, scoring, reporting, and database updating. This approach is most suitable for larger organizations with more mature competency applications in place, or it can be done more economically on an outsourced basis.

Recommendations

The value of an assessment program lies not with the method of administration but with the accuracy of the competency model(s) and the validity of the assessment instrument. A batch approach the first time around, executed as a stand-alone application or done over the Intranet, can reduce project development time and cost while delivering equivalent results.

Does the Model Reflect What Is or What Should Be?

The generally continuous nature of organizational change creates another question. Chapter 1 provided a brief history of the TQM movement and introduced continuous quality improvement (CQI). The premise of CQI is that processes are always being evaluated and incrementally improved by everyone in the organization. The goal is to deliver an ever-increasing level of quality and customer satisfaction. Similarly, reengineering creates temporary periods of radical change. This environment of periodic large change and continuous small change as shown in Figure 2-1 generates benefits for the organization but creates significant challenges in designing a competency application.

The issue is deciding to what processes are competencies going to be built, current activities or coming improved versions? The primary concern is that competency-related development efforts will document broken or inefficient processes. Even if the process is not broken, the "if it ain't broke, break it"

Figure 2-1. Improving the organization.

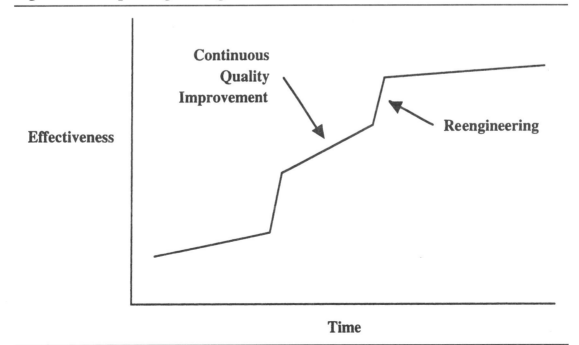

proponents will still worry about locking in current processes. This is because, unless HR is very careful, the competence movement can become a massive impediment to change.

Competency modeling adds another layer to HR processes. It operates alongside the performance management/appraisal system that already takes up significant supervisory and HR resources. Competency modeling also formalizes employee assessments. This makes it more difficult to experiment with alternative processes, titles, and work assignments, and to keep employees who are involved in the trial covered by the existing assessment system.

An example is the competency model for today's marketing professional. Marketing is rapidly changing in an e-commerce world. Table 2-1 gives some examples of how old activities are being replaced. These new Web-based marketing activities still don't appear on many job descriptions, and few, if any, show up in competency models or assessments. So for the organization just getting into e-commerce, how should competencies be written up for marketing professionals? Should current activities be documented, or should Web-based content be covered? And if Internet content is included, who in the organization is qualified to create the model and its corresponding assessment for something the organization isn't doing yet? (It may even be difficult to find outsiders capable of creating appropriate Web-based competency models.)

Finally, who is qualified to assess workers on something they are not yet doing? Management has no experience in setting standards with new processes. Self-assessment will not work, because this is questioning into ignorance. Outside assessment may be possible, but this is not likely to be a viable long-term solution.

Recommendations

The best time to initiate a competency project is during a planned CQI or reengineering of existing work processes. (Installing the human resources module of an ERP package can be just such a time.) The fear that competency-based applications may stifle organizational change is a very real one. Competency-related applications are always at risk of either getting out of synch with actual processes or becoming busywork administrative overhead. By linking competency application development to new projects, change is facilitated rather than slowed.

Table 2-1. Changing marketing activities.

Traditional	E-Commerce
Public relations	Web-casting
Writing brochures	Authoring Web pages
Writing sales letters	Writing e-mail, fax blasts
Direct mail techniques	Listservers
Sales support	Direct selling
Print advertising	Banner advertising

The concept of competence needs to be an integral part of all design decisions. As alternatives are evaluated, decide whether proposed competency standards are realistic, obtainable, and appropriate. How do new processes drive competency needs, and how do available employee competencies drive process options? How can competencies anticipated for new processes be identified, assessed, and developed?

The process improvement or reengineering team, with assistance from HR, is in the best position to create competency models for upcoming processes. Relatively stable processes can be analyzed and modeled as a continuous responsibility of the human resources department.

What Should the Expectations Be for Competency Project Time?

It is essential that management's expectations concerning competency-based HR applications be realistic. Many operations-oriented managers, inexperienced with these efforts, assume that competency modeling and assessment are activities with classic start and finish dates. Instead, competency is more of a successive approximation application, exhibiting a substantial learning curve with the possibility of a relatively mature state reached only with stable processes.

Experience shows that it takes about three cycles to have an acceptably reliable competency model and assessment. This is particularly true for an organization's first attempt. Later projects can benefit from the experience curve and can meet requirements faster.

Assuming that the assessment is done annually, the first year is taken up with the model development and an initial assessment. The focus here is on getting a selected workgroup or department assessed for development needs and linking those needs to existing development resources. Managers must initially be trained in how to interpret reports and counsel employees on their individual needs. Institutional reports should also indicate what additional developmental resources are required.

The second year typically shows a refinement in the model and assessment. The results also improve. Managers have greater comfort levels and familiarity with the process, having by now gone through one round of employee competency counseling. The development activities identified previously have been completed and actual benefits can be discussed. Managers can review last year's feedback and compare it to this year's requirements. New development activities, identified in the first year as needing to be created, should now be online and available for workers to utilize.

By the third year, unless there are significant changes in processes or in the organization chart, competency-based HR applications should be reaching a level of relative maturity. At this stage, continuing efforts should consist more of maintenance than development. The competency model, assessment, and development resources are not being philosophically and operationally redesigned; they are being tweaked and adjusted as needed due to changes in positions and processes.

Recommendations

Some competency-based HR applications may beat this typical three-year rule of thumb, and some may lag it. But it is important for management to understand that competency-based HR applications are multiyear development projects. There will be immediate benefits the first year, but the organization will typically require several rounds of improvement before reaching acceptable levels of accuracy and results.

Minor dissatisfaction with the first round is not unusual. Weak areas are readily apparent. Most organizations immediately see that there are things that they need to do differently the next time around. This is normal and healthy. The organization's leadership must understand that they need to make the commitment to stay the course for multiple cycles until the desired results are obtained.

How Will the Results Be Used by Management?

Competency-based HR applications have the potential to create fear and skepticism within an organization. Any change can be frightening, and competency is a major shift in the philosophy of assessing employees and identifying required development activities. Even workers in well-led organizations can come up with all sorts of spurious explanations for why management might be interested in looking at competencies.

Perhaps management has just latched onto the next fad. The entire competency effort can be dismissed with a "this, too, shall pass" attitude on the front line and from managers. All it may take is to wait out management's inevitable disillusionment with the current batch of consultants or for the sponsoring leader to move on.

Perhaps executives are looking to downsize the organization. This may be the way management is going to rank employees and sort out the keepers from those who will have their futures freed up. An honest self-assessment may be a form of organizational suicide, or a candid 360-degree rating of a coworker may be murdering someone else's career.

Perhaps this is how raises and promotions will be determined. It is not enough to have generated positive business results; employees are now going to have to show job competence through a series of useless forms.

Perhaps this is a giant power grab by HR. Headquarters staff will own employee assessment standards and the measurement process. Shouldn't qualifications and promotions be determined by line managers?

Such speculations tend to circulate in the absence of a clear message from management at the very start of a project. Executive leadership must make it clear that competency assessment is intended to raise the skills of the organization's employees, and that they will target learning and development activities specifically to those who require them. The end result is that everyone should be better prepared to succeed at work rather than be punished for what they don't know.

Recommendations

Everything depends upon the trust level that exists in the organization and on the quality of individual leaders. The lower the trust level, the lower the willingness to be candid and accurate in assessments. The lower the trust level, the more open and thorough the communications must be on what management intends to do with the data.

This is why it is so important to keep the competency assessment process separate from the performance management process. No matter how much management insists that assessments will only be used for determining development activities, employees will not believe it if the assessment results are handed back along with annual appraisals and raises.

A more comfortable approach for employees is to have management schedule the assessment process to start directly after the appraisal process. This way the assessment does not drive the appraisal rating; rather, the appraisal provides input for development needs. Competency assessments could be completed within two to four weeks of the appraisal—or even earlier with Intranet-based administration systems. This separates the appraisal from the assessment, yet it is early enough in the year to provide input for scheduling development resources.

What Are the Desired Outcomes for the Organization?

This is the classic question involving business results. What added value or positive impact is the organization working to attain with its competency-based HR applications? Possible outcomes include the following.

✧ *Meet vendor requirements.* The competency application may be a requirement of a quality certification program. For example, an ISO 9000 certification is considered to be essential by many manufacturers in Europe. In the United States, parts suppliers must have their ISO 14000 certification to be qualified as vendors for the major automobile manufacturers. Bidders for U.S. Department of Defense contracts are urged to utilize the People–Capability Maturity Model. In these cases, the competency application can be a requirement for staying in business.

✧ *Enhance the marketing position.* Competency-based applications can also improve the stature of an organization. Winners of the Malcolm Baldrige National Quality Award and related state quality awards are promoted nationally and within their communities. Even without awards, competence efforts can be highlighted in an organization's marketing materials and used to enhance its stature and competitive position.

✧ *Hiring effectiveness.* Competency-based efforts can have a positive effect on hiring and turnover. Improved recruiting and selection processes deliver employees who are more qualified for their new jobs. This has the potential to decrease turnover, a measure that can be tracked before and after the application is deployed.

✧ *Better internal placement.* Similarly, positions can be filled more effectively with properly qualified internal candidates. Employees who are ready to move up can be readily identified and promoted. Employees who want to move up but are not qualified can be steered into necessary development activities. The result is more of the right people in the right jobs.

✧ *Training/development efficiencies.* Organizations that train employees by title or by workgroup may be wasting a lot of productive time. Thirty-year employees may not need to be sitting next to new hires in some training class mandated by management. The goal for developing employees is just-in-time, just-as-needed. The immediate result of individual assessments is an easy win. Fewer people are involved in development they don't need, which means that the costs of developing people may go down.

✧ *Increased productivity.* Productivity can be improved three ways. First, enhanced selection of employees results in better across-the-board performance on the job. Second, time wasted in unnecessary development activities is converted to productive work time. Third, existing employees receive the development they want and need to be more effective in their jobs.

✧ *Better organizational performance.* Competency-based HR applications can contribute to the overall performance of the organization, although they are hard to isolate as a direct cause. They can deliver extremely large paybacks by helping organizations identify people who can help capture market share, shorten time to market, raise the level of customer service, be more innovative, improve efficiencies, and make better decisions.

So there are a number of attractive reasons for organizations to implement competency-based HR applications. Development team leaders must have a clear understanding of what business results top management wants to generate with the project. The team can continually ask questions such as:

"Will this help us eliminate one day of wasted training?"
"Will this help us identify people who can bring our products to market faster?"
"Will this help us find the right person for this job?"

"Will this satisfy quality requirements on personnel qualifications?"
"Will this drive customer satisfaction and profitability?"

These questions become the fundamental reality check in making process design and content decisions.

Recommendations

Make certain to get a clear message from top management concerning the expected organizational outcomes. Keep those outcomes in focus during the development process, and use them as checkpoints in making decisions in order to stay on target. Having everyone understand what management wants from the project, and why, helps to reinforce the message that management "really means it."

What Are the Desired Outcomes for Employees?

Competency-based HR applications deliver a number of beneficial outcomes for frontline employees. These need to be understood and communicated. Possible outcomes for individuals include:

✧ *Understanding position requirements*. Competency applications require a thorough grasp of the processes and skills/knowledge required to meet position performance standards. Employees don't have to wonder what they need to know and what they should be doing on the job.

✧ *Can get needed training*. Competency assessments let employees indicate, in a low-risk manner, where they need help in getting their job done. It also lets them establish where they meet qualifications and where they need not waste time in unnecessary development activities.

✧ *Easier to show qualifications*. When targeted business goals are not being met, the question arises whether the problem is people, processes, or uncontrollable outside factors. Competency assessments, along with the appraisal system, make it easier to show whether individual employees are properly trained and qualified. Where workers are not qualified, the assessment shows that this is an organizational development problem, not an individual performance problem. Either way, the initial look is at competencies and qualifications rather than at individuals' motivation and success.

✧ *Ability to prepare for the new/next job*. Performance appraisals require that an employee be in a job for a period of time before the review takes place. Workers can be appraised only for jobs they have held. This is totally inadequate in promotion planning. An advantage of competency assessment over simple performance appraisal is that competencies can be determined for jobs to which an employee aspires.

For example, a frontline employee who is interested in moving up can be assessed based upon the qualification standards for a supervisor. Any gaps can be addressed with development activities, if appropriate. Then when the organization has a supervisory position to fill, employee assessment records can be searched to locate all frontline workers who are qualified for the position. This allows employees to put themselves into a candidate position for the next job. They can prove their competence ahead of time, rather than being judged subjectively or on factors outside their control. Competency applications provide a straightforward way to say objectively, "I'm ready."

✧ *More rational personnel decisions.* Using competency assessment information, recruitment, hiring, placement, and promotion decisions are made much more objectively. Employees are hired, assessed, developed, and promoted based upon objective competencies rather than subjective preferences or unrelated factors such as seniority. This helps the truly qualified individual rise to the top, and allows others to become qualified if they are willing to take advantage of available development opportunities.

✧ *More competent coworkers.* If everything works as intended, the overall competence of the workforce is enhanced. This is both an organizational benefit and an individual one. Everyone's work is simplified if coworkers are competent and qualified to complete their part of the process. Checking, error correction, and rework are reduced. Internal service is improved and working conditions are enhanced.

✧ *Healthier, more competitive employer.* The final individual outcome of competency-based HR applications is one of job security. The healthier the organization is, the more resources there are for employees. The stronger the organization is as a competitor, the safer everyone's position is. And the more the organization is growing, the more job opportunities open up in the form of new positions and available promotions.

Assessment of competence makes it easy for the qualified worker to stand out and difficult for the unqualified worker to hide. Competency-based HR applications help migrate the responsibility for employee qualifications from management down to the individual worker. All employees get the information they need to determine their job qualifications and to fill in their gaps. They also have the opportunity to get themselves prepared ahead of time for the next promotion.

Recommendations

There are strong competence-related payoffs for both the organization and the individual worker. Make certain this "What's in it for me" message gets out to frontline workers as early in the development process as possible. This sell-in is critical, especially if there is an attitude of distrust or skepticism in the organization.

Competency applications can be positioned as a way to address existing concerns about unfair assessments and subjective personnel decisions. Competency concepts bring a management-by-fact approach to a formerly subjective personnel process.

How Will Success Be Measured?

Potential wins abound for competency applications. But that is all they are unless there is a measurement process in place to determine project success. As said earlier, the old adage states, "If you can't measure it, you can't manage it." Measurement of competency-related outcomes can be problematic.

A great danger is that projects can move well into their delivery cycle before anyone begins talking about the measurement of results. At this point it is often too late. To determine the delta caused by a change such as competency modeling, there must first be a baseline for comparison. So measurement must start before project implementation, and it is often conducted concurrently with competency application development.

Measurement of competency applications is similar to the measurement approaches used with other HR applications, such as training. These range from simple satisfaction feedback to complex organizational performance measures. It all depends upon the resources an organization wants to put into the effort. Measurement approaches include the following:

✧ *Project fulfillment*. The simplest measurement approach is a review of the project plan. Possible evaluation questions include:

"Were all development activities completed?"
"Were they completed on time?"
"Were they completed within budget?"
"Were all promised deliverables provided?"
"Did they include the promised content?"
"Were reporting and counseling steps completed by the involved parties?"
"Were organizational reports generated?"
"Were they used by the appropriate resource departments to make individual development planning decisions?"

In other words, regardless of effectiveness, did the development team do what it said it would do within the given parameters? This establishes what and how much was done. The remaining challenge is to determine how effective these efforts were. There are a number of additional qualitative measurement approaches.

✧ *Anecdotal sampling*. Interviews can be conducted with a cross-section of employees who were assessed, and with supervisors and managers who conducted counseling sessions. Their anecdotal feedback can be summarized and reported back to the development team and top management. This is the easiest measurement to conduct and has the least objective validity. The participants are the least likely to possess the competence expertise required to effectively judge the project. They also lack the organizational perspective to evaluate whether management's desired outcomes were achieved.

✧ *Project team formal evaluation.* The internal development team can review the project's success. This is a formal internal review or debriefing of the project to identify what went well, what should be stopped, and what should be included for the next iteration. Again, the project team may not possess the competence expertise required. It is analogous to being an internal ISO 9000 implementation team member versus being an external ISO 9000 certified lead auditor. The qualification to judge is very different from the qualification to do.

✧ *Expert evaluation.* Internal or external experts on competence can review the project and its outputs to determine its overall effectiveness. Judgments are typically based on benchmark experience with other organizations and on how this project compares. Some experts may already have developed their own measurement philosophy and approach, one that has been proven valuable in practice. For example, this chapter is a checklist of issues that must be taken into account in designing competency-based HR applications. As such, it can readily be used to evaluate past and present development efforts.

✧ *Performance impact.* At this stage measurement becomes more objective. Performance improvements compared to baseline measurements are used to show the value of competency applications. For example, the performance impact of selecting employees by competency versus using traditional methods could include:

> Higher average sales per person
> Reduction in departmental turnover
> Lower errors per 100 lines of program code
> Reduction in training costs
> Higher acceptance rate for job offers

The measures listed above show the impact on performance of the competency-based HR application. But they are still one level removed from business results.

✧ *Improvement in business results.* A competency application must support the ultimate business goals of profitability, competitiveness, market share growth, rising efficiency, faster time to market, and increasing customer satisfaction. Ideally, competency outcomes can be linked to these business results. For example, reduction in turnover lowers costs, which contributes to profitability. Lowering programming errors increases efficiency and speeds time to market. Higher average sales increases efficiencies.

Measuring the results of competency-based HR applications is the only way to be able to prove success to top management. This requires measurement of current performance at the time the project is started, followed by a second measurement after the application is implemented and has had time to affect the workforce. By building measurements into the project from the start, the application can be designed to facilitate the collection of performance data.

Recommendations

Bring up the topic of measurement early in the development cycle. Get baseline performance numbers before making any changes so that there will be a "before" set of numbers from which to work. Make decisions as to the type of measurement data that will be collected. It may be one of the above, or it may include any combination of these elements.

What Are the Desired Deliverables?

As HR processes begin to be redesigned around competencies, the issue of outputs becomes important. Project deliverables may change frequently during the life of the development effort, but they should be considered as early as possible. Deliverables can include the following.

✧ *Competency model.* The heart of every competency-based HR application is the position competency model. This is typically comprised of twenty or more individual competencies that workers must possess to be qualified for the position. Models can also be created for entire workgroups, with more than one job covered.

✧ *Position standards.* Position standards are the required levels for each competency for each job. Where a workgroup model is being used, standards for single competencies will vary by position.

✧ *Assessment instrument.* This is the measurement tool that will be used to determine levels of competency. The design decisions concerning assessment approaches and instruments are covered later in this chapter.

✧ *Gap reports.* The organization is interested in identifying gaps between employee competence and position standards, and then addressing them with related development resources. Gap reports by individuals are necessary for personal development planning. Summary gap reporting can be used to evaluate workgroups or entire organizations.

✧ *Individual development plans.* The value of an automated process is in connecting groups of databases. Individual gap reports can link assessment results with the enrollment database and with position curriculums. The result is a customized individual development plan listing resources to address any competency gaps identified by the assessment.

✧ *Individual career development plans.* Employees can be assessed for positions to which they aspire, then they can also see what they need to do to become qualified for the promotion. In competency applications in which a single assessment is used for entire sets of positions within a workgroup, this is simply a request for a different report. The data already exists. In applications with unique assessments by position, this means filling out an assessment for each new job.

✧ *Resource deployment plans.* The aggregate report of all employee gaps provides information on development resources needed. Training departments can create development resource schedules for the coming year and form attendee invitation lists for those who need specific resources to address their individual gaps. This way development is provided only as needed.

✧ *Development topic requirements.* Initial assessment efforts usually identify some areas of organizational need where there are no existing resources. Where justified, HR can begin the development process to provide resources that will eliminate the gaps observed and formally add them to the course schedule or online learning system.

There are also one-time opportunities, such as when line managers ask HR, "We've got a regional meeting coming up, and there is a half-day of time where we can insert some development. What should we do?" The assessment database can be analyzed for this workgroup to determine what are the most prevalent and important needs for the entire workgroup. Then a customized development solution addressing one or more specific competencies can be provided for such situations.

✧ *Resource effectiveness feedback.* A major concern in organizations is determining the effectiveness of development resources. Consider training as an example. There are five classic measures of training effectiveness: attendee ratings, end-of-class testing, delayed testing after the attendee has returned to the workplace, interviews with coworkers for observed behavioral changes, and measurement of improvements in business results. An assessment process allows organizations to create a brand new kind of resource effectiveness measure.

Competency assessments can be linked with gap resources and the training administration system. If an employee has a gap for a competency and attending a seminar is indicated, then the organization can track the effect of that seminar on competencies with questions such as: "How many employees have attended this class but are still ranked below standard for any competencies it addresses?" or "How many employees meet standards for this competency without ever having availed themselves of the relevant resources? Are the resources even necessary?"

Assessments give HR a new tool with which to evaluate development resources. Asking these questions and using reports from the assessment administration system, HR can fine-tune its inventory of development activities.

✧ *Online learning links.* As more organizations move to interactive Intranet-based implementations, a new direct linkage between assessment and development resources can be created. It is relatively simple to link an Intranet-based assessment to online learning materials. When a gap is identified, even during the assessment session, employees can immediately be referred to the appropriate development catalog or to online courseware that addresses the competency content. This is the ultimate in real-time assessment and remediation.

Recommendations

The best way to look at deliverables at this stage is to highlight what the organization wants to be able to do. The detailed reports and screens required will come later in the design. But the overall functionality needs to be considered early on.

Who "Owns" the Process?

Quality concepts teach that every process must have an "owner." A process owner is defined as someone who has responsibility for the overall success of the process, and who is also responsible for its continuous improvement. Process owners can improve processes on their own, or they can request to form a process improvement team if the task is complex enough and the potential benefit great enough.

Competency applications are certainly complex enough to justify a team development approach. But a common problem in many organizations is that there is not clear project ownership. Is HR leading the effort? Is this a line function driven by the management of those being assessed? Certainly, a range of individuals from many departments will be involved. But whose appraisal will be negatively affected when there is an unproductive outcome? The person (or department) with this responsibility must also have the authority to own the process.

Recommendations

The professional knowledge and skills required to own an assessment process are not typically found in line operations. Line managers and frontline workers provide subject matter expertise and are essential in the creation and evaluation of competency models and assessment instruments.

An assessment application development process potentially requires skills in consulting, formal team facilitation, job analysis, assessment authoring, test creation, development resource administration, database programming, and online systems development. Expertise in these areas is likely to be found distributed across many administrative staff functions. Because so many departments are affected in competency application development, the process owner is best centrally located rather than remotely based. Professionals within HR or training often are logical candidates for assessment process ownership.

Which Workgroup(s) Will Be Targeted in the Project?

In their enthusiasm over core competencies, many organizations embarked on wide scale implementations of a competency process. As discussed in Chapter 1, a core competency approach cannot substitute for individual position competency models. Core competencies are too general to be valid for hundreds or thousands of individual positions.

Developing competency-based HR applications is an ideal candidate for a targeted pilot implementation. The organization is experimenting with wide-scale change, adding a process roughly the scope of its performance appraisal system. There are issues of culture and climate to manage. Administrative procedures and integrated computing systems have to be developed. This can be better managed and controlled by working with a single department or workgroup at the beginning. Ideal candidate workgroups have the following characteristics:

✧ *Multiple levels.* The initial application should present an opportunity to develop competency models for jobs at several organization levels. This could include frontline workers, supervisors, and middle managers (those who have supervisors reporting to them). These represent significantly different kinds of work activity. It is also helpful to have a mix of line and staff functions in the group. This creates the opportunity to model administrative and support positions.

✧ *Management commitment.* It is hard to overemphasize the importance of management support for competency-related development projects. If top management within the workgroup "really means it" and supports the effort enthusiastically, then middle managers and supervisors who are capable of sinking the project are given proper incentives to succeed. The ideal candidate is a leader who volunteers his or her department for the pilot.

✧ *Good culture and climate.* Choose workgroups that have a well-established culture and a healthy climate. Make certain that there are no leadership dysfunctions or hidden agendas within the department. Workgroups with positive quality climate, satisfaction, or leadership feedback survey results make good candidates for competency projects.

✧ *Structured job positions.* A common error is to start with a department that has extremely complex, interdependent jobs. This complicates identifying and building the competency model and the assessment instrument, particularly when the development team is in the early portion of its learning curve. Search for workgroups that have relatively structured job positions and duties. This helps shorten the model development time and minimizes issues of assessment validity and accuracy. The goal of the pilot program is to establish organizational processes on competencies. Other departments, models, and assessments can be added relatively easily once the overall system is up and running.

Recommendations

Choose the pilot workgroup with care. The development team can greatly complicate its job by choosing a workgroup whose positions cannot be readily modeled. The result is that the team can do everything right and still come out wrong.

Who Will Be Involved in Development?

The first guideline is that the team should include all the potential stakeholders. This means that groups such as HR, organizational development, strategic planning, industrial engineering, training, information technology, legal, management development, customers, suppliers, and the targeted workgroups may need to be represented.

There are also a number of additional skills that should be represented, some of which currently may not be available in the organization. (The first application of competency concepts is the selection of the development team.) The team must be able to perform job analysis, create assessment instruments and tests, design and automate processes either in batch mode or over the Intranet, and set up assessment counseling processes.

This is a good point to discuss the issue of using professionals versus "talented amateurs." Many organizations make the mistake of assuming that teams can substitute for lack of knowledge or skills. For example, a team might be assembled to build a customer survey. But when none of the members have a professional background in survey design, question writing, or statistical analysis, the resulting survey may have problems with response dimensions, questions, and ultimate reliability.

As one development team member put it, "No matter how many of my neighbors I get together, I still can't build an atom bomb." Numbers are not equivalent to knowledge. One nuclear physicist is more valuable than a block's worth of neighbors. Similarly, would patients rather have a team of business people perform brain surgeries, or just one neurosurgeon?

The analogy holds for competency development projects (and it will hold for self-assessment and 360-degree assessment). Bringing stakeholders together does not guarantee that the development team will have the competencies it needs for the project. The team needs qualified professionals in competency-related development. These can be developed internally, hired, or contracted for with vendors, consultants, or outsourcers.

Recommendations

An early development team activity is to take a realistic look at its own internal competencies, then model the requirements needed for the development project. Team members must make a candid assessment of their capabilities as either professionals or talented amateurs. Gaps must then be filled either through development activities or additional help from inside or outside resources.

Who Will Perform the Assessment and upon Whom?

The most critical factor in the success of a competency-based HR application is the competency assessment. It does not matter how exhaustive the model is, how finely detailed the reports are, or how dutifully HR processes are executed; if the measurement methodology is not accurate, the project is a waste.

Two requirements for an assessment are validity and reliability. *Validity* means that the competencies measured are the ones necessary to drive desired business results. *Reliability* means that the measurement instrument accurately captures the true competency levels of employees. (Quality experts would say that the measurement needs to be "free of random error.") In practice, validity and reliability mean that outside factors influencing the assessment must be minimized.

The issue here is who should actually perform the assessment, and who is going to be assessed. There are a variety of approaches ranging from simple self-assessment to complex tests, and everything in between. These can be used singly or in combination to provide results that meet an organization's desired standards of reliability. As with nearly every other aspect of competency-based HR applications, there is a correlation between effort and results. Higher reliability requires more design and implementation sophistication. Following is a range of possible approaches along with the issues they create.

Curriculum Assessment

The simplest method of assessment is to create training curriculums by position. An employee is considered qualified when the course sequence is completed. Qualification is maintained through periodic refresher courses and new training seminars. Examples include schoolteachers needing continuing education credits, nurses needing seminars to stay licensed, and computer-support professionals needing course attendance to become certified.

Curriculum-based systems are attractive because they are easy to track and administer. Attendance records are kept as a normal part of the training enrollment system, and so it is a minor upgrade to add curriculum information and query capabilities to the database. Many training administration software vendors already offer this as a standard function in their systems.

The major weakness is one of accuracy. The attendee's presence in training is considered to be the measure of competence. (Curriculum-based assessment is also known as the BIS—bottoms in seats—method.) Attendance does not guarantee any level of competence.

Creating a curriculum and tracking its completion is an easy first step in adding in competency concepts. Many of the required elements are already in place—seminars, interactive courses, learning activities, and formal mentoring or on-the-job development. In order to create course content and sequences, organizations must begin thinking about what employees in various positions have to know and be able to do. It encourages standardization of methods and performance. It gives everyone common terminology and processes. It starts the employee competence database effort. It gets HR professionals and line managers thinking about what development needs employees have with respect to completing the curriculum.

In general, a curriculum-based competency application provides at least a minimal level of functionality and reliability. Better than doing nothing, it is a start that can be improved upon in a CQI sense.

Self-Assessment

This is currently the most popular method of assessment with early adopters, and therefore requires a thorough analysis. With this approach, employees rate their own competencies by completing some sort of assessment instrument.

The process is quite attractive. It makes intuitive sense since employees know their own needs best. Create a competency model, then survey employees as to where they rank on a continuum scale by competency. This is comfortable to implement. Administration is straightforward. The process is quickly automated and the data is readily compiled.

The primary concern with self-assessment is that of reliability. First, are employees qualified to assess themselves accurately? This approach assumes that employees, based solely on their own work experiences, can reliably rate their level of competence to some absolute scale. The implicit assumption is that every employee naturally possesses the knowledge, ability, and integrity required to assess levels of workplace performance reliably.

The problem is analogous to an organization involved in ISO 9000 quality certification. If individual organizations going through the process were qualified to judge their own status, there would be no need for ISO 9000-certified lead auditors. Similarly, companies could set their own bond quality ratings. Banks could perform their own FDIC audits. There would be no need for colleges to assign grades. Students could announce that they had learned course content at the level they desired and then assign themselves appropriate grades. Gymnasts could assign their own scores as they dismounted the apparatus.

Employees are not trained HR professionals. They were probably not involved in the development of the competency model for their position. In essence, the process is "questioning into ignorance." Employees may not have the experience or the overall workplace perspective to rate their competencies on any beginner/expert style of continuum. Depending upon their own skills, they may not have the insight to understand what truly excellent competence is. (They don't know what they don't know.) This is particularly true of workers at the lower competency levels. They are likely to be the least qualified to provide accurate assessments.

The next problem is consistency. With a self-assessment, particularly when no specialized training in how to complete the assessment has been provided, there is likely to be little consistency among individuals. For example, customer satisfaction survey expert Bob Hayes wrote about asking ten people to tell him the meaning of the word "some," using a number from one to ten. Their answers ranged from "three" to "seven."[3] Imagine employees faced with competency questions such as, "Rate your knowledge of routing and delivery methods: None/Some/Competent/Superior/Expert." Without a thorough understanding of what each word means in general, and what it means for that specific competency, employees with equivalent actual competency often rate themselves quite differently.

A third problem is motivational bias. One cause may be coercive or punitive managers, who are immediately apparent when the results come in. Their subordinates may be reluctant to report competency gaps accurately. The direct reports of one such manager responded to line items only when they could mark "Expert" and left the remaining competencies blank. Another common situation is that of respondents marking "Expert" on every competency, fearful of indicating any perceived weaknesses.

A variation of motivational bias is where employees see the assessment linking to promotion opportunities. They try to "game" the system by figuring out what management wants to see, not only for their current position, but for identifying those ready for promotions. This is prevalent in implementations where management has not clearly communicated exactly what the expected outcomes are for the competency application.

A final problem is perceptual bias. Some individuals cannot accurately see themselves as they really are. One such category is "pronoids," people who overestimate their competence. (Paranoids have delusions of persecution. Pronoids have delusions of acceptability.) Others, due to a lower self-image or higher perceived work standards, underrate their competence. Either way, the assessment responses and resulting development plans are out of line with actual needs.

So self-assessment, while convenient and intuitively logical, has significant potential for reliability problems. At the very least employees must be totally comfortable with the process and its ultimate value to them. They must be clear that the data is going to be used only for development. Assuming that the instrument is properly written—and this is a very large assumption—employees must be formally trained in what all the terms mean and how the instrument should be filled out, and given a large number of examples. Finally, administrators should be alert for any indication of management/supervisor problems that are causing bias in the self-assessments.

360-Degree Assessment

Whereas traditional performance appraisal is a top-down process in which supervisors or managers evaluate subordinates, 360-degree feedback refers to seeking input from others in the workplace, including superiors, coworkers, subordinates, and even customers. In a competency application, this means that anyone in the organization who has interacted with an employee could potentially complete an assessment on that individual.

360-degree assessment is often considered superior to self-assessment. Similar to teams, the belief is that a group view provides a better gauge of an individual's competence. First, the team approach to assessment is thought to eliminate any blind spots or bias existing in self-assessment. Second, it is felt that teams make better decisions than individuals because members synergistically supplement each other's efforts.

This is commonly illustrated in training seminars through a type of group decision-making exercise, such as the "Survival" series. These exercises require team members to solve problems individually first, then through group consensus. The resulting answers are compared to experts' correct answers, and decision-quality scores are computed. In almost all cases, the team will generate a better solution than any of its individual members.

It is possible for 360°-survey approaches to deliver these advantages. Good examples are managerial feedback exercises completed in conjunction with leadership training programs. Differences in self- and 360-degree assessment are readily measured by having both the team and the individual complete assessments. When the results are compared, a leader's self-assessment often shows significant differences from the team's perception.

A 360-degree approach shares many of the advantages of self-assessment, and it makes even more sense. Intuitively, if a person's self-analysis is useful, then a group of second-party opinions must be even more valid. Many organizations are already involved in some form of 360-degree feedback and have achieved a level of workplace acceptance for the process. Administratively, 360-degree assessment is relative easy to set up, circulate, and tabulate, and it can be automated readily.

Yet there are serious concerns. The problem of a respondent not having the qualifications to assess competencies accurately is multiplied. Coworkers have less knowledge about the jobs of others than those performing them. For example, in the case of subordinates assessing managers, the subordinates may not have ever had any managerial experience or training, and they therefore have no real basis upon which to make the assessment. What is the validity of individuals assessing coworkers when the assessors (1) may only interact with the person, (2) may never have actually done the job, (3) don't necessarily understand the processes involved, and (4) have never been trained in assessing others?

Consistency is an even bigger problem with 360-degree assessment because of an increase in the level of complexity. Assessment application designers now have two areas of consistency to worry about. Respondents have to be internally consistent in their own ratings of different coworkers, and they also need to be externally consistent with other respondents in assessing individual coworkers. Multiply this by several coworkers whose specific competencies have to be assessed for their unique positions, and maintaining consistency quickly exceeds the capabilities of a typical person.

360-degree assessment introduces a different kind of motivational bias. The assumption is that respondents altruistically assess their coworkers in order to help them identify developmental needs. This assumption of goodwill may not be justified. Workers are being asked to assess people who may be their competitors for upcoming promotions. This introduces a very real conflict of interest, one in which a respondent may have a personal interest in the outcome of others' assessments. This is a difficult temptation for even the most objective coworker to handle. While there may be no conscious effort to lower a competitor's assessment, the potential for bias cannot be ignored.

Outside the business world, conflict of interest is usually eliminated whenever it is identified. Legislators put their assets into blind trusts so that their voting is not affected by personal gain or loss. Judges recuse themselves when they discover a possible conflict of interest with a case they are trying. Smart parents never umpire their own child's ball game. In these situations, the existence of a potential conflict, while not necessarily affecting the outcome, taints any result, and the same holds true for having potential workplace competitors assess each other.

Finally, perceptual bias still exists with 360-degree techniques. The only thing respondents are truly expert on concerning their coworkers is their own feelings. In many 360° systems, respondents are not really assessing competencies, they are merely indicating how satisfied they are with a coworker's interaction with them. Even with careful efforts in the creation of competency models and instruments, a 360°-assessment process can quickly deteriorate into little more than a satisfaction survey ("Rate your coworker on communications skills" or "This individual's conflict management skills are . . .").

360-degree assessment is a common tool for many organizations, but its basic assumptions can be challenged. Without significant support and validation processes built into a competency application, 360-degree assessment can deliver results with only minimal validity. At best, consistency must be continually monitored and managed. In an unhealthy organizational culture, 360-degree techniques can turn the workplace into a war zone where coworkers can take anonymous shots at each other and at management. In either case, these are significant challenges to assessing competencies successfully.

Testing

This assessment technique is a conceptual leap from the subjective to the objective. It is a standard method of establishing minimum competencies for many professions, such as automobile drivers, lawyers, real estate agents, professional engineers, insurance agents, brokers, CPAs, pilots, physicians, and actuaries. Yet despite the popularity of testing in professional certification and licensing, it has been slow to catch on internally in many organizations.

Part of the overall reluctance to implement testing may have been due to everyone's lengthy school experience. The work world was seen to be the end of regurgitating facts and the beginning of actual performance. Now, however, testing is becoming more and more acceptable as a means to ascertain workplace knowledge and competence.

Testing addresses many of the concerns about self- and 360-degree assessment. Where assessment by individuals provides an opinion, testing potentially provides a measure of what the respondent knows and can do. The test becomes a standardized tool with an objectively measured result. Motivation and perception bias are no longer an issue.

Testing shifts the responsibility for reliability and consistency from the distributed respondent to the centralized test author, because reliability is now totally dependent upon the quality of the instrument. This can cause problems, of course. On the difficult/easy scale, writing valid test questions is very difficult. It is not a skill the typical HR department possesses. It is far easier for HR staff to write general competency questions with a rating dimension for a response.

Further, new factors come into play with testing. Testing gets an organization into the education business, where it is often far behind its K–12 or university cohorts. Unlike the educational system, few organizations have processes in place to assist individuals with special needs. Testing for competence hurts people who are not good test-takers. And some workers may be physical, visual, or auditory learners rather than textual learners.

Similarly, testing tends to unfairly underrate employees with learning and perceptual disabilities. The test, as a verbal instrument, must deal effectively with cultural issues of perception, comprehension, vocabulary, use of words and sentences, and English as a second language. Any disconnect between the construction of the test and the comprehension of the respondents reduces the validity of the results.

Another major concern with testing for competence is in thoroughness. Today's case-worker positions require a wide range of general knowledge in addition to a mastery of position-specific facts and processes. Testing cannot provide the same overall perspective used in self- or 360-degree assessment. An individual or coworker may well understand the overall competence of someone on the job, whereas a test establishes only how much someone knows about what is asked. Testing is a statistical sampling technique where the subset of information tested is assumed to accurately reflect the total body of knowledge and skills a worker possesses.

For example, a network administrator needs to have an extensive general knowledge of personal computing and server software. Study guides for the Microsoft Certified System Engineer (MCSE) exams contain literally thousands of pages full of facts and procedures. Six tests, each approximately one hour long, can cover only a miniscule portion of what MCSEs need to know to be effective. Yet candidates can pass tests by answering as few as thirty questions on something as complex as "Implementing and Supporting Windows NT Servers." This has led to what information technology professionals call "paper MCSEs"—people who are certified but cannot do anything useful because they have not had any real experience with networks.

Position tests require far more development time and resources to create than do assessment instruments. They demand a higher level of educational and competency professional expertise from the author. Done correctly, test assessments provide a more objective, accurate, and consistent measure of the relevant competencies. Many organizations will shift to testing as their competency assessment applications mature and improve.

Business Results

The next higher level of competency measurement involves looking at actual business results generated by the individual. The emphasis must be on individual business results rather than the results of workgroups or the organization. The assumption behind this approach is that business results measure competence in people. For example, salespeople who make assigned quotas are considered to be more competent than salespeople who do not meet their goals.

The attraction to management of this approach is that it provides a direct link between competence and desired business outcomes. There is a *Field of Dreams*-style assumption: "If they are competent, results will come." Since results are the evidence of competence, normal business data becomes the assessment.

The flawed assumption is that there is a direct cause-and-effect relationship between competencies and business results. Employees do not have total control over their processes and are not solely responsible for outcomes. Therefore, using business results as an assessment means that people are being measured based on factors not addressed by their competencies. This is clearly unfair.

An even bigger danger is that this approach appears to be a performance appraisal, not a competency assessment. The definitions in Chapter 1 explained that competency assessment ascertains whether an employee is qualified to do the job. Competency does not mean actual performance. Appraisal and compensation systems are already in place for that purpose.

The effect of competency-based HR applications on business results is best analyzed at levels above the individual. Before-and-after studies of workgroup performance can be completed. For example, researchers studied the effects of using competencies as employee selection criteria rather than traditional methods.[4] As shown in Table 2-2, they found that the more complex the job, the greater the benefits of using competencies to select superior employees. This is a valid use of business results to measure the effects of competency-based HR applications at a group level. Attempting to use business results for individuals moves the application away from competencies and interferes with the existing performance appraisal process.

Many organizations begin with simple curriculum models and course attendance records. They then move to simple individual or 360-degree assessment. Next they incorporate testing, starting with seminars and courseware and, ultimately, assessment instruments.

The pace of this migration is often driven by technology. Batch systems are giving way to interactive applications. A few leading-edge organizations are now putting the entire competency-based HR system on their Intranet. This online availability of applications facilitates the administration of assessments and tests across the entire organization.

Recommendations

The best competency applications should utilize a range of assessment techniques, from individual assessments to testing. The approach may depend upon competencies being measured. Self- or 360-degree assessment may continue to be used for soft skills. Information and process mastery will require interactive applications, delivered either on internal Intranets or by outside service providers over the Web. Ultimately, the assessment process will close the loop with development in real time. Competency applications will be integrated into the online learning system. When individuals identify a shortfall in required competencies, they will immediately be sent to the appropriate learning content site.

How Are Assessments Validated?

The previous sections covered the concerns about the reliability of self-assessments and 360-degree assessments. If these methods are going to be used, then decisions have to be made about how responses will be validated. Again, there

Table 2-2. Business results of using competencies as selection criteria.

Job	Productivity
Low complexity	+19%
Moderate complexity	+32%
High complexity	+48%

is a range of choices depending upon the degree of reliability desired and the resources available to execute at that level.

No Verification

The easiest approach is to defer the issue. Employee assessment of competencies is certainly more valid than no assessment at all. Developers may initially wish to concentrate on creating accurate competency models and their associated assessment questions. The decision to include a verification step can be made after the first set of responses is tabulated.

Informal Verification

A simple examination of results can provide a basic validity check. One approach is to select ten recognized superstars and ten obvious strugglers and examine their assessment responses in detail. See if their responses reflect their relative competency levels. Look at the variation in responses for each competency. Are results skewed high or low? Is the range wide or narrow? Also examine summaries by manager. Data from groups that have negative environments will be skewed to the high end, or will be incomplete due to questions not answered or assessments not turned in.

  If there are concerns about the process, have informal conversations with a wide range of people being assessed. Their off-the-record comments will provide good indicators of what is going right or wrong with the entire process. A careful investigation can often deliver as much benefit as a time-consuming and costly formal validation process.

Survey Employees

Useful data can be gathered by openly asking employees their opinions about the reliability of the assessment. This is best done shortly after the feedback sessions have been completed and the individuals assessed have had an opportunity to talk to each other about the process. The survey should be confidential, with no employees' responses identified by name. When there are trust issues with management, this survey is best tabulated by third parties outside the organization. Figure 2-2 shows an example of a straightforward survey on reliability.

Managerial Validation

Another way to provide a check on accuracy is to have the manager or supervisor also assess the employee. Managers can use the same instrument as the employee, or they can fill out a simplified assessment by category rather than by competency. Managers and employees then meet to work through their differences until both agree on the assessment responses.

Figure 2-2. Assessment reliability survey.

You recently completed a self-assessment of your competencies for your current job. The goal of the assessment process is that all employees will receive the development resources they need. The HR department is working to insure that self-assessments are as accurate and reliable as possible. This confidential survey will help HR continue to improve the assessment process.

Please respond to the following statements using this scale:

     5 = strongly agree
     4 = agree
     3 = neither agree nor disagree
     2 = disagree
     1 = strongly disagree

☐ I believe that the assessment results will be used for development purposes only as promised.
☐ I believe that I will not impact my performance rating by indicating any development needs on the self-assessment.
☐ I filled out the self-assessment as accurately as possible and did not rate myself higher than actual.
☐ I believe my coworkers filled out their self-assessments as accurately as possible and did not rate themselves higher than actual.

Comments:

Thank you for your assistance in completing this survey. All responses will be kept in complete confidence. Responses and comments will be tabulated and reported as a group without identifying the source of any individual input.

360-Degree Validation

Similar to managerial validation, 360-degree feedback can be used as validation rather than as the actual assessment. Optionally, where communications and culture are good, the individual and the coworkers who did the validation assessment can work through any variances, usually in a facilitated team meeting. The difference between 360-degree validation and 360-degree assessment is that here the individual still has the ultimate authority to specify the response.

Audit Sampling

This approach is similar to the Internal Revenue Service's compliance audit program. Here a representative subset of respondents is contacted and asked to verify every line item of their assessment. This can be done either in person or over the phone. The size of the subset can be determined either statistically based on desired confidence levels or behaviorally based upon data closure; i.e., no real change in results is generated from adding more samples.

The goal is to have the assessment expert/auditor provide the standardization to determine what the true assessment should have been. Errors high or low can be identified, and overall accuracy statistics can be computed. For example, an organization might discover that 85 percent of responses were accurate, with 60 percent of the errors caused by ratings higher than actual and 40 percent of the errors caused by ratings lower than actual.

The names of those audited are not released. All the organization is concerned about is estimating the accuracy of assessment responses. In an environment of CQI, problem areas can then be addressed in the next assessment instrument.

Recommendations

Organizations may wish to utilize several of these techniques concurrently, particularly in the early stages of a new application. Informal validation is always useful. Managerial validation is an excellent way to gain leadership's involvement and buy-in. Audit sampling involves experts in the assessment process, people who truly understand the model and are qualified to administer it. The audit generates measurable quality data that can be used to track assessment validity over time in order to facilitate improving the instrument continuously. Each of these makes its own unique contributions to the assessment process and has a place in most competency-based HR applications.

How Is the Project Going to Be Communicated to the Organization?

Adding competency-based processes to HR applications is a change of major proportions. Anything this significant and far reaching is likely to create a large amount of activity on the rumor mill, much of it driven by uncertainty, fear, and anxiety. Perhaps it is too much to hope that everyone will be enthusiastic about new competency-based HR applications, but they should see the value of committing to the effort. It is essential that all present and future stakeholders "mean it" if the development project is to be successful.

Recommendations

Informally, urge development team members to communicate with their peers and departments about the project. Organizationally, use both formal and informal communications tools. Create a positive buzz about the project and its benefits to all participants. Keep focusing on how the applications will make all the HR functions more effective. Provide updates as to the project status.

If warranted, share as much information as possible. One organization placed the first draft of its assessment instrument on the wall, then put an electronic copy on the server and invited everyone in the pilot department to e-mail back comments and suggestions. Show screen layouts around and get future users' reactions to any interactive systems. In general, make the project extremely open and accessible. This is the best way to eliminate concerns about motives, and it also can improve the ultimate solution through early feedback from frontline employees who will be completing assessments.

Sample Project Plan

In 1995, the Anheuser-Busch Learning Center (BLC) embarked on a competency modeling and reporting project for its field sales department. This consisted of personnel who call on Anheuser-Busch (A-B) wholesalers, large national accounts, and retailers across the United States. The department consisted of ten regional offices with supervisors and frontline personnel deployed in home offices throughout the country. Here are the decisions they made in designing a program that was very successful in meeting their desired outcomes.

1. *Does the organization really mean it?* Project approval came directly from the vice president of sales. A-B allocated significant budget and personnel to the effort.

2. *Is the goal quality or excellence?* A-B chose a quality approach. It wanted to help every employee meet position standards. Employees were to be assessed to standards by position and have their competency gaps identified. Then individual development plans were to be created.

3. *Is the development effort continuous or periodic?* Development was periodic. The department had just undergone its first major sales reorganization in nearly twenty years. Time was going to be required for the department to digest the changes and adapt all its processes, so the model was assumed to have some stability for the next several years.

4. *Is the assessment a rolling process or a batch one?* The entire assessment process was periodic. Assessments were completed near the end of the calendar year. The data was then used to create course calendars for the following year, to identify potential attendees, and to provide input for creating or acquiring new development resources.

5. *Does the model reflect what is or what should be?* Due to the recent reorganization, the challenge was to document the new "what is."

6. *What should the expectations be for the competency project time?* Total development time for the initial project was approximately eighteen months. This was on time, and deadlines for the first assessment were met. Continuous improvement was anticipated. (Over a period of four years, the assessment instrument had minor modifications made before each succeeding annual assessment.)

7. *How are the results going to be used by management?* Managers did a superb job of positioning the process and executing to their promises. Assessments were kept separate from well-established performance appraisal and salary administration systems. Assessment results were clearly used by the BLC to provide more targeted development resources.

8. *What are the desired outcomes for the organization?* Sales department employees at A-B were a mix of recent hires and old hands with more than twenty years of experience. A-B wanted to eliminate wasted training and to know what new training to develop. The project was financially justified by the projected elimination of a single wasted day of training per person per year. Any increases in effectiveness were considered to be added value.

9. *What are the desired outcomes for employees?* At the time of the project, performance expectations for the sales positions in the new organizational structure were not clearly defined. A side benefit of creating competency models was the identification of competency standards and tasks for the new positions. Other benefits were curriculums for the new positions so that sales employees would know what courses they should be attending. The summary reports given to individuals included relating gaps to available courses and the creation of a development plan that supported their specific market objectives for the coming year. Finally, employees could ask to be mapped to a position they aspired to so that they could see what was needed to become qualified for that promotion.

10. *How will success be measured?* First, development project goals were met. Assessments were completed, reports were tabulated, printed, and distributed, and counseling sessions with managers were held. The entire process fed the enrollment system and the R&D process for creating new development resources. The only other feedback was informal. Due to the frequency of promotions and moves between regions, the A-B sales department is a highly networked system. The general opinion about a project can usually be readily determined with a few well-placed phone calls. Key managers and frontline individuals were contacted for feedback on the overall attitude and effectiveness of the program.

11. *What are the desired deliverables?* The system generated these reports for individuals: assessment to standards summary, gap report with associated development resources, curriculum status, market plan, and manager's validation summary. The organization utilized customizable reports indicating gaps by competency and development resources needed. All organizational reports could be selected down to individual attendee in order to create invitation lists.

12. *Who "owns" the process?* The project leader was an assistant on the vice president's staff. In the latter stages of development, ownership was shifted to the BLC for administration and any further updates.

13. *What workgroups will be targeted in the project?* The A-B project included all field sales personnel except for administrative assistants in regional

offices. The regional structures were identical, and there were ten different professional and managerial positions to model.

14. *Who will be involved in the development?* The project was initially managed by the vice president's staff assistant. The development effort was headed by an experienced project manager in the BLC. The job analysis effort was led by a manager in the A-B corporate organizational development department. Employees from other departments were utilized as needed. An outside consultant was used to help create the assessment instrument, to program the relational database used for tabulating results, to administer the assessment, and to prepare and distribute reports.

15. *Who will perform the assessment, and upon whom?* A-B chose to use self-assessment for this initial implementation. There was some concern about reliability, but this was shown not to be an issue. Instructions were provided with the assessment, and phone support from the consulting firm was available to employees.

16. *How are assessments validated?* The list of competencies was divided up into categories, each containing five to seven line items. Managers were reluctant to fill out complete assessments on each of their people, so a shorter assessment form asking managers to assess subordinates only by category was created and tabulated. This became the basis for discussions when managers met with subordinates to do development planning. At that time, managers went over employees' assessment inputs item by item.

A-B found that, in general, bias was not an important issue. Employees generally rated themselves lower than did their managers. Employees said they were excited at the opportunity to receive training and saw the assessment as a way to obtain their fair share. Managers admitted that they did not have enough detailed knowledge of the subordinate's actual competencies.

There were a few instances of managers who did not have the right trust environment with their employees. Assessment summary reports quickly highlighted these situations. Employees were contacted, had the process again explained to them, and then filled out another self-assessment.

17. *How is the project going to be communicated to the organization?* A-B has a history of utilizing field sales panels made up of frontline personnel and managers. Membership on this panel is considered to be positive recognition and is assigned on a rotating basis. The field sales panel was kept up to date on the project. In addition, as part of the job analysis, A-B brought in focus groups for each of ten jobs for a three-day analysis and input session. The attendees represented nearly one-sixth of the field sales staff, which meant that the entire sales organization was aware of the effort from the beginning.

Next Steps

A-B has now converted the original periodic, paper-based, batch-mode competency application into an electronic form for its corporate Intranet. This will be discussed in more detail in Chapter 9.

Anheuser-Busch's implementation is not a model for other organizations. It is a sample showing the decisions made by one company in its first implementation, begun before Intranet technology was widely available. The issues covered in this chapter have been identified through experience and can prevent many serious problems later on. Figure 2-3 shows a design decision worksheet for stepping through the questions and options described in this chapter.

There are a multitude of possible paths in working through this chapter. Making decisions as a group will keep the design team focused on the desired outcomes, minimize later problems, and speed project cycle time. Once these decisions are made, the work of building competency models can begin.

Learning Points

1. There are important design decisions that must be made at the very start of a competency project in order to eliminate later problems.
2. The first implementation should be done right or not at all. This means management has to commit to it, communicate it, fund it, support it, and execute it. Management may also have to change the organization's culture in order to make it work at all.
3. All the anticipated outcomes must be clear. This includes quality or excellence, management and individual outcomes, and measures for success.
4. Logistics have to be determined, such as selecting the development team, planned project length, periodic or rolling development and administration, current or future process competencies, deliverables, project leadership and involvement, groups to be assessed, and assessment methodology and validation.

Notes

1. Jerry B. Harvey, *The Abilene Paradox and Other Meditations on Management* (San Francisco: Jossey-Bass Publishers, 1996), 13–15.
2. Philip B. Crosby, *Quality Is Free* (New York: New American Library, 1980), 15.
3. Bob E. Hayes, *Measuring Customer Satisfaction: Development and Use of Questionnaires* (Milwaukee: ASQC Quality Press, 1991), 51.
4. J.E. Hunter, F.L. Schmidt, and M.K. Judiesh, "Individual Differences in Output Variability as a Function of Job Complexity," *Journal of Applied Psychology* 75 (1990): 28–42.

Figure 2-3. Design decisions worksheet.

1. Does the organization really mean it? (How management is going to prove it.)

2. Is the goal quality or excellence?	☐ Meets standards	☐ Variable grading
3. Development effort?	☐ Periodic	☐ Continuous
4. Assessments performed?	☐ Periodic	☐ Continuous
5. Model which processes?	☐ Current	☐ What should be

6. Management's expectations about the project (schedule, development resources, improvements, continuing resources):

7. How are results going to be used by management (improvement process, separate from appraisals)?

8. What are the desired outcomes for the organization?

☐ Meet vendor requirements   ☐ Better internal placement
☐ Enhance the marketing position   ☐ Training/development efficiencies
☐ Hiring effectiveness   ☐ Increased productivity
☐ Other: ☐ Better organizational performance

9. What are the desired outcomes for employees?

☐ Can get needed training   ☐ More rational personnel decisions
☐ Easier to show qualifications   ☐ More competent coworkers
☐ Ability to prepare for the new/next job   ☐ Healthier, more competitive employer
☐ Other:

10. How will success be measured?

☐ Project fulfillment   ☐ Expert evaluation
☐ Anecdotal sampling   ☐ Performance impact
☐ Project team formal evaluation   ☐ Improvement in business results
☐ Other:

Figure 2-3. *(continued)*

11. What are the deliverables?
 	
     ☐ Competency model   ☐ Individual career development plans
     ☐ Position standards   ☐ Resource deployment plans
     ☐ Gap reports   ☐ Development topic requirements
     ☐ Individual development plans   ☐ Online learning links
     ☐ Other:

12. Who "owns" the process?
13. What workgroup(s) will be targeted in the project? (Good candidates offer: multiple job levels, management commitment, good culture and climate, and structured job duties.)
14. Who will be involved in the development?

15. Who will perform the assessment, and upon whom?
 	
     ☐ Curriculum assessment   ☐ Testing
     ☐ Self-assessment   ☐ Business results
     ☐ 360-degree assessment   ☐ Other:

16. How are assessments validated?
 	
     ☐ No verification   ☐ Managerial validation
     ☐ Informal verification   ☐ 360 validation
     ☐ Employee surveys   ☐ Audit sampling
     ☐ Other:

17. How is the project going to be communicated to the organization?

Sources of
Competency Information

Position models are at the heart of every competency-based HR application. They are living GIGO (garbage in–garbage out) test factories. No matter how sophisticated the assessment, no matter how intricate and timely the on-line administration, the results are useless if models are not accurate and complete representations of their relative positions. Get this wrong and the competency application is doomed.

Not surprisingly, competency modeling is very hard to do. It falls well outside the comfort zone of most HR professionals because it is not a standard part of their skill set. HR practitioners do not have any experience at formalized competency modeling. There are no modeling courses in college curriculums and no competency professional certification programs. There are few public enrollment seminars and conferences. Everyone is talking about competency applications, but finding an organization with a mature implementation in place is difficult.

Fortunately, HR professionals have many skills that are transferable to building competency models. In addition, there is a wide range of position-related documentation that can be utilized in identifying competencies. What is required is a process that can be followed to create valid models. As usual, there is not a single best process to recommend. Everything depends upon the situation, available information, people and financial resources required, and how rigorous management wants the effort to be.

Everything Is Based on Processes

The basic tool for generating competency models is the concept of processes. As Figure 1-4 showed, processes are made up primarily of activities (rectangles) and decisions (diamonds). Activities require skills, and decisions require knowledge. Thus, continuing questions for the design team are:

1. What does the employee have to be able to do?
2. What does the employee have to know to do it?

The answers are much easier to determine when there are flowcharts for job processes, but this is rarely the case. Therefore, the design team, along with subject matter experts, managers, or position holders, will have to step through major process activities to determine necessary competencies. If an item is not related to a specific process step, then it is not a valid competency.

Categorizing Competencies

Getting started in competency modeling is always difficult. The design team finds itself sitting in a room asking, "Now what do we do?" The best way to search for competencies is with a top-down approach, from general to specific. The top level of this approach is to step through the categories of position competencies and begin building the list. The first of these categories is often taken for granted yet should receive careful consideration when building models.

By Assumption

Certain competencies are assumed to be present in every employee. Closely related to "conditions of employment," these address issues such as behavior, ethics, and work habits. Many development teams do not take time to discuss these as candidates for their competency models because they are assumed to be traits that every worker has. The reason to consider them here is that the competency model will ultimately be expanded beyond employee assessment and development into the areas of candidate identification, selection, and hiring/promotion. At this level these necessary competencies cannot be assumed; they must be verified. Even if they don't make their way into the models used for employee assessment, they may ultimately need to be part of those used for employee acquisition.

Consider "honesty" as a potential general competency. It is an attitude that affects the job. It correlates to performance. There are numerous ethics instruments used in industry to test for honesty so it can be measured to response norms. And honesty can be developed or improved through programs such as open book management or ethics training. So, theoretically, Honesty could be included in a universal competency list for employees.

The opposing argument is that honesty is a trait that all employees should bring to the workplace. It is a condition of employment that either exists or does not exist in the personality of the individual, and it should not be included with trainable items such as Punch Press Operations. People do not have to be trained or developed for honesty as adults. It is either there or it is not.

The value of this argument occurs in reframing the discussion to understand where honesty fits into a job. The team can ask, "What situations occur on the job where honesty is even an issue?" or "When do employees on this job have to make decisions that might be affected by their honesty?"

For example, service representatives are trained to present their products in the best possible light. So what is the answer when a customer asks, "Have you been getting a lot of trouble calls from other buyers?" An honest response is not very flattering to the organization, "We've been deluged with complaints about this product . . ." A more positive reply might be, "I don't know the exact call volumes, but we're aware of the problem and are working on a rapid fix. Let me have your name and number, and we'll get back to you as soon as we have a resolution."

So what starts as an honesty issue is transformed into a complaint handling skill that is a strong candidate for a customer service representative competency model. In this way, Honesty might generate a group of derived competencies, all identified by figuring out when the service employee would have to think about conveying raw information versus coming up with a more service-oriented spin. Similar discussions can be generated by borderline assumptive competencies such as diversity sensitivity, stress management, work-at-home productivity, or time management.

Additional assumptive competencies can be generated by examining issues from a negative viewpoint. While the final model should contain positive definitions of competencies, it is a useful idea generation technique to discuss employee dysfunction. Candidate topics might be gossiping, personal business at work, negative attitudes and moodiness, unwillingness to change, playing favorites, thinking only about the department's welfare, not taking the extra step for customer service, or not taking responsibility for quality improvement. These are typical attitude problems from the "Won't Do" category in Figure 1-3. As such, they are not good candidates for competencies, but they can still generate other possibilities.

Take gossiping as an example. This could lead into a discussion of skills for recognizing and handling sensitive information. Unwillingness to change might link to knowledge of process measurement, analysis, and improvement techniques. Playing favorites may stimulate a conversation about decision-making criteria and methods. Personality issues such as moodiness are harder to link but still create opportunities for discussion about how these behaviors affect job performance or how they might relate to Communications Skills competencies.

The main goal in this section is to determine where to draw the line first for employee assessment applications, then for hiring/promoting. This is both a philosophical and a systems decision, and one that is greatly affected by the industry involved. Supermarkets have an enormous problem with shrinkage due to delivery person and check-in clerk collaboration. Many chains require that all employees complete psychological honesty tests before being hired. New employees then attend follow-up training on ethics and business controls during their orientation period. On the other hand, someone taking an office job and shuffling papers all day may never receive any specific training on ethics.

Whatever the approach, the decision should be a conscious one made by the development team. If competency modeling is going to be utilized throughout HR processes, then assumptive issues will need to be addressed somewhere, if not in the competency models used for individual assessments.

By Law

Government and its associated regulatory agencies create requirements that apply to all workers. For example, the Civil Rights Act of 1964 specifies that discrimination with regard to age, race, color, religion, sex, national origin, handicap, or veteran status is illegal. (Several states have statutes that add to this list.) In 1980, the Equal Employment Opportunity Commission issued Final Guidelines as an amendment to the *Guidelines on Discrimination because of Sex*.[1] Its definitions of three types of sexual harassment have since been upheld and further defined by Supreme Court rulings.

A host of other legislation affects the workplace, including:

Age Discrimination in Employment Act, as Amended
National Labor Relations Act
The Federal Wage Garnishment Law
Occupational Safety and Health Act
Immigration Reform and Control Act
Employee Polygraph Protection Act
Worker Adjustment and Retaining Notification Act
Pregnancy Discrimination Act

These acts, coupled with regulations from a wide array of agencies such as the Securities and Exchange Commission, National Labor Relations Board, Environmental Protection Agency, Occupational Health and Safety Administration, and the Internal Revenue Service, are massive potential sources for competency line items because of government-dictated processes that must be followed. This requires not only knowledge of the regulations but also an understanding of how to comply with them and report the results.

Other governmental regulations apply to specific industries. For example, a trucking company must follow strict rules for handling hazardous materials. Tractors and trailers have to be properly marked. Drivers must be certified by class of material. Warehouses have to pass inspections of the physical plant and procedures. Materials must be properly packaged, labeled, and handled. Routes may be controlled, and there may be special driving rules, such as stopping at railroad tracks. Specialized record keeping and reporting is required. The cost for noncompliance can be enormous in terms of health and welfare, actual damages, legal fees, and regulatory fines. These massive sets of rules and regulations must ultimately find their way into the competency models for trucking company jobs, including managers, administrators, supervisors, loaders, and drivers.

Regulations thus provide a source of position competencies for every worker in the United States and for workers in specific industries. It is impossible to include everything the government mandates without making the model unwieldy, but major items such as proper job interview procedures or sexual harassment guidelines and responses may well find their way onto nearly every competency model in the organization.

By Industry

Individual industries have their own professional competency models and assessment approaches. These range from official licensing to unofficial industry group guidelines and certifications. As was pointed out in Chapter 2, many industries require practitioners to pass state-sanctioned licensing examinations, including:

Real estate sales agents and brokers
Insurance sales agents
Securities sales agents
Professional engineers
Lawyers
Police officers (must also pass academy coursework)
Firefighters

Other industry organizations provide certification programs that, while not official in a legal sense, establish for the consuming public that an individual has achieved a certain level of professional expertise. These programs are usually sponsored by trade groups or associations, and they can require a term of industry experience, a specified level of education, self-study or completion of a set curriculum, and passing of a certification examination. There are literally hundreds of industry-wide examples, such as:

Certified Administrative Manager
Certified Speaking Professional
Certified Life Underwriter
Certified Wood Flooring Installer
Certified Financial Planner
Certified Residential Specialist

There are potentially thousands of vendor certification programs, usually for usage, maintenance, and repair of products. This is particularly prevalent in the computer industry, where hardware manufacturers train and qualify repair technicians on their computers and peripherals. Software vendors have even more extensive certification processes. The Microsoft Certified System

Engineer designation requires passing six exams and can take twelve months to complete. Novell has its Certified Netware Administrator and higher-level Certified Netware Engineer sequences. Visit a personal computer store's repair department and there will be technician certification wall plaques from IBM, Compaq, Hewlett-Packard, and Toshiba among numerous others.

Finally, industry groups can provide other nonofficial material that is useful in investigating competencies. These might take the form of publications covering ethical guidelines or professional standards. This documentation is particularly helpful because it recommends industry best practices that professionals should follow.

Certification programs provide an excellent source for general industry competencies. The sponsoring government department, vendor, or trade association has done much of the preliminary work. Their study materials and sample exams provide great input to position models and assessment instruments and can save the development team a significant amount of work.

By Organization

Enterprise-wide documents provide the next general source of competency information. At the top level are vision, value, and mission statements. These reflect the overall philosophy of the organization, where it is headed, what it does, and how it should act. There may not be anything detailed enough to generate a specific competency line item, but these statements should be reviewed for possible content.

For example, one of the corporate values of a high-growth manufacturer is "We will set aggressive goals and significantly exceed them." If their salespeople are not performing at 200 percent of quota, management thinks something is wrong. Therefore, universal competencies such as Creativity, Problem Solving, Reengineering, Change Management, and Process Improvement might be indicated for this firm.

IBM's corporate motto was "Think." Its classic values, originated with Thomas Watson, were respect for the individual, excellence, and customer service. These values generated competency requirements in dealing with employees, in creating products, and in providing service. When Lou Gerstner took over IBM, he commented publicly, "The last thing IBM needs right now is more vision."[2] He refocused IBM on execution in the marketplace and on profitability. IBM became much less employee-friendly and much more efficiency-minded. In today's market, with low-end and midrange computers turning into commodities that can be purchased directly over the Internet, and with profit being driven out of the hardware business, services are the big growth opportunities for computer manufacturers such as IBM. The organizational competencies that employees will bring to their jobs need to reflect the changing overall vision and mission of the company.

Vision, mission, and value statements may not provide very many competencies to an individual position's model, but these statements should still receive some attention from the design team. The statements can help establish an overall theme for the model, as with IBM. They will also be useful when it comes to tightening up the model. Going back to the organization's basic statements provides additional input for the keep/cut decision.

By Workgroup

Another category level is the workgroup. In many organizations, departments have their own versions of vision, value, and mission statements. These can be used just like the organizational statements to provide input for competency line items. Departments may also have specialized procedures and documentation that apply only in situations unique to their workgroup. This could be caused by jobs that require travel, entertaining customers, handling money, working with sensitive information such as personnel or R&D data, clean room operations, equipment operation, and so on.

Workgroup-level competencies are more common in organizations with hybrid job structures, such as self-directed work teams or case worker teams. Here everyone in the department may need to be qualified to do anyone's job. Workgroup-level competencies are also required when the model is designed to let multiple titles be assessed using a single instrument. Again, the benefit of this approach is that any employee can be evaluated for a different position without having to complete a new assessment. Management can also query the database at any time to find out who is qualified for an upcoming open position and then create a candidate list.

By Background Information

A special category of competency input has to do with background knowledge. What general business, industry, or company information is required to meet job standards? Do technicians need to understand both binary and hexadecimal number systems for today's numerically controlled manufacturing machinery? Probably not, but this is covered in many basic programming concepts courses.

Conversely, do drivers need to know how a limited slip differential works? Although it might be helpful in bad weather to understand which wheels have traction, this is not part of the licensing exam. It is useful but not required background information. As far as the state license bureau is concerned, the car is a black box that magically transports people from place to place. No general knowledge about automobile mechanics is required. Drivers do not even have to show that they can operate both automatic transmission and stick shifts. All that matters is that licensed drivers can pass license and eye exams and can operate just one car correctly.

Design teams have been forced to rethink the general knowledge and skills assumed to be present and that usually get omitted from a competency model. This is a particularly important issue when the model will be extended to hiring and promotion decisions. For example, many managers have commented, "I don't know what the schools are doing these days. Nobody knows how to write any more." Yet few organizations assess writing skills in candidates and employees, nor do they have plans to begin doing so.

A major chemical company offered a series of personnel development courses on an optional sign-up basis. Fees were very reasonable and were paid by the employee's department. To the surprise of the HR department, of fifteen or so courses offered each term, the only two that always had full enrollments were basic math and basic reading skills, both of which were taught by grade school teachers. There were a large number of employees that had been hired without the necessary minimum skills to do their jobs. When courses became available, employees quickly signed up.

Another organization found itself in a difficult situation when it hired a young woman for a sales position. After a two-week orientation process, she was asked to deliver some information to a customer location. When she asked, "What bus goes there?" the manager realized that she didn't have a driver's license. It never occurred to anyone in the hiring process that a person could not drive, so no one ever asked about it.

While background competencies such as reading, writing, and driving may not be important enough to end up on a position list, they may be critical on a hiring competency list and must at least be evaluated. These questions must be considered, "What general knowledge and skills are we taking for granted or overlooking? Are they important for employees to possess, and can they be improved? If so, are they worth including in the competency model and assessing?"

There is also a wide range of organizational background information to be considered. Does every employee need to know the organization chart and what every department does? Do employees need to know what is in the policy manual so that they can look things up when they have questions? This is important in understanding where to go for necessary information and where to send others who need something the employee cannot provide.

What about details of other departments? Do Kellogg's employees outside the plants need to know how cereal is made? It may not be essential, but it is helpful in differentiating various brands of breakfast food. Do all Monsanto employees need to know how their chemicals are manufactured? Probably not, so this is not taught to everyone.

Design teams need to consider the general industry and organizational background information that is required for a position. They have to decide what information to include everywhere, what to exclude in the position model but include later for the hiring/promotion version, and what can be assumed to be present and excluded everywhere.

These external and internal categories—law, industry, organization, workgroup, and background knowledge—are often overlooked in the design team's eagerness to get down to the details. Analysis by category identifies issues that would not arise by looking solely at positions and helps identify the larger issues common across individual job models.

Using Position Documentation

Organizations typically generate a large amount of people and process documentation that can be reviewed when creating competency models. There is more material available than a design team would typically want to examine in depth. In selecting documentation sources to use, the design team should look for what is most complete, what is considered most accurate, what is readily available, and how long it will take to review it.

In utilizing documentation, keep in mind the fifth design question from Figure 2-3, which focuses on whether to model current or planned processes. Existing documentation reinforces current processes, since future processes are not likely to have much infrastructure supporting them. In an environment of rapid change, research and customer feedback documentation may be the only available resources in designing new processes.

Industry Research

Academic journals, trade publications, and business periodicals are sources for leading-edge concepts that can find their way into competency models. Research articles require a hypothesis–test–conclusion format to get published. This focuses content on useful questions that should be answered or on common misconceptions that need to be corrected. Articles in trade and business publications usually include examples of what successful organizations are currently doing. The result is a good indication of what current best practices are and what new processes may need to look like. All this can find its way into position competency models.

For example, there has been significant research through the years on what is necessary for success in selling. Researchers Marvin Jolson and Lucette Comer identified a "mutually exclusive and collectively exhaustive partitioning of tasks that must be accomplished in all selling jobs."[3] Data was gathered from 77 sales managers who completed questionnaires evaluating 202 saleswomen of industrial products, supplies, and services. The sales managers rated performance based upon six "functions of selling." They were:

1. *Prospecting:* identifying and qualifying new customers for the firm's products
2. *Contacting:* getting in the door and making good first impressions
3. *Probing for needs:* establishing the prospect's requirements
4. *Stimulating desire:* making the actual presentation
5. *Closing:* asking for and getting the order

6. *Retaining activities:* retaining the sale and developing an ongoing relationship with the customer

According to the authors, "These functions are universal and have been used previously to measure selling performance across widely different selling jobs."

A somewhat different selling model is found in a trade publication, *Sales and Marketing Management* magazine.[4] Author William Keenan, Jr. listed sales competency examples developed by William Schiemann & Associates:

  ✧ Responding to changing markets
  ✧ Communicating with customers
  ✧ Establishing and maintaining long-term relationships
  ✧ Self-development

The article went on to discuss a company that identified 39 sales competencies and 174 sample behaviors that were subsequently integrated into forecasting, appraisal, and compensation systems. A company representative also confirmed an observation from Chapter 2 about assessment validation, "We often find that the salesperson tends to be more critical of his competency gaps than the sales manager would be."

These articles are good examples of available research that can be applied to competency modeling. The two articles above were discovered by a client performing a search for sales skills information published within the last twenty years. No matter what the industry or position, a rigorous search effort, perhaps conducted by third-party experts using library-based academic, business, and general article indices, trade publications, and Internet searches, can generate excellent results.

Vendor Information

A resource that is often overlooked is vendor publications. A manufacturing plant, for example, may be making a ten-year commitment to its production-line equipment vendor. The supplier must have extensive support materials and processes in place to help buyers install, run, and maintain the complex equipment. These training courses and reference materials can be ideal in developing competencies for production jobs.

At a higher level, many suppliers have extensive R&D operations that issue marketing and reference documents about their industry and products. Maintenance departments issue lists of frequently asked questions (FAQs), operating guides, and productivity tips. These, too, can provide help identifying useful competencies for a position model. Vendor sales representatives can be asked to track down this information or to provide contact names to the project team.

Customer Feedback

A very powerful source of information is customers. Since customer satisfaction is one of the top three measures of quality, customers—both internal and external—should have input to the competency modeling process. Continuing with the sales example, surveys of customers generate very different competency results than do surveys of sales managers. In fact, the top sales behaviors indicated by sales professionals are rarely listed by customers.

Accurate buyer preference data has been around for many years. In the late 1970s and early 1980s, *Purchasing* magazine published results of an annual contest in which readers were invited to nominate outstanding sales representatives.[5] Respondents were asked to identify the top three characteristics of these reps, and the winners and their customers were later interviewed. The authors performed a content analysis of the surveys from 1977 through 1983 and tabulated the frequencies for traits that were mentioned by buyers. The long-term averages are shown in Table 3-1.

In the table, traditional sales call behaviors as identified earlier in this chapter take a back seat to customer-focused issues of product application, use, service, support, and assistance. Note that traits #2, #4, #7, and #10 refer to category-level general competency issues. Note also that the only traits related to the sales call that made the *Purchasing* list were #8 and #9. None of the "mutually exclusive and collectively exhaustive partitioning of tasks that must be accomplished in all selling jobs" were listed, nor were the softer traits from the *Sales & Marketing Management* model mentioned. This research is nearly twenty years old, has been validated repeatedly by later research, and is still being ignored by many sales organizations. It shows how important competencies can be missed by not asking customers for their input.

Additional ideas can be obtained by reviewing any of the organization's formal customer survey results. Satisfaction measurement is a rather circular process, with customers providing feedback on survey line items and their responses being used to develop competencies and priorities. Yet survey analysis

Table 3-1. Sales competencies desired by customers.

Sales Trait	Average Percent Mentions
1. Thoroughness and follow-through	65
2. Knowledge of his/her product line	59
3. Willingness to go to bat for the buyer within the supplier's firm	54
4. Market knowledge and willingness to keep the buyer posted	41
5. Imagination in applying his/her products to the buyer's needs	23
6. Knowledge of the buyer's product lines	18
7. Diplomacy in dealing with operating departments	16
8. Preparation for well-planned sales calls	12
9. Regularity of sales calls	9
10. Technical education	7

can lead to identifying new competencies. For example, in a 1994 survey, research firm ISDI asked *ChemicalWeek* magazine readers to rank the importance and their satisfaction with supplier performance in fifteen areas.[6] The two areas ranked high in importance but low in satisfaction were:

⟡ Responsiveness to problems or requests
⟡ Long-term commitment to the industry

This leads development teams to a discussion of which competencies address these two elements. Long-term Commitment to the Industry may well be an organizational core competency that will not appear on a position model. But designers need to understand issues related to Responsiveness to Problems or Requests. This could be addressed by individual competencies such as Time Management, Project Management, Customer Database Operation, Record Keeping, or Prioritizing and Scheduling.

Thus, formal customer survey results are very helpful in identifying new competency candidates, with one reservation. The limitation of survey feedback is that sometimes customers do not know what to ask for. Surveys measure only how the organization is doing on what it does. So this can be another instance of reinforcing existing competency models at the expense of continuous improvement. It is the role of the development team to also link satisfaction issues to current or new competencies in a position model.

These are great examples of why it is critical to include customer input in the competency research effort. Customers can have a very different view of requirements. Although the sales examples in this section reference external customers, the design team should not overlook internal customers from other departments. They can provide input that is equally valuable to the modeling effort.

Regulations

Written regulations, when applicable, are essential sources of competency information. Refineries have extensive documentation on procedures for replacing a valve. Accountants have voluminous reference material available from the Federal Accounting Standards Board on the proper handling of nearly every imaginable financial transaction. Land surveyors follow established industry practices before officially stamping a survey or a set of plans. Regulation reference materials, while often overwhelming in size or scope, can provide important insights into what competencies employee must bring to the job.

Certification Requirements

Professional certification programs are excellent sources for position competencies. Someone else has already done much of the generic competency model development. These programs are usually the result of extensive research by a team of association, educational, or trade professionals. The resulting certification standards, assessment processes, and study materials highlight skills and knowledge that are required for certification.

For example, the Certified Administrative Manager (CAM) program, sponsored by the Academy of Certified Administrative Managers, requires the following:

- ✧ Have three years of management experience.
- ✧ Possess high standards of professional and personal conduct.
- ✧ Exhibit leadership ability.
- ✧ Made a contribution to administrative management effectiveness.
- ✧ Pass a series of five examinations measuring knowledge in financial, personnel, information systems, administrative services management, and management concepts.
- ✧ Write a 2,500-word response to a case study problem.

Table 3-2 shows the areas of expertise included in each of the five CAM examination categories.[7] These provide an extensive source list for possible competencies required of administrative managers throughout an organization. The challenge is to convert this general expertise list into specific competencies. Also, items such as Security (10) may need to be refined. Does this refer to safety of employees, physically securing buildings and equipment, or maintaining confidential information? Compensation (48) has many different sub-specialties. Does this refer to designing salary levels and brackets, creating incentive plans, or salary administration?

Some of the areas of expertise, such as Micrographics (12) or Consulting (70), may not be significant enough for inclusion in a final model. Others, such as Controllership (36) or Programming (62), may be so general as to be of little help in identifying specific competencies. Regardless, reviewing any relevant industry or professional certification programs can provide a proven list of potential competencies.

Quality Programs

Another source of generic workplace information can be found in quality recognition programs such as ISO 9000/14000, the Malcolm Baldrige National Quality Award, and state quality awards. The quality application is a document that helps identify competency requirements. In the 1997 Baldrige criteria, "6.1 Management of Product and Service Processes/b. Production/Delivery Processes/(1)" required "a description of key processes and their principal requirements."[8] These descriptions and requirements provide direct input into position competencies.

Similarly, "2.2 Company Strategy/b. Human Resource Plans/(1)" requires a response for the following elements, "changes in work design and/or organi-

Table 3-2. Expertise areas of certified administrative managers.

A. Administrative Services
    10. Security
    11. Forms analysis and management
    12. Micrographics
    13. Record systems/retention
    14. Reprographics
    15. Facilities management
    16. Office environment and design
    17. Energy conservation
    18. Word processing
    19. Telecommunications
    20. Mail systems
    21. Office supplies management
    22. Office services
    23. Photocomposition
    24. Purchasing

B. Financial Management
    25. Non-profit financial management
    26. Taxes
    27. Budgeting
    28. Financial analysis
    29. Asset management
    30. Leasing
    31. Contractorship
    32. Cash management
    33. Mergers and acquisitions
    34. Capital budgeting
    35. Financial management (small business)
    36. Controllership
    37. General accounting
    38. Public accounting
    39. Auditing
    40. Cost accounting
    41. EDP conversions
    42. Investment management

C. Personnel
    43. Human resources planning
    44. Personnel policy
    45. Performance evaluation
    46. Government compliance
    47. Manpower development and training
    48. Compensation
    49. Labor relations
    50. Safety and health
    51. Employee benefits
    52. Job descriptions and specifications
    53. Personnel audits
    54. Recruitment
    55. Executive recruitment

56. Personnel testing
57. Retirement planning
58. Outplacement

D. Information Systems

59. Systems analysis and design
60. EDP operations
61. Manual systems
62. Programming
63. Computer security
64. Systems interface

E. Miscellaneous

65. General management
66. Insurance
67. Business education
68. Government (specify area)
69. Sales/marketing
70. Consulting
71. Other (not listed above)

---

zation to improve knowledge creation/sharing, flexibility, innovation, and rapid response." Processes and strategy elements contained in the response to this section lead to possible competencies that affect processes and the ability to drive change.

State quality awards are often based upon national criteria but are adopted for specific applications. The 1997 Missouri Quality Award–Education closely follows the Baldrige criteria of the same year. The "6.2 Management of Education Support Processes and Business Operations/a. Management of Education Support Processes" response must address:

1. How key requirements are set, taking into account the needs of students and faculty;
2. A description of the key educational support processes and their principal requirements and measures; and
3. How the school ensures that educational support processes are performing effectively; and how the education support processes are evaluated and improved. Describe how each of the following is used or considered: (a) feedback from students, families, and faculty; (b) benchmarking; (c) peer evaluation; and (d) data from observations and measurements.[9]

Again, the Missouri State Quality Award application will discuss methods for determining process requirements, descriptions of key processes with their corresponding requirements, and measurement techniques to very specific performance levels. This content highlights many possible competencies, including benchmarking, 360-degree assessment, and data analysis techniques.

ISO 9001 specifications are a similar source of required competencies.

Processes are addressed in section "4.9 Process Control." Employees must be able to follow documented procedures for production within standards, installation and service of equipment, monitoring and control of output, and approval of output. This implies competencies in actual production, in operating test equipment, and in understanding the decision criteria for passing or rejecting output.

Finally, organizational quality programs and documents provide specific input for competencies. For example, in initiating its quality program in preparation for making a Baldrige award application, Momentum Distribution, Inc., identified six basic competencies for its entire workforce:

1. Competitive Benchmarking: finding and implementing the best business practices.
2. Quality Improvement Processes: a nine-step quality improvement process.
3. Problem Solving: an eight-step problem-solving model.
4. Measures of Quality: statistical process control tools such as charts, graphs, and flowcharts.
5. Cost of Quality: using a simple costing model.
6. Inspecting for Quality: a flowchart for quality inspection.[10]

By definition, these competencies are part of every position model that Momentum might develop for its employees.

Quality improvement efforts are always excellent sources of competency information because they require organizations to document goals, processes, performance, and results.

Using Process Documentation

The lesson of quality is that everything revolves around processes. If processes are designed efficiently and are performed without defect, then the organization will be successful. Process documentation is therefore one of the most important sources of competency information, and it comes in many forms.

Procedure Manuals and Flowcharts

In today's world of customized service and processes performed by generalist case workers, the classic procedure manual is becoming obsolete. It simply takes too long to document processes that evolve with frequent reorganizations and changing customer demands. Procedures that are locked in writing or embedded into interactive administrative systems are also seen as poor customer-satisfaction approaches. Yet where this information is available, it is a good resource for competency design teams modeling current systems.

As discussed in Chapter 1, process flowcharts are excellent resources. They are a common by-product of process improvement teams, where flow-charting the existing process is one of the initial steps in continuous improvement. The flowchart helps quickly identify the knowledge and skills required to complete a process. This information can be quite extensive. One manufacturer has six hundred factory flowcharts completed, with a remaining three hundred under development. They detail every production and maintenance process at all the plant locations and can be used to create operations competency models.

Another type of process documentation is the value-added flowchart. Unlike a regular flowchart that highlights activities and decision points of a process, the value-added flowchart lists process steps from the point of view of a thing going through the process.[11] The idea is to shorten up process cycle time and to increase customer satisfaction by identifying when no value is being added to the products, paperwork, and information flowing through a system. When no value is being added, those steps are candidates for elimination.

Procedure manuals and process flowcharts, when available, are very useful for documenting competencies for current operations. In the case of a process improvement team's proposed flowchart, they can be used to develop competencies for upcoming workplace tasks.

Time Logs

Where detailed position information is not available, and management does not have a strong opinion about what the future will require of the position, the only alternative may be to document the current position in detail. One common tool is a time log, an approach used in time-management analyses. Building time logs requires that employees write down everything they have done in a representative workweek, usually in fifteen-minute increments.

The strength of this approach is that there is a very complete list of activities. In conversations, most workers cannot remember everything they do each day, and recall even less for an entire week. The time log captures everything. Potential weaknesses revolve around accuracy. The week being measured may not be typical due to special projects or one-time activities. Employees may resent the record-keeping burden and refuse to keep continuous records. Instead, they just complete the entries at the end of the day with something that looks reasonable. Finally, the fifteen-minute increment may not be applicable in today's environment, where employees rarely work more than five minutes on anything before being interrupted. The alternative, five-minute increments, may be even less likely to be accurately filled out.

Time logs, when filled out completely and accurately, generate an extremely large amount of data for the design team to analyze. Going through each log, consolidating activities, capturing the elapsed times, and then analyzing the data for implied competencies put a heavy burden on the design team. But time logs are one of the most accurate, objective ways to document "what is" for positions.

Job Task Analysis

A more hands-on approach involves sending job analysis experts out to observe and investigate how people work and what they do. More than the traditional industrial engineering/time-and-motion study efficiency experts, job task analysis (JTA) requires competency professionals who can document what is being done in a position and take a conceptual step backwards to identify what competencies are required of that employee.

The resources required to perform a JTA are highly position and employer dependent. Some organizations send out a group of two or three analysts and study multiple workers in the same position. They feel that this increases the validity of the competency model by expanding the study base and analyst viewpoints. Other competency modeling development teams have a single JTA expert who provides position studies. A more structured job, such as a call center representative or a factory worker, may require studying fewer individuals. An unstructured position, such as a repair technician or plant supervisor, may require analyzing a wider range of employees.

Time required is also highly variable. The JTA study time can last hours, days, or weeks, and the elapsed time could be months. Everything depends upon the work cycle, i.e., how long it takes to see everything someone does in a position. This may require multiple visits at different times, such as during a typical workday or during end-of-month closings. Position tasks may vary according to factors such as seasonality or the availability of part-time workers. The JTA professional must either perform studies during these times or else determine what is done, and therefore required, using traditional methods like interviewing or documentation review.

A possible weakness of JTA is that an observer becomes part of the work system being analyzed. Employees are tempted to "game" the observer in order to keep the demands they face as low as possible. Workers might change their pace, throw in extra steps, or change methods while being observed. This is where JTA professionals must be experienced enough to detect when they are not getting a realistic view of the position.

Given a qualified analyst or analysis team, JTA can be an extremely accurate method of developing competency models. There is a standardization of approach, methodology, and analysts. Data is acquired first-person, on-the-job, with no intermediaries or documentation that might not be accurate. Consequently, JTA can make a good primary technique, or a strong validation approach when using other methods in this section.

Customer Contact Maps

Every time an organization contacts a customer through its people, processes, or products, it generates what Jan Carlzon of SAS Airlines called "moments of truth.''[12] Carlzon wrote that each of his ten million customers contacts an average of five SAS employees with a typical contact time of fifteen seconds each. This results in about fifty million moments of truth where SAS employees have to prove themselves to customers.

There are other contact points for SAS customers, driven by factors such as the quality of the in-flight magazine or meal, the flying experience, the accuracy of television monitors showing flight times, length of ticket lines, or condition of the equipment. Carlzon points out that when customers see a coffee ring on the pull-down tray, they begin to wonder about how the jet engines are maintained.

A common quality tool for studying customer service is to build a customer contact map. This is a list of every instance in which a customer, internal or external, is "touched" by the organization, department, or position. This includes categories such as face-to-face conversations, inbound and outbound phone calls, mailings, paperwork, brochures, advertising and promotion, processes, and pickup or delivery of products.

The value of contact maps is similar to value-added flowcharts that follow "things" through the system. Contact maps provide a different way of looking at processes—totally customer focused. The question to ask in using customer contact maps to identify competencies is, "What do employees need to know or do to be able to satisfy the customer for this particular contact?" The answers often give new insights into required service competencies and their relative importance to customers and to the organization.

Using Existing Documentation

Today's environment requires organizations to document job requirements and standards in order to legally hire and terminate employees. While this documentation often varies widely in how accurately it represents the current job or how specifically it addresses possible competencies, it is another important source of information. (One of the potential outputs of the modeling process is often an improvement in position documentation.)

Job Descriptions

Job descriptions are an obvious source for competency input. When job descriptions are well written, possible competency requirements can be readily determined. Consultants Roger and Sandra Plachy[13] recommend that job qualification evaluations include this basic information:

1. *Knowledge.* What does the employee need to know, and how will the necessary skills be acquired?
2. *Information processing.* How must the employee mentally use the information?

3. *Scope of responsibility.* What decisions must the employee be able to make?
4. *Interpersonal communications.* What are the contacts with others, and what are the reasons for those contacts?
5. *Impact on results.* What goes wrong when the employee makes an error?
6. *Description of controls.* What exists to prevent errors?
7. *Confidential and sensitive information.* What is available to the employee?
8. *Scope of financial responsibilities.* What is the employee's responsibility for expenditures and funding/revenue?
9. *Environment.* What is the level of physical and mental stress, strain, and exposure on the job?
10. *Supervisory/management responsibility.* How does the employee direct the work of others?

These factors can then be linked to specific competencies. Examples of converting job descriptions to competency models will be shown in Chapter 4.

Union Contracts

Collective bargaining agreements are not popular sources of competency information but can be similar to job descriptions in defining exactly what a union employee is expected to be able to do. The value lies not with the various sections on employment practices but with the rules for what each union position can and cannot do under the current agreement. It may even be beneficial to temporarily involve a contract expert with the design team in developing a competency list.

Departmental Planning Documents

Many organizations go through extensive planning processes near the end of each year. September or October productivity can be near zero while departments review current-year plans and get ready for critical budgeting meetings with management about the following year. The presentation and reporting requirements can be quite extensive and involve an exceptional amount of detail about upcoming projects.

Departmental planning documents, when they are truly used by the organization, are helpful in a changing environment. The goals and projects they describe are sources for modeling "what is to be" for the coming year.

Performance Plans

Performance plans are the individual's equivalent to departmental planning documents. They break the department's plans down into people-level activities and assignments. They highlight what each employee is expected to accomplish for the coming year and at what level each is expected to perform—all competency-related issues.

Appraisal Forms

In some organizations, an individual's performance plan created in the beginning of the year becomes the appraisal form used at the end of the year. The performance appraisal is made against the stated plans for the year. In other organizations, a standardized appraisal form is used for all distinct classes of employees, such as exempt and nonexempt workers. Either approach provides important input similar to that of the performance plan, where individual line items can suggest a related group of competencies required.

Personnel Development Resources

The organization's training and development resources provide excellent competency information. Learning activities are targeted at improving performance on the job. The research that was conducted during curriculum, course, or learning product development, and the goals and competencies documented in the student materials, are often already in a competency format and ready to be used in a model.

Training Curriculum

Many organizations, whether early in the competency modeling effort or else required by regulatory agencies, have developed position curriculums. Some curriculums can be organization-wide. For example, the Momentum Distribution Company developed the following training modules as part of its quality implementation. Employees went through this curriculum at the inception of Momentum's quality program, and the target for new hires is to complete the programs within six months. The curriculum included:

- ✧ Overview of the Momentum Quality Plan
- ✧ Overview of the Malcolm Baldrige National Quality Award
- ✧ Interactive Skills
- ✧ Visioning
- ✧ Goal Deployment
- ✧ Competitive Benchmarking
- ✧ Quality Improvement Processes
- ✧ Problem Solving and Measures of Quality
- ✧ Application Project

In Momentum's philosophy of operation, the quality topics addressed by these courses are competencies required of all Momentum employees and appear on every position model.

Development Resource Learning Points

Whether part of a curriculum or an optional training or learning resource, the major learning points of a development resource are essential inputs to position competencies. Simply reviewing the course or activity goals can point to important competencies. Online and in-person training documentation is a must-review source of competency information. Design reviews, learning goals pages, summary screens or sheets, and attendee tests are all extremely useful in building competency models, and they also provide essential information in authoring the competency assessment.

Many organizations struggle with identifying potential position competencies, yet they fail to take advantage of the wealth of institutional documentation they already possess. A common team question is, "Where do we start?" The easiest, and least expensive, answer is to collect a complete set of relevant position documentation, evaluate whether or not it is an accurate reflection of the job to be assessed, then use it to build the competency list.

Using Interviews

Using documentation is a hard-information approach to developing competency models. It is driven by data and processes captured in regulations, surveys, manuals, plans, contracts, procedures, and courseware. In many organizations, all this paperwork exists, but it is so different from reality as to be useless. Seen as non-value-added overhead and an administrative headache, keeping paperwork up-to-date is an easy task to skip. This means that the only available source for competency items is often soft information gained from interviews, focus groups, and customer conversations.

The first challenge in utilizing soft information is maintaining validity and accuracy. The problem is similar to that of self-assessment. Those involved in a process may not have the ability to step away and analyze it for competencies required. This is a professional skill for which frontline workers have not been trained. Design team members will have to make the link between participant feedback and competencies.

The second challenge is in sorting through the mountain of data that soft-information investigations create. At an average speaking speed of 150 words per minute, interviewees generate 6,000 words per hour. (This assumes they speak two-thirds of the time and the interviewer speaks the remaining third.) Interview ten workers for an hour each and the verbatim results could fill a medium-size business book. Multiply this by different jobs in a department, and suddenly the design team is creating an encyclopedia of raw competency data.

One large organization brought focus groups together at the beginning of its model building research. Ten positions from one department were to be modeled, and it was decided to invite ten position holders each. The groups generated over two thousand different competency entries for their single department. The design team had to create a specialized database in order to track the entries, and even then the data was nearly incomprehensible. The sorting, analysis, and consolidation process took nearly three months of elapsed time and many hours of team discussion. Therefore, design teams must keep in mind that if a soft-information approach is to be used, steps must be taken to obtain enough data to be reliable but not so much that there is overkill.

The best approach with interviewing is to adopt a minimalist attitude. Additional interviews or meetings can always be held later to gather more data. In the example above, the organization might have been better served if the design team had first conducted simple phone interviews with two or three people on each job, and then made the decision on whether to utilize a multiday focus-group approach.

Interviewing, if used, should be done periodically during the project. First, it generates better results. Instead of getting all the data up front and then showing the competency model and assessment instrument to jobholders for a final check right before rollout, feedback should be continuous. Problems are identified and corrected immediately during the development. In competency projects, the jobholders are the "customers," and the more often they can be involved in design, review, and validation efforts, the better the results. This sounds like simple advice, something almost too obvious to mention, but it is frequently ignored by design teams.

Spreading interviews out during the life of the design project can also be more time efficient. Instead of spending days with worker focus groups at the beginning of a project, perhaps a series of interviews done at the start can deliver nearly the same value. A summary of these initial conversations can be given back to the interviewees for review, and early-model versions can be shared with jobholders. The total amount of investigation time may be less than that used up front with focus groups.

Regardless of the approach, the question with interviewing is always, "How much is enough?" While there is no absolute right number of interviews that guarantees completeness in a soft-information situation, a good behavioral guideline is "closure." This means that closure is reached when the same topics keep coming up and when interviews are no longer generating significantly new information. Closure for a relatively stable job might occur after only one or two interviews. Conversely, closure for a multilocation case worker position may not be achieved even after ten or more interviews.

Design teams will likely have some element of interviewing included in the project, if only to involve all of the stakeholders. As usual, the breadth and depth of the interview schedule depend on the time and resources available, and on the individual requirements of the competency models.

Customer Interviews

Contact mapping is an inside-out look at customer needs. Interviews (along with formal surveys) are an outside-in, customer-driven look at competency requirements. The advantage of interviews is that organizations often learn far more by speaking with customers than by surveying them. First, many customers will not bother to complete a written survey. Second, many who do return the survey do not bother to write in any comments because either the survey does not spark any ideas or they have too much to say to put it all in writing. Granted, people are difficult to reach by phone these days, but when contact is made with the help of a few open questions, customers can convey a wealth of good ideas in just a few minutes during a phone call.

A common question is whether customer interviews should be conducted by the organization or by an independent third party. There are also various pros and cons for each option, such as internal versus external and blind versus identified approaches. In traditional customer-satisfaction research, using outside firms with a blind approach ensures the least bias. Outside firms calling on behalf of an identified client may still get more candid feedback than internal callers receive. For pure satisfaction research, an organization may therefore want to use a third-party service.

Customer interviews in a competency context have very different purposes. The caller is asking about needs, not performance. Because the goal clearly is customer service rather than "How are we doing?" there is no worry for the customer about hurting the current sales or service representative. In addition, an organization can create customer goodwill by asking about needs. Finally, the interview requires a caller who is completely knowledgeable about the position in question, the customer's industry, and the products/services being provided. For these reasons, customer interviewing for position modeling purposes is best done by an employee-caller who is qualified to discuss specific products and customers, reacts to what is being heard, and recognizes competency-related information when it comes up. This is probably going to require someone who either is on the design team or is specially trained for the interview process.

It helps to be very open and up front with customers about the purpose of the interview. The caller can state something like this: "Hi, I'm Barbara Wilson with the HR department at CooperComm, Inc. We're working to improve the quality of products and services you receive from us and would appreciate it if you could spend a few minutes talking about where we could improve. In particular, we're interested in the competencies of our people and what you want to see from them. Could I get your input on a couple of quick questions?"

"Think of your best [job title]. What do they do that makes them the best?"
"Think of your worst [job title]. What do they do that makes them the worst?"
"What do you look for in a good [job title]?"
"What competencies do they need to do that?"
"Where does our [job title] rate on that best-to-worst scale?"
"What competencies should our people improve upon?"

Note how the questioning sequence does not jump right into a discussion of competencies. Customers need help in identifying the boundaries of behavior across all the vendors that they deal with before they can provide feedback on a specific organization. Note also that the results are going to be anecdotal rather than objective. If objective numbers are required, a formal customer survey should be done instead.

Some organizations prefer to start with a higher-level approach and work downward to detailed competencies. Here are the general questions one organization asked its customers:

"What are the challenges facing you in your business?"
"How well are we meeting your needs?"
"What are other companies/suppliers doing to meet your needs?"
"What can we do to better meet your needs?"

These questions do not necessarily generate specific competency information as with the first set. Instead, the design team will have to analyze the stated customer needs to determine which competencies address them.

Customer interviews are prime sources of competency information and are strongly recommended for every competency-based HR application development project. Informal customer input is also very helpful in fighting the "documenting broken processes" problem. Customers will provide strong input into what should be and into what competitors are doing. This is critical to helping the organization meet its desired business outcomes.

Supplier Interviews

Suppliers provide another outside viewpoint, similar to customers, but with a push-through approach. Suppliers have a larger perspective of the marketplace or industry because they deal with a wide range of an organization's competitors. Suppliers are interested in making certain their customers are successful with their products, or that their downline supply chain partners are maximizing sell-through.

Getting candid feedback from a supplier is a bit more complicated than getting it from customers, since the supplier does not want to irritate its customer—the organization. In order to not play favorites, the supplier must also be circumspect about what other customers—the organization's competitors—are doing to be successful.

The question flow is similar to that used with customers:

"Think of your best customer. Why does it have the best success with your product?"
"Think of your worst customer. Why does it have so little success?"
"Where do we rate on that best-to-worst scale?"
"What would you do if you were us to get the most out of your product?"
"What competencies do our people need to do that?"
"What would you recommend we do to get our people into that best category?"

Again, the recommended approach is to be straightforward. Tell the supplier about the competency modeling effort. Depending upon the amount of business being done between the organizations, some suppliers may even be willing to offer resources or personnel for the effort. The design team should not focus on what competitors are doing but on what the vendor believes the most effective procedures are and what is required to complete them.

Employee Interviews

The best/worst approach works equally well with employees. A small group of successful employees can be interviewed. Questions could include:

"What does your job require you to know and do?"
"To what do you attribute your success?"
"What are you particularly good at that drives your business results?"
"What competencies do you think someone in your position needs?"
"What should we be doing for others in your position to help them become more effective?"
"What can we do now to help you become more effective?"

Next, a group of less successful employees can be interviewed. Questions for someone who is newer on the job could be:

"How prepared for the job were you when you began?"
"What didn't you know or understand that you should have?"
"Knowing what you do now, what would you tell someone just beginning?"
"How could we have better prepared you for the job beforehand?"
"What competencies do you think someone in your position needs?"
"What can we do now to help you become more effective?"

These responses can then be analyzed to identify the supporting competencies. As was discussed in "Self-Assessment" in Chapter 2, employees may not be able to step outside their positions and analyze them from a competency standpoint. This may require someone higher up in the organization.

Supervisor Interviews

Supervisors are an important source of information. Theoretically, they should have the best perspective of anyone concerning competencies required for a position. Supervisors may have previously worked in the position being analyzed. Supervisors should be involved in the hiring process. Supervisors deal with customers and with customer service issues. And supervisors are the final link in conveying management concerns to frontline workers.

Supervisors can be asked:

"Think of your best employees. Why are they more effective?"
"Think of your worst employees? Why are they struggling?"
"What competencies do people need to succeed in the [title] job?"
"Are your new hires properly prepared for the job?"
"What does it take for them to develop required competencies?"

Supervisors can provide the most candid interviews of any group. They have a very difficult position at the bottom of the management chain and are on the front line for product, service, and people problems. As a result, they are very often focused on the practical competency issues that will immediately improve business results.

Competency application design teams will want to include some form of interviewing throughout their research. Interviews not only provide position research data, but they also help keep employees informed about the project, its goals, and its progress. Interviewing involves many people outside the design team and helps to create an atmosphere of consensus. Interviews can also provide early warnings of potential problems, either in overall process dysfunctions or in the specifics of a competency model. Design teams must not only "walk the talk," they must "talk the walk" by keeping the organization involved and informed.

Using Teams

A more structured method of gathering competency information is to utilize focus groups or work teams. This provides the advantage of individual input with the consistency and structure of a group activity. Focus groups are also much more expensive, requiring an organization to assemble a team of employees at a single location for several days, and to provide the group with a trained facilitator familiar with team operations and competency modeling.

The focus group should contain cross-functional skills. Candidates for team membership are: employees holding the position, a competency project design team member, an HR professional with job analysis experience, a trainer for related courses, a supplier, a customer, and an industry or HR consultant. Experience has shown that it can also be helpful to include an employee in a different position who is not a stakeholder. The outside perspective often brings new ideas and viewpoints to the team. Ideally, the team should consist of five to seven individuals plus a facilitator.

After completing normal team-building and rules activities, the focus group can then be directed to provide the following:

- ✧ Tasks list
- ✧ List of responsibilities
- ✧ List of projects
- ✧ Customer contacts
- ✧ Decisions
- ✧ List of competencies required
- ✧ List of measures

The initial goal for the group is to develop a complete list of tasks for the position under analysis. The group can use any of the documentation sources described earlier in this chapter, in addition to their own experience. Tasks can be identified by building lists that document what is currently being done: responsibilities, active projects, customer contacts, and decisions. The ultimate goal is to capture all knowledge and skills required for the position.

As long as the group is assembled, it is also useful to discuss measurements for the tasks identified. This will be needed in building an assessment instrument for the position.

Using Benchmarking

Interviewing provides informal feedback on the best and worst performers in an organization. To obtain more objective data with this approach, the competency model design team can conduct a formal benchmark of those employees exceeding and falling below performance standards. Studying the links between actual business results and competencies often provides a radically different view of required model elements.

Continuing the sales competencies example used earlier in this chapter, researcher Larry Craft helped general agents and managers at a major life insurance company analyze their most successful salespeople.[14] Using a personality profile questionnaire, insurance professionals identified as top performers scored high in:

✧ *Emotional intensity:* the salesperson's sense of urgency or drive toward short-term goals.
✧ *Intuition:* the degree to which a person relies upon experience and feelings to make a decision, as opposed to complex analysis of subject matter.
✧ *Assertiveness:* an individual's ability to control the actions of others.

Top performers were characterized as "high ego drive" individuals. Craft recommended that organizations train these trailblazer individuals and provide them with ready support for their questions and problems.

A related benchmarking study used expert modeling techniques similarly to analyze superior insurance salespeople.[15] Expert modeling requires documenting—in writing, audiotape, or videotape—everything the salesperson does. Notes are made during and directly after sales calls. A five-year study of top producers found that:

1. Top salespeople almost never follow a canned, step-by-step sales call.
2. Top salespeople are more customer-oriented than product-oriented.
3. Top salespeople vary their speech to mimic customers' patterns.
4. Top salespeople use stories and metaphors to make their points.
5. Top salespeople learn how prospects make buying decisions in order to understand how to sell to them.
6. Top salespeople are flexible enough to change a prescribed selling approach if the customer is ready to buy.

These models are not only different from what customers and managers identified, they are radically different from each other. This shows the anecdotal nature of soft-information approaches—even relatively structured ones such as expert modeling. It also illustrates the importance of using a variety of input sources and viewpoints. Internal views tend to focus on selling activities and external views concentrate on service factors. Competency-model designers must take both sets of data into account.

Using Established Models

A final resource for identifying competencies is simply to use a completed model obtained from an outside source. An organization undergoing significant change may see little value in documenting current processes, and it may want competency models to support a quick transition to new modes of operation. This requires seeking information from outside the group of stakeholders.

Management Directed

The competency model may be driven by the dictates of top management. If the organization decides to expand markets or offer additional products or services, new competencies will by necessity be required.

For example, Iomega Corporation, maker of Zip®, Jaz®, and Clik!™ removable mass storage drives for personal computers, saw annual revenue increase from $170 million to over $1.7 billion in three years—one of the fastest growth rates in the history of computing. Iomega's strength during this period was its consumer focus and execution, supported with a hip attitude, unique advertising, and splashy colors and designs. Data was called "stuff," and an assortment of eye-catching characters were used in print and media advertising and point-of-sale merchandising pieces at retail.

In order to continue Iomega's growth, top management realized that it would have to be successful in convincing large enterprise organizations to adopt its drives as standard features for all PCs. This required a completely new set of competencies affecting software solutions, component design, customer support, product rollout, marketing, advertising, public relations, and enterprise sales. Information could no longer be "stuff"; it was now mission-critical data. Instead of catchy graphics, selling now revolved around issues of total cost of ownership, return on investment, end-user productivity increases, worldwide support infrastructure, and product line families and plans. Competencies in these areas became part of the mix by management mandate.

Many organizations struggle in building competency models because they do not understand that, in some situations, management must make a decision. For many new ventures (such as building competency models), data does not already exist, no systems are in place, and no industry models are available. As was seen with the various sales skills models in this chapter, there may be many possible approaches for success in a position, all with a measure of validity. Someone in management must set the direction, explain what the organization needs to be doing, and turn the design team loose. Then the issue changes from trying to discover what the organization should be doing into building a model for what management is leading the organization to do. Often this is the only way to move forward with the competency modeling design process.

Third-Party Models

The number one request of competency-model development teams is, "Does somebody already have a model for this position that we could start with?" There are a number of organizations that provide completed competency models for a variety of positions. (These are detailed in Chapter 10.) Existing models exhibit a wide variation in approach, thoroughness, and measurement styles. This is both their strength and weakness. The various styles give the design team many ideas for proceeding, but the existence of so many options may also make it much more difficult to select which approach is best for an individual organization.

Some organizations may be willing to accept existing models, knowing their limitations, in order to minimize development efforts. Lacking the necessary expertise, personnel capacity for development team activities, or a budget for consultants, small- and medium-size organizations can at least get started by utilizing models created by others.

Most organizations prefer to develop custom models for their positions. There is simply too much at stake. Significant standardization can still take place with a custom process. The design team will find that there is a group of foundational competencies that are common to all positions in the organization. This may make up half to two-thirds of individual competency-model line items. Then there will be competencies that are common within workgroups. In the final analysis, only about one-fourth of all competencies may be specific to a single position. So while the first model is difficult to create, there quickly are economies of scale in developing succeeding models both within the workgroup and for other departments.

The initial reaction of a design team, after seeing all the potential sources of competency information, is to be overwhelmed. A key point is that not all of the sources in this chapter need to be used. What teams must do is to select their research approach by design rather than by default. The research phase must support the accuracy and validity of the overall modeling and assessment process. Figure 3-1 contains a reference checklist of the competency resources discussed in this chapter.

This chapter completes the research portion of the book. Design teams should now have a common vocabulary and purpose. Critical decisions about the project have been made, and all desired competency reference information has been gathered. The team is now ready to begin actual competency modeling by building a position model consisting of competencies, competency definitions, standards by position, and an assessment.

Learning Points

1. Once the key design decisions are made, the next step is to begin researching existing information related to position competencies.
2. There is an overabundance of sources for competency information. Design teams need to develop a research plan to determine what is available, what is valuable, and what will be reviewed in detail.
3. There are important benefits to utilizing different viewpoints. This means involving as many outsiders as possible such as employees, customers, vendors, suppliers, advisors, and trade groups.
4. Competency modeling is a continual process of balancing "what is" with "what should be."
5. It is important to not overlook basic competencies that may not appear in position assessment applications but that are needed for hiring/promotion applications.
6. The various sources of competency information will often support widely differing models for similar positions. A design team is still necessary to select what is right for an individual organization.

Figure 3-1. Source of competency information worksheet.
"Everything begins with processes."

Categories
- ☐ By assumption (conditions of employment)
- ☐ By law
  - ☐ Statutes
  - ☐ Regulations
- ☐ By Industry
  - ☐ Licensing
  - ☐ Trade/government certifications
  - ☐ Vendor certifications
- ☐ By organization
  - ☐ Vision/value/mission statements
  - ☐ Core competencies
- ☐ By workgroup
- ☐ By background information
  - ☐ General
  - ☐ Industry
  - ☐ Organization

Position Documentation
- ☐ Industry research
- ☐ Vendor information
- ☐ Customer feedback
  - ☐ Needs analyses
  - ☐ Satisfaction surveys
- ☐ Regulations
- ☐ Certification requirements
- ☐ Quality programs
  - ☐ Malcolm Baldrige
  - ☐ ISO 9000/14000
  - ☐ State quality program
  - ☐ Internal quality program

Process Documentation
- ☐ Procedure manuals
- ☐ Process flowcharts
- ☐ Value-added flowcharts
- ☐ Time logs
- ☐ Customer contact maps

Existing Documents
- ☐ Job descriptions
- ☐ Union contracts
- ☐ Departmental planning documents
- ☐ Performance plans
- ☐ Appraisal forms

Personnel Development Resources
- ☐ Training curriculum
- ☐ Development resource learning points

Interviewing
- ☐ Customers
- ☐ Suppliers
- ☐ Employees
- ☐ Supervisors

Teams
- ☐ Focus groups
- ☐ Cross-functional teams

Benchmarking
- ☐ Superstars/benchwarmers
- ☐ Expert modeling

Established competency models
- ☐ Management directed
- ☐ Third-party models

7. The goal at this stage is to gather as much competency-related information as is useful. The include/exclude decision on individual competencies comes later.

8. Sometimes the model will not be developed or derived; it will be mandated by management in order to support new strategic plans.

Notes

1. Equal Employment Opportunity Commission, *Guidelines on Discrimination Because of Sex*, 29 CFR Chapter XIV Section 1604.11 Sexual Harassment (10 November 1980).

2. Robert Faletra, "We Need a Leader," *Computer Reseller News*, 26 July 1999, 18.

3. Marvin A. Jolson and Lucette B. Comer, "Predicting the Effectiveness of Industrial Saleswomen," *Industrial Marketing Management*, February 1992, 71–72.

4. William Keenan, Jr., "Manager's Handbook: Person-to-Person," *Sales and Marketing Management*, December 1993, 30.

5. Alvin J. Williams and John Seminerio, "What Buyers Like from Salespeople," *Industrial Marketing Management* 14 (1985), 75–78.

6. Elizabeth S. Kiesche, "CW-ISDI Survey: Customers Satisfied—Barely," *ChemicalWeek*, 6 April 1994, 68–72.

7. Academy of Certified Administrative Managers, *The Directory of Certified Administrative Managers* (Willow Grove, Pa.: Administrative Management Society, 1984), 1–4.

8. National Institute of Standard and Technology, *1997 Criteria for Performance Excellence: Malcolm Baldrige National Quality Award* (Gaithersburg, Md.: U.S. Department of Commerce, 1997), 15.

9. Excellence in Missouri Foundation, *1997 Criteria for Performance Excellence and Application Forms— Education* (Jefferson City: State of Missouri, 1997), 29.

10. Momentum Distribution, Inc., *Continuous Quality Improvement* (Bellevue, Wa.: Momentum Distribution, 1992), 6–7.

11. Rath & Strong Management Consultants, *TIME: The Next Dimension of Quality* (New York: American Management Association, 1993), 18-minute video.

12. Jan Carlzon, *Moments of Truth: New Strategies for Today's Customer-Driven Economy* (New York: Harper Collins, 1989), 3.

13. Roger J. Plachy and Sandra J. Plachy, *Results-Oriented Job Descriptions* (New York: AMACOM, 1993), 30–32.

14. "Questionnaire Helps Identify Top Sales Producers," supplement to *Personnel Journal*, June 1993, 6.

15. Kenneth Friedenreich and Donald J. Moine, "Winning Sales Strategies for the 1990s," *Insurance Review*, January 1990, 26–29.

Building Competency Models

As Chapter 3 showed, there is no shortage of source information in creating competency models. Design teams are typically faced with information overflow. There are potentially hundreds of competencies—major and minor—that contribute to success in any job. The true value-added task, assuming accurate and complete position information has been gathered, is building a workable list of position competencies that will drive desired business results.

This chapter presents examples that illustrate the process of competency list generation and final item selection. It utilizes a variety of sources from the research methods in Chapter 3 and concludes with a sample competency model for a small workgroup containing different titles. This working model will be used throughout the discussion of CMAR and is already entered into the Competency Coach software included on the CD-ROM disk accompanying this book.

The first step is to create a list of position competencies that are required for a worker to be qualified to perform a job to established standards. In practice, this means identifying what it takes to complete every process done in the position. This long list of competencies is prioritized, then pared down to a more manageable and measurable size, keeping required and critical competencies in the model.

Size of a Competency Model

The first question in creating a competency list is, "How many competencies should be in the model?" As is the case with this entire development project, there is no single answer. While some experts recommend no more than twenty to thirty position competencies, organizations have implemented very effective systems with seventy or more.

The size of a model depends on several of the design factors discussed in Chapter 2. If the model has been built for multiple jobs in a workgroup, it will by necessity be larger than if built for a single position. Case-worker position models will be more complex than for workers in heads-down administrative jobs. Curriculum-based models are quite simple. Models for union jobs may also be well bounded. It all depends on the individual situation.

In the beginning, the design team should not worry about the size of a competency model. Much like a brainstorming exercise, the initial goal should be to identify every possible competency required for a position. The primary objective is thoroughness. In the initial identification stage, many organizations inadvertently or purposely omit critical competencies. Nothing should be ruled out at the start.

A model can be consolidated and prioritized later to determine which competencies need to be measured individually. Anheuser-Busch identified over two thousand specific line items of knowledge and skills required for its entire field sales force. These were later whittled down to seventy-four competencies. The consolidation process is time consuming but relatively straightforward. It is a matter of correctly defining competencies and establishing priorities, a process that will be covered in Chapter 5.

Reviewing the Guidelines for a Competency

The first check for a valid competency is to use the general definition. To review from Chapter 1, a competency must have these characteristics:

1. Requires knowledge, attitudes, and/or skills that affect the job
2. Correlates with job performance
3. Can be measured against standards
4. Can be improved

These criteria should be used throughout the development project when discussing whether to include various competencies in a model. Any item that does not meet all four of these requirements is not a valid candidate.

Organizing Competencies into Hierarchies

Another issue is determining how to group and separate competencies on a list potentially containing thousands of line items. The investigation process results in a hierarchy of competencies. The best way to keep relationships straight is to use outlining terminology. For example, Sexual Harassment is a main category (parent) of competency that is too general to evaluate and measure. Underneath it in the hierarchy might be Knowledge of Employer Complaint Procedures, Investigating Incidents, Counseling Targets, and Disciplining Offenders (child) competencies. Related areas such as Communications Skills or Diversity (siblings) are categories in their own right.

Competency interrelationships do not always fit into a clear parent-child relationship. Sometimes a competency fits in multiple categories; for example, Sexual Harassment/Investigating Incidents might also apply to HR or service groupings. The design team needs to decide how deeply to pursue such hierarchies and how interrelated to make them. This depends upon how much time is available to the team, how thorough an assessment will be required, what the value is of the additional items, and what effects these competencies will have on the length and reliability of the assessment instrument. The line has to be drawn somewhere.

Using an Existing Competency Model

Valid competencies must have equally valid definitions, otherwise assessment becomes impossible. Following are examples from two different sources, a general competency list from the U.S. government and content from a typical training seminar. The U.S. model contains a wealth of ideas on possible competencies but requires additional work editing definitions. The course material is more specific but needs to have its competencies identified.

Office of Personnel Management Model Example

Crisp Publications, a business books and training materials vendor, offers a paper adapted from U.S. Office of Personnel Management information. It lists and describes these fourteen major business competencies:

1. Communication (oral, written, listening)
    A. Effectively expresses ideas and facts in a succinct, organized manner
    B. Makes clear and convincing oral presentations
    C. Considers and responds appropriately to ideas and thoughts expressed by others
2. Flexibility
    A. Remains open to change
    B. Adapts behavior and work methods in response to new information, changing conditions, or unexpected obstacles
3. Conflict Management
    A. Resolves conflicts, confrontations, and disagreement in a positive and constructive manner
    B. Strives for win-win solutions
    C. Works to minimize negative personal impact
4. Creativity and Innovation
    A. Develops new insights into situations and applies innovative solutions to make organizational improvements
    B. Designs and implements cutting-edge programs and processes
5. Customer Focus

     A. Anticipates and meets the needs of clients

     B. Achieves quality end products

     C. Advocates and takes action for improving services

6. Process and Product Improvement

     A. Assures that effective internal controls are developed and maintained to ensure the integrity of the organization, products, and services

     B. Continually improves the quality of products and services

     C. Identifies simpler, faster, less costly processes for achieving high-quality results

7. Initiative (decisiveness, self-direction)

     A. Demonstrates belief in own abilities and ideas

     B. Is self-motivating and results-oriented

     C. Recognizes own strengths and weaknesses

     D. Makes sound, well-informed decisions

     E. Perceives the impact of decisions

     F. Commits to action to accomplish organizational goals

8. Managing and Developing Others

     A. Ensures that staff are appropriately selected, utilized, appraised, and developed

     B. Motivates and guides others toward goal accomplishments

     C. Rewards people for efforts and achievements and ensures they are treated in a fair and equitable manner

     D. Empowers people by sharing information, knowledge, skills, power, and authority

     E. Develops lower levels of leadership by pushing authority downward and outward throughout the organization

     F. Coaches and mentors others

9. Diversity

     A. Recognizes the positive influences of diverse cultures, viewpoints, and behavioral and learning styles

     B. Adapts leadership styles to a variety of situations

     C. Builds a workforce that includes and values diversity in race, gender, culture, and other aspects of individual differences

10. Leadership (providing vision and direction, fostering commitment)

     A. Inspires and challenges others

     B. Takes a long-term view and initiates organizational change for the future

     C. Builds commitment to the vision with others

     D. Identifies opportunities to move the organization toward the vision

     E. Works with others to build vision

11. Team Building

     A. Manages group processes

    B. Encourages and facilitates cooperation, pride, trust, and group identity

    C. Fosters commitment and team spirit

    D. Works with others to achieve goals

12. Financial Management

    A. Prepares, justifies, and administers budgets for program areas

    B. Plans, administers, and monitors expenditures to ensure cost-effective support of programs and policies

    C. Monitors, oversees, and controls revenue-generating activities

13. Project Management

    A. Determines objectives and strategies

    B. Develops plans and organizes resources for implementation of projects

    C. Coordinates with other parts of the organization to accomplish goals

    D. Monitors and evaluates the progress and outcomes of operational plans

    E. Anticipates potential threats or opportunities

    F. Synthesizes large amounts of information into important points

14. Relational Influence

    A. Considers and responds appropriately to the needs, feelings, and capabilities of others

    B. Develops networks and coalitions with others who have mutual interests or goals

    C. Develops networks and coalitions with others who have complementary skills and knowledge

    D. Gains cooperation from others to obtain and share information and accomplish goals

    E. Builds consensus and finds mutually acceptable solutions

    F. Persuades others and influences outcomes

    G. Develops and maintains awareness of external factors that affect the organization*

This is a very useful reference and will benefit from some refinement. A design team utilizing this list can modify these definitions to fit the CMAR framework. Following are steps that can be taken to make the transition:

✧ *Develop hierarchies.* Line item 1A illustrates a possible hierarchy of competencies: Communication–Oral Communication–Presentations–Persuasive Presentations (or Clear Presentations). It might be more understandable to present the model in this format.

*Debbie Woodbury, *General Business Competencies* (Menlo Park, Calif.: Crisp Publications, 1997), 1–3. Reprinted with permission: Crisp Publications, Inc., 1200 Hamilton Court, Menlo Park, CA 94025.

❖ *Qualifications focus.* These definitions read more like appraisal criteria than a competency model. In this book, a competency is a *qualification* to perform, not the actual performance. For example, 1B is written, "Makes clear and convincing oral presentations." Recasting this as a competency definition, the result might be, "Can give presentations using the six steps of persuasion."

❖ *Measurability/objectivity.* According to the rules for a valid competency, items such as 1A must be measurable. "Clear" and "convincing" are perhaps suitable words for a general feedback instrument but not for competencies. Adding the phrase ". . . using the six steps of persuasion" makes the line item measurable. (The six steps might be content from an "Effective Presentations" workshop offered to employees.)

Similarly, 3B, "Strives for win-win solutions," addresses effort made, not competence to perform. Striving is not achieving, nor can striving be objectively assessed. Words such as those used in 2A "Remains open . . . ," 7E "Perceives . . . ," 11C "Fosters . . . ," and 13E "Anticipates . . ." all present the same concern.

❖ *Compound line items.* Note that the rewritten definition for 1B omitted "clear." 1B is a compound line item mentioning both clarity and persuasiveness. While related and probably interdependent—it is hard to be persuasive if the presenter is not clear—they are two separate issues. If both are to be included in the model, they initially deserve their own line items. Otherwise, which element will an assessment question be addressing? Definitions 1A-C, 2A, 3A, 4A-B, 5A and C, 6A, 7A-D, 8B-C and F, 10A-B, 11B-C, 12A-C, 13A-B and D, and 14A and D-F all contain compound elements that may need to be addressed.

A good example of avoiding potentially compound line items is 14B and 14C. These correctly separate the closely related issues of coalitions of those with mutual goals and complementary skills. Whereas definitions with compound items are acceptable at this stage, the design team must be careful not to carry line items with multiple competencies into standard-setting and assessment steps.

The benefit of using models such as this Office of Personnel Management list is in generating ideas for possible competencies. What are the competencies required for the 3C, "Works to minimize negative personal impact," line item? This links back into categories of Communications, Managing and Developing Others, Leadership, Team Building, and possibly Diversity. Competencies such as Listening, Logical Decision Making, Process Improvement Skills, and Employee Counseling can be generated from considering "negative personal impact."

Training Materials Example

Training materials are excellent sources of competency information. If properly researched and designed, they address competencies that drive specific employee performance factors. Course design documentation and leader/student materials provide direct input to a model. For example, a CooperComm, Inc., course in negotiating for bank loan officers has the following business results goals:

1. Raise loan yields.
2. Raise loan security (lower defaults and losses) by obtaining better terms and conditions.

The seminar has these learning goals:

✧ Provide analysis tools to better prepare for negotiation situations.
✧ Provide strategy tools to help determine negotiation approaches.
✧ Provide tactical tools to conduct negotiations sessions.
✧ Help attendees link tools and skills back to the job.

The student manual contains these course chapters:

1. Multi-Form Tendencies: A Four-Type Personality Model
2. Decision Making under Risk
3. Win/Lose Decision Making
4. Negotiating Leverage
5. Negotiating Tactics
6. Managing Concessions
7. Planning Checklists

Since Negotiating is a category-level general topic, information contained in this course can be used to develop child competencies not only for the loan officer position but for other bank jobs that require negotiations skills. Derived competencies and definitions could include:

✧ *Multi-Form Tendencies*. Can identify the four-type personality tendency of others. Knows strategies for effectively dealing with each type. Can mediate personal tendencies to fit style of others.
✧ *Decision Making under Risk (Framing)*. Knows the differences in decision making with gains versus losses. Can reframe gains to losses or vice versa. Knows the six Framing decision-making keys.
✧ *Win/Lose Decision Making*. Knows the three types of win/lose negotiations. Can identify wins for negotiating partners. Can develop negotiating strategies to leverage potential wins.
✧ *Negotiating Leverage*. Knows the three categories of leverage and the thirteen individual leverage types. Knows the six truths concerning leverage. Can recognize the leverage approaches of others. Can develop strategies utilizing available leverage.
✧ *Negotiating Tactics*. Can recognize by category the fifty-five negotiating

tactics when encountered. Knows their approach, emotional goal, and which Multi-Form styles are affected. Can develop strategies utilizing tactics when necessary.

✧ *Managing Concessions.* Knows the five-step concession cycle. Knows the nine rules for making concessions.

✧ *Planning Checklists.* Can use the organization negotiations-planning checklists to manage a negotiating effort.

Unlike many line items from existing competency models, these definitions are written correctly by a CMAR professional. Difficulties in tapping into the extensive commercial databases of competencies are twofold. First, the commercial model may have been built on a different set of design assumptions. Second, the generic models must be made specific to the organization's actual position. Third, the model will often introduce poor practices, such as compound competencies, performance-like language, or subjective terms.

Experience has shown that adapting existing models has not proven as useful as many design teams hoped, especially for white-collar positions. In addition to having to go through hundreds of competencies and definitions to determine their applicability to individual positions, the design team still needs to do significant editing. Either way, much original writing needs to be done to end up with a valid list.

Examples of Identifying Competencies

Following are examples of how to use the information sources from Chapter 3 to generate potential competencies.

Customer Research

Customer satisfaction surveys provide extremely important input in the competency modeling process. The rankings of behaviors and service elements indicate competency issues and gaps. The *ChemicalWeek* sales satisfaction survey referenced in Chapter 3 determined the importance of fifteen organizational sales performance factors in the chemical industry.[1] Here they are listed in the order of importance to buyers:

1. Performance of products
2. Consistency of product quality
3. Ability to deliver product on time
4. Honesty of salespeople
5. Response to problems or requests
6. Long-term commitment to industry
7. Ease of doing business

8. Ability to accept short lead times
9. Efforts in developing relationships
10. Efforts in responsible care
11. Reputation
12. Efforts in product stewardship
13. Knowledge of business
14. ISO 9000 certification
15. Frequency of in-person visits

Some of these criteria are driven by the company and might be candidates for overall core competencies, such as #1–3, #6–8, #11–12, and #14. The remainder are all candidates for a sales representative's or support technician's competency model. Honesty is a good example of an attitude competency rather than knowledge or a skill. Responsiveness might generate additional competencies in Time Management and Knowledge of the Organization.

In the absence of a definition, items such as "responsible care" may require a bit more research to understand exactly what customers were thinking about when they evaluated this line item. The same might be said of "developing relationships" and "product stewardship." These rather indefinite terms can mean different things to various customers, and they require clarification before they can be understood in the context of competency modeling.

Expert Modeling

The expert modeling study of insurance salespeople introduced in Chapter 3 uncovered a list of face-to-face selling behaviors versus the more general characteristics evaluated by chemical purchasers.[2] Top producers were found to have these approaches in common:

1. They never followed a canned, step-by-step sales call.
2. They were more customer-oriented than product-oriented.
3. They varied their speech to mimic customers' patterns.
4. They used stories and metaphors to make their points.
5. They learned how prospects made buying decisions in order to understand how to sell to them.

Resulting insurance sales competencies might include sales call flexibility, knowledge of the customer, communications sensitivity, selling features and advantages, using "for instances," and questioning techniques to determine buying criteria.

Vision/Values/Mission Statements

General competency information can be uncovered by studying an organization's foundational statements. These are often a primary source of core competencies rather than position competencies, but they can indicate individual items that should appear in every model for the organization. Following is an example set of vision/values/mission statements from a consumer goods distribution firm. This is adapted from a mid-size, family-owned company selling to retailers ranging from large chains to small stand-alone stores.

✧ *Vision statement.* We will lead the competitive marketplace of the future for the benefit of the customer, employees, management, suppliers, and successors of the company.

✧ *Values statement.* We will act with honesty, integrity, and thoughtful management. We will offer opportunities to our employees through training, education, advancement, and compensation. We will exceed the expectations of both suppliers and customers with the quality and reliability of our service. We will add value to our customers' business.

✧ *Mission statement.* Help our customers satisfy their customers and maximize available profits by selling our products.

The vision statement focuses on leadership. This could generate competencies such as Competitive Knowledge, Understanding the Retailer's Business, and Consumer Preferences. The vision statement also speaks to an inclusive attitude going beyond the organization. This might suggest additional competencies, such as Distributor Industry Knowledge, Supplier Knowledge, and Customer Satisfaction Focus.

The values statement highlights Ethical Behavior and Developing People. Quality and reliability indicate a competency in Total Quality Management. This mission statement, like the vision statement, links to Understanding the Retailer's Business.

Organizational statements are helpful in identifying general, core competencies that can be refined, and that may possibly make their way into position models. They are a good place to begin in making certain that basic competencies are included where needed.

Training Curriculum

Other general information comes from position training curriculums. For example, the AAIM Management Association in St. Louis has developed a curriculum that indicates a range of general manufacturing competencies. AAIM offers a series of courses in three fundamental manufacturing competency categories (course length in days is shown in parentheses):

1. Quality
   A   Core Concepts of World-Class Quality (1)
   B. Statistical Process Control (2 1/2)
   C. DOE: Design of Experiments Overview (1/2)
   D. PFMEA: Failure Mode and Effects Analysis (1)

    E. QFD: Quality Function Deployment (1)
    F. Six-Sigma Manufacturability (1)
    G. Reliability Tools (1)
  2. Supply Chain Management
    A. Kanban Materials Management and Demand Planning (1 1/2)
    B. World-Class Supplier Management (1)
    C. Supplier Certification (1)
    D. Flow Velocity Manufacturing (1)
    E. Advanced Flow Velocity Manufacturing (1)
  3. Process
    A. Process Improvement Reengineering (1)
    B. Problem Solving and Decision Making (1)
    C. Project Management (1)
    D. ISO 9000 and QS Overview(1/2)
    E. Machine Quick Changeover (1)
    F. Basic Blueprint Reading (1)
    G. Total Productive Maintenance (1)
    H. 5 S (1)
    I. Safety Management (1)
    J. Total Asset Utilization (1)
    K. Daily Management (1/2)

The AAIM recommends that members take at least one day in each competency area plus two days of electives to achieve a fundamental level of manufacturing knowledge. "Mastery" status requires an additional five days of electives. Design teams can use this curriculum, plus the instructional design research behind each course, to identify competencies for a manufacturing position model. For example, a job focusing on manufacturing efficiency might require competencies in:

   ✧ Six-Sigma Manufacturability (Quality fundamental)
   ✧ Flow Velocity Manufacturing (Supply Chain Management fundamental)
   ✧ Machine Quick Changeover (Process fundamental)
   ✧ Advanced Flow Velocity Manufacturing (elective)
   ✧ Total Asset Utilization (elective)

A related position in manufacturing management might add these competencies for a mastery level of knowledge:

   ✧ Core Concepts of World-Class Quality (elective)
   ✧ Daily Management (elective)
   ✧ Safety Management (elective)
   ✧ World-Class Supplier Management (elective)
   ✧ Kanban Materials Management and Demand Planning (elective)

A manufacturing competency model then flows directly from the learning points of this series of courses. This way a design team can leverage the curriculum development efforts of other organizations and vendors to help identify unique competencies required in specialized positions.

Licensing Programs

Licensing criteria provide an even more detailed set of professional competencies. For example, states require engineers and land surveyors to possess certain education credentials, pass licensing examinations, and meet experience and continuing education standards. The topics covered by testing are excellent starting points in building an accurate technical position model.

For example, the National Council of Examiners for Engineering and Surveying (NCEES) lists the following description for the Industrial Engineering Principles and Practice of Engineering examination:

1. *Facilities:* site selection, plant layout, equipment, material handling and waste management systems, packaging equipment, capacity analysis, and power service and other utility requirements
2. *Manufacturing:* products, manufacturing processes, maintenance procedures, operations sequencing, machine grouping, robotics, automation, and value engineering
3. *Production and inventory systems:* forecasting, production scheduling, project scheduling, production control, resource planning, logistics, and distribution
4. *Work systems and ergonomics:* measuring work, methods analysis, incentive and other payment plans, workplace design, human-machine interfacing, and industrial hygiene and safety
5. *Quality assurance:* quality assurance plans, reliability analysis, control procedures, capability analysis, quality aspects of design
6. *Management and computer/information systems:* organization design, staffing plans, productivity, human resources, computer systems analysis and design, specification of computer equipment, and computer communications protocols

NOTE: The examination is developed with problems that will require a variety of approaches and methodologies, including design, analysis, application, and operations. Some problems may require knowledge of engineering economics, probability and statistics, and operations research techniques.[3]

This description covers general topic competencies such as Forecasting or Workplace Design and also mentions cross-functional techniques such as Engineering Economics or Operations Research. It is highly unlikely that any one industrial engineering position would require all of these competencies. And the topics are too general at this level to generate individual competencies that could be assessed.

Design teams can use lists of this type to quickly identify potential competency categories for an industrial engineering position. Items that do not pertain to the position being considered can be readily eliminated, and categories that do apply can be developed in further detail. For example, Human Resources under Management and Computer/Information Systems might be refined to require project management Personnel Allocation and Balancing. An assessment question could then be created for this specific position competency.

Vendor Certifications

Vendor certification programs provide another level of detail in searching for position competencies. Here manufacturers want to make certain that customers or service suppliers are capable of properly operating, maintaining, and repairing products. The vendors are very knowledgeable about what it takes to be successful with their products and what competencies to include in their training and assessment programs.

An extensive and difficult certification program is the Microsoft Certified Systems Engineer (MCSE) designation. MCSEs are qualified to plan, implement, maintain, and support information systems effectively in a wide range of computing environments, using the Microsoft Windows NT Server and the Microsoft BackOffice integrated family of server products. MCSE certification requires passing a series of six tests, four required and two electives, covering a massive amount of network-related information. An example course sequence for an IT professional interested in creating a Windows NT 4.0 track might be:

1. Microsoft Windows NT Workstation 4.0
2. Networking Essentials
3. Implementing and Supporting Microsoft Windows NT Server 4.0
4. Implementing and Supporting Microsoft Windows NT Server 4.0 in the Enterprise
5. Implementing and Supporting Microsoft Exchange Server 5.5 (elective)
6. Internetworking with Microsoft TCP/IP on Microsoft Windows NT 4.0 (elective)

Microsoft organizes the content of each course into the following standard sections: planning, installation and configuration, managing resources, connectivity, monitoring and optimization, and troubleshooting. (Details on test competencies are available on the Microsoft Web site at http://www.microsoft.com/mcp/mktg/choices.htm.)

For example, Installation and Configuration competencies for the Microsoft Windows NT Workstation 4.0 examination are:

✧ Install Windows NT Workstation on an Intel platform in a given situation.
✧ Set up a dual-boot system in a given situation.
✧ Remove Windows NT Workstation in a given situation.

- ✧ Install, configure, and remove hardware components for a given situation.
- ✧ Use Control Panel applications to configure a Windows NT Workstation computer in a given situation.
- ✧ Upgrade to Windows NT Workstation 4.0 in a given situation.
- ✧ Configure server-based installation for wide-scale deployment in a given situation.

These are very specific competencies that are objective and can be assessed. While the certification examination may not cover every single one of these situations, an MCSE can be expected to know how to complete these tasks. A design team building a competency model for Windows NT Server network administrators can use Microsoft's knowledge requirements to develop a competency model at whatever level of detail required. The team might even simply specify that the administrator must possess an MCSE designation and let Microsoft's test become the assessment.

Employee Manual

Guidelines in employee publications contain relevant competency information for various positions. As an example, the Server's Handbook of a small restaurant chain describes the organization's focus and approach to food service. Principal concerns for all associates are:

1. The guest comes first. There are literally thousands of dining alternatives where guests can eat, so we must make each experience in our restaurant an extraordinary one.
2. We serve high quality foods. We use quality ingredients, time-consuming preparation methods, and cook to order.
3. We are fast and accurate. We need to service our customers within their time expectations and requirements. We also need to make certain that what is delivered to the table is exactly what our guests ordered, cooked exactly the way they want it.
4. We will maintain cleanliness standards. Cleanliness is more than just meeting legal requirements. We maintain a clean restaurant for our guests and for ourselves. The perception of our restaurant can make us or break us.
5. We listen to our guests and associates. Our customers continuously tell us what they want, how we are doing, and what we need to improve upon. Our frontline associates also have good ideas on how we can improve ourselves.
6. We will treat each other with mutual respect. People are more productive when they are treated with dignity and respect.
7. We work as a team to satisfy our guests. To work at our best, we cannot work alone. No task is "not my job" when it means the customer is not properly served.

This list introduces organizational core competencies such as Quality Food. There are also several attitude and intent issues, such as a Customer-First Focus and Respect for Coworkers. Yet the following individual competencies might result from a review of this handbook:

✧ *Cleanliness.* Knows health department regulations for restaurants. Know operational procedures regarding cleanliness. Knows prescribed method of hand washing and when hands must be washed.
✧ *Listening.* Follows recommended communication style when conversing with customers. Knows procedure for recording guest feedback and suggestions.
✧ *Restaurant Knowledge.* Knows responsibilities and tasks of other members of the restaurant team. Can temporarily fill in as needed.

Employee handbooks, reference cards, or posters often distill overall operational information down to what is really important to an organization. This information can be very useful in getting started on a competency model.

Process Flowchart

Process flowcharts, if up-to-date and accurate, are ideal sources of competency information because they indicate the step-by-step method to complete a process. A flowchart's format makes it very easy to identify the knowledge and skills required by simply looking at diamonds (decisions requiring knowledge) and rectangles (activities requiring skills.) Figure 4-1 shows documentation for a climate-controlled warehouse inspection.

This deceptively simple flowchart actually represents sophisticated and critical competencies. In this process, the temperature of products is an important quality issue. Spoilage could mean actual customer damages, a reduction in customer satisfaction, or a cost in lost product. There also may not be a one-to-one correspondence between thermostat settings and warehouse temperature. Thermostats can be inaccurate, and, in addition, the operator of this process must understand the airflow and leakage characteristics of the warehouse in order to know which thermostat to set at what level for a uniform warehouse temperature. An inefficient setting can mean higher energy bills, and uneven cooling could still ruin product.

According to the flowchart, operators competent in this process must know:

✧ Product temperature requirements (diamond #1)
✧ Targeted set points for each thermostat (diamond #2)

They must also be able to complete the following activities:

✧ Correctly measure product temperature (rectangle #1).
✧ Accurately read the thermostat and its historical charts (rectangle #2).
✧ Properly reset/adjust thermostat settings to uniformly change the warehouse temperature (rectangles #3 and #4).

Figure 4-1. Climate-controlled warehouse monitoring process.

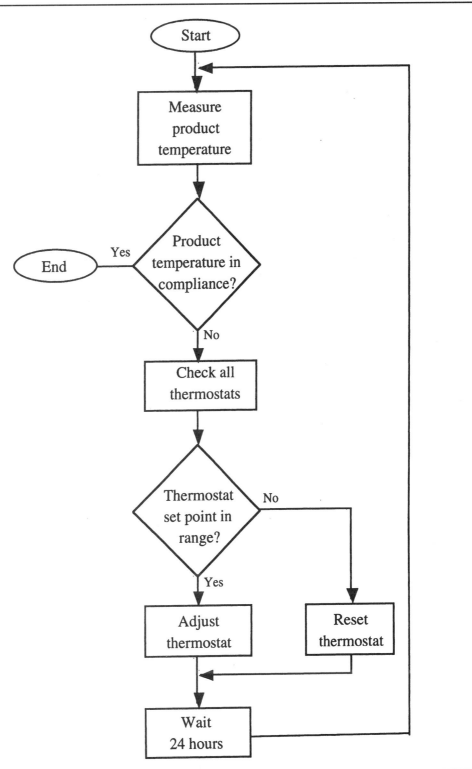

One complication not shown in this example is that a typical process chart rarely applies to just one position. Designers must make certain to separate out who does what in the process. This will be illustrated in the next example.

Value-Added Flowchart

Value-added flowcharts document processes in a different way. They follow an object through the operation and record the steps in handling and modifying it. While this is very useful in identifying non-value-added steps, it makes the task of mining the chart for competencies more difficult. The analyst must pull knowledge and activity information out of the flowchart and must also understand who is involved in each step, which are details the value-added flowchart may not contain.

Table 4-1 shows "before" and "after" steps for a simple appraisal process. The process improvement team felt that quarterly appraisals were too frequent and that the form was too involved. They also believed that the department manager did not have enough personal knowledge to appraise employees and

Table 4-1. Value-added flow analysis.

Current Quarterly Performance Review Process

Activity	Time in Hours	Value-Added?
Employee completes form	1.00	VA
Supervisor completes form	2.00	VA
Manager reviews evaluation form	0.50	NVA
Human Resources reviews form	0.50	NVA
Make corrections	0.50	NVA
Employee and evaluator review form	1.00	VA
Recommendations for the coming year	1.00	VA
Review each quarter	1.50	VA
TOTAL	8.00	
Total for 20 employees	160.00	

Proposed Semiannual Review Process with New Form

Activity	Time in Hours	Value-Added?
Employee completes form	0.33	VA
Supervisor completes form	0.66	VA
Human Resources reviews form	0.33	NVA
Make corrections	0.16	NVA
Employee and evaluator review form	0.50	VA
Recommendations for the coming year	0.50	VA
Review every six months	0.50	VA
TOTAL	3.00	
Total for 20 employees	60.00	
TIME SAVED	100.00	

VA = value-added
NVA = non-value-added

that the task should be fully delegated to the supervisors. The results of these proposed changes are: more effective appraisals, a savings of one hundred hours of departmental time, and a faster cycle time by (1) eliminating non-value-added steps while appraisals sat on the department manager's desk waiting to be reviewed and (2) eliminating another set of potential edits.

The new form and process flow change the competency models for several positions. Supervisors will be required to have the same level of appraisal competence as the department manager does now. With the greater gap between formal performance discussions, supervisors will also have to be better at providing regular feedback to subordinates. The manager will no longer need to have sufficient personal knowledge and experience with frontline personnel and operations to validate appraisal contents, but will need to be better at coaching and counseling supervisors through the appraisal process. HR will have greater responsibilities, becoming solely responsible for checking appraisals to make certain that supervisors follow organizational guidelines.

Value-added flowcharts are common organizational change tools because of their simplicity and ability to generate immediate improvements. Competency application developers should be aware of any current or past process-improvement team activity and make use of their analyses and flowcharts to help refine position models.

Job Description

Job descriptions, when accurate, complete, up-to-date, and well written are essential sources of competency information. There can be almost a one-to-one correspondence between the job description and the position model. Following is a sample job description in the results-by-duty format of HR consultants Roger and Sandra Plachy.

> *Job Title:* Advertising Manager
> *Job Purpose:* Promotes product/service by defining, developing, and implementing advertising and sales promotion programs.
> *Essential Job Results:*
>
> 1. Defines advertising objectives, campaigns, and budgets by studying marketing plans; consulting with product and market managers.
> 2. Selects internal/external media vendors by determining production requirements.
> 3. Achieves advertising financial objectives by preparing an annual budget; scheduling expenditures; using combinations of internal/external resources; analyzing variances; initiating corrective actions.
> 4. Ensures supply of promotional literature by monitoring inventories; keeping product information current.
> 5. Develops advertising and sales promotion programs by utilizing

media advertising, direct mail, trade shows, publicity, point-of-purchase, and audiovisual presentations.

6. Completes operational requirements by scheduling and assigning employees; following up on work results.
7. Achieves advertising financial objectives by preparing an annual budget; scheduling expenditures; analyzing variances; initiating corrective actions.
8. Maintains advertising staff by recruiting, selecting, orienting, and training employees.
9. Maintains advertising staff job results by counseling and disciplining employees; planning, monitoring, and appraising job results.
10. Maintains professional and technical knowledge by attending educational workshops; reviewing professional publications; establishing personal networks; participating in professional societies.
11. Contributes to team effort by accomplishing results as needed.*

This format greatly simplifies the design team's task. Along with the standard organizational competencies appearing on every employee/manager model, this job description might include the following additional competency definitions. (Comments are shown in parentheses.)

1. *Advertising Campaign Design.* Can research information from marketing plans and input from product and market managers. Can develop objectives, activities, timeframes, resource requirements, and budgets. (Note the addition of several planning elements.)
2. *Vendor Selection.* Can develop production requirements, identify performance criteria, evaluate, and select media vendors. Can make inside/outside vendor analysis. (This result was raised to a competency criteria level, with inside/outside made a separate competency.)
3. *Financial Management.* Can prepare an annual budget. Can utilize the ERP system to schedule and track expenditures and take action on variances to budget. ("Internal/external sources" was eliminated because financial management is in-house for this example.)
4. *Promotional Literature.* Can develop a promotional literature plan. Can determine content and formats for publications. Can develop and execute processes for keeping information up-to-date. Can maintain availability of all materials while controlling inventory costs. (The creation of the content, design, and item mix are the critical issues here.)
5. *Advertising and Sales Promotion Programs.* Can develop programs utilizing media, direct mail, trade shows, publicity, point-of-purchase, and multimedia presentations. Can determine mix to maximize effec-

*Reprinted from *Results-Oriented Job Descriptions* Copyright© 1993 Roger J. Plachy, et al. Reprinted by permission of AMACOM, a division of American Management Association, New York, N.Y. All rights reserved. http://www.amanet.org.

tiveness and cost-efficiency. (The advertising manager must be able to do this *well*.)

6. *Operations Management*. Can assign work, schedule employees, and monitor results. (This issue might better be covered by standard line items included on all managerial competency lists.)
7. *Advertising Financial Management*. (This item, while addressing a slightly different issue, should be consolidated with #3. Perhaps change the first sentence in #3 to, "Can prepare an annual budget for internal operations and advertising expenditures.")
8. *Staff Management*.
9. *Staff Performance*. (#8 and #9 also are issues better covered with standard language for all managers.)
10. *Professional and Technical Knowledge*. Is up-to-date on latest research, concepts, and techniques of advertising and promotion. (The actual methods of staying current are not the concern of a competency model.)
11. *Team Contributions*. Can perform in one or more of the productive team roles. (This is a valid job description item, but not a competency item. Again, the competency designer should be alert for performance words such as "accomplishing." Competency measures qualifications to perform on a team, not whether or not the advertising manager actually contributes to teams.)

This is how a well-written job description can be used to create additional position-specific competency line items.

Performance Plan

Performance plans, similar to job descriptions, are another valuable course of competency guidance. Properly written, the plan describes performance objectives for an employee. These can then be converted into competency form for the model. As an example, the performance plan for a salesperson working for a major equipment manufacturer included these items. (Comments are shown in parentheses.)

1. Make sales quota.
2. Make install quota. (Installations could take place as much as 18 months after the sale, so quotas were tracked and compensated separately.)
3. No order correction after entry.
4. No order cancellation after official confirmation.
5. No configuration rework while on the factory floor.
6. No order shipped and uninstalled.
7. No emergency component shipments required for installation.
8. Monthly forecasts within $+/-$ 5 percent of actual results.

9. Sales force automation database kept up-to-date.
10. Monthly sales and account reports submitted on time.
11. Accurate travel expense reports submitted within two weeks of return.
12. Accurate monthly expense reports submitted by the fifth of the following month.
13. Individual account goals are the following: (these are often listed from the objective measures to the subjective goals by account).
14. Personal goals are the following: (training and development, self-development, education, professional growth, etc.).
15. Participate in process improvement teams and/or with individual suggestions.
16. Adhere to all policies as specified in the Employee Manual.

Here is how these performance plan items might link to a competency model. Items #1 and #2 require competencies such as Personal Selling, Complex Account Selling, Industry Knowledge, Customer Knowledge, Product Line Knowledge, and Solutions Selling. Items #3 through #7 link to mastery of the administrative order entry and tracking system, with the focus being on eliminating costs of errors or rework. Items #8 through #12 involve keeping management properly informed and feeding the accounting system in an accurate and timely fashion. Item #13 is where detailed sales planning is reported for each major account in the territory. Item #14 focuses on personal development and could link to the proper completion of an assessment and development planning process. Item #15 requires competencies in the organization's quality programs, such as team skills, measurement and analysis of data, and process improvement techniques. Item #16 requires an understanding of all Employee Manual issues, such as values, ethics, treatment of coworkers, and administrative procedures.

This relatively simple individual performance plan helps identify a significant list of potential position competencies for this large-equipment salesperson. Note that it is not particularly strong at identifying competencies by law, by industry, or by organization categories.

A Working Model of Competencies

Following is the working model set of competencies for a white-collar office environment. This model is organized by competency category and competency. Definitions follow the rules listed earlier in this chapter except for several compound line items. The model was designed to cover manager, team leader, administrator, salesperson, and technical support positions.

1. *General Information*
    1-1. *Organizational Information.* Knows information transmitted during the new employee orientation process. Knows contents of the New

Employee Manual. Has basic knowledge concerning the organization's structure (organization chart), departments, and responsibilities of those departments. Knows where to go to find employment-related information.

1-2. *Basic Industry Knowledge.* Understands the employer's industry and marketplace. Knows and can access industry information sources such as industry analysts, trade journals, and online references.

1-3. *Policies and Procedures.* Knows organizational guidelines covering behavioral and financial policies and procedures. Knows contents of the Employee Manual.

1-4. *Legal Review and Approval.* Knows when legal approval is required for activities such as outside communications, rights, contracting, document retention, and personnel decisions.

1-5. *Diversity.* Can work with any employee without bias. Is sensitive to the values and behavioral differences between cultures represented at the employer. Knows the three-step response when observing bias in the workplace.

1-6. *Sexual Harassment.* Knows the three EEOC definitions of illegal sexual harassment. Knows the employer's complaint and reporting procedures required when observing a harassment incident. Can use the six levels of harassment and the harassment offender stereotypes to communicate harassment incidents.

2. *Management/Leadership*

2-1. *Planning.* Can perform needs and SWOT analyses. Can operate project-planning software to manage activities and on-time execution. Can use the software's output to solve scheduling problems and improve the quality of results.

2-2. *Leadership.* Can direct others. Can empower subordinates and delegate responsibility and authority. Can facilitate the development of vision, value, and mission statements. Can create a learning environment.

2-3. *Ethics.* Knows the contents of the organization's Code of Conduct booklet. Can apply the code to everyday work situations.

2-4. *Interviewing.* Knows the legal restrictions on interview questions. Can create a structured interview process for a position.

2-5. *Performance Planning.* Can create a performance plan based upon the job description, real-world analysis of required work tasks, and development needs of the employee. Can link the plan activities to the business goals of the workgroup.

2-6. *Performance Reviews.* Knows the legal restrictions on conducting reviews. Can use the performance plan to structure the review. Can use the review to identify the development needs for the next performance plan. Can conduct career-planning counseling with an employee.

2-7. *Salary Administration.* Knows the salary administration policies and guidelines.

2-8. *Coaching.* Can perform work task coaching with an employee. Can use the four-step coaching cycle in developing employee skills.

2-9. *Counseling.* Knows the six-step change procedure in counseling employees. Can use the Counseling Statement form to document performance or attitude gaps and establish next steps. Can create a success opportunity to help an employee improve.

2-10. *Open Book Management.* Can read and interpret the organization's balance sheet and income statement. Know the key measures of the workgroup and can use them to improve performance.

3. *Sales/Marketing*

3-1. *Account Planning.* Can use the organization's customer relationship software system to track account status. Can use the system to identify, segment, and prioritize opportunities. Can use the system to prepare accurate forecasts.

3-2. *Complex Account Selling.* Can identify the account buying influences and how to sell to them. Can create tailored sales messages for each buying influence. Can create a calling plan that moves the account forward to a buying decision.

3-3. *Product Strategies.* Knows the strategic messaging and sales approaches for all products. Can identify new sales opportunities. Can determine which products are best for specific customers and situations. Can execute a territory sales plan for meeting sales quotas.

3-4. *Sales Call.* Can execute a No Push Selling sales philosophy. Know the three valid sales call goals. Knows the Multi-Form five-step sales call process.

3-5. *Questioning.* Can ask open and closed questions. Can question to identify explicit customer needs. Can use questioning to assist customers in identifying their needs.

3-6. *Competitive Activities.* Knows competitors' strategies, target markets, business proposition, and products. Can track the current competitive activity in the territory. Can create strategies and plans to counter competitive efforts.

3-7. *Negotiating.* Knows the six-step negotiating process. Can analyze partner Multi-Form Tendency, adapt strategies and tactics accordingly, and complete an offer/counteroffer sequence that minimizes concessions.

3-8. *Territory Administration.* Knows how to accurately complete tracking reports such as the weekly Call Report and monthly Market Activity Report. Can utilize a time management system to track and meet deadlines, appointments, and commitments. Can maintain territory records that are sufficient for a new representative taking over the territory.

3-9. *Trade Shows.* Can set up a trade show booth according to company display guidelines. Can execute the special tradeshow sales conversation.

4. *Technical*

    4-1. *Product Knowledge.* Can explain each product's intended market, features, and general advantages. Knows and can explain products' feature differentiators over competition. Can demonstrate and operate products. Can install and maintain products.

    4-2. *Service Knowledge.* Can explain each service's intended market, features, and general advantages. Knows and can explain services' feature differentiators over competition. Can perform the services in the workplace.

    4-3. *Contracting and Consulting.* Can identify opportunities for internal and external contracting and consulting process. Can develop a Scope of Effort and design a Phase 0 study. Can lead the contracting process.

    4-4. *Project Management.* Can create plans for completing complex projects involving multiple resources and personnel. Can utilize project management software to perform tracking, resource allocation, and cost budgeting. Can use the results of project management software to resolve project problems.

    4-5. *Training.* Can determine training needs and goals. Can evaluate current training effectiveness. Can create training program content. Can perform any of the five-level analyses of training effectiveness.

5. *Administration*

    5-1. *Personnel Policies.* Knows the contents of the Personnel section of the Policy Manual. Can apply the Policy Manual to work situations.

    5-2. *Budgeting.* Can monitor and track workgroup financial and operational performance to budgets. Can use the online accounting and budgeting ERP system.

    5-3. *Expense Reporting.* Can utilize appropriate forms to capture and report expenses. Can allocate expenses to proper expense codes. Can post expenses to the online system.

    5-4. *Order Entry.* Can complete order forms for products and services. Can enter orders into the online system.

    5-5. *Financial Justification.* Can identify cash flows and perform break-even or payback analysis. Can compute discounted NPV, RIO, and IRR calculations. Can create life-cycle cost estimates.

    5-6. *Statistics.* Can compute statistical measures and present them graphically. Can utilize ratio analysis to make business decisions.

6. *Personal Computing*

    6-1. *Operating System.* Can utilize the operating system to perform daily tasks. Can customize it to maximize personal productivity.

    6-2. *Word Processing.* Can type at least 30 words per minute. Can create and format documents.

    6-3. *Spreadsheets.* Can create and format spreadsheets.

    6-4. *Presentations Software.* Can create text-based presentations. Can utilize graphic elements when and where appropriate.

    6-5. *Database Management Software.* Can create and operate a database.

6-6. *E-mail*. Can send messages and file attachments to others. Can archive messages for later retrieval.

6-7. *LAN Access*. Can store and access information on network servers. Can create shared documents.

6-8. *Mainframe Access*. Can operate the ERP applications for my workgroup. Can retrieve mainframe data and port it into desktop applications.

6-9. *Internet Access*. Can access and browse the Internet. Can download files and upload files.

7. *Personal*

7-1. *Assertiveness*. Can use assertive verbal skills. Can recognize manipulation when encountered and respond assertively.

7-2. *Nonverbal Communications*. Can observe and interpret nonverbal information. Can modify personal nonverbal communication to improve effectiveness.

7-3. *Conflict Management*. Can use a process to minimize conflict. Can adapt personal communications to remain in control while dealing with conflict.

7-4. *Creativity*. Can use creative techniques to generate ideas.

7-5. *Change Management*. Can utilize organizational change programs and data. Can create a climate conducive to change. Can contribute to continuous improvement efforts.

7-6. *Decision Making*. Can apply individual and team decision-making techniques.

7-7. *Effective Meetings*. Can conduct a meeting that meets effectiveness guidelines. Can perform in necessary team roles.

7-8. *Humor*. Can utilize humor to improve communications and results.

7-9. *Listening*. Can listen effectively to maximize comprehension and retention. Can utilize systems for retaining vocal information.

7-10. *Memory*. Can use memory techniques to retain important information.

7-11. *Presentation Skills*. Can present effectively using established guidelines. Can organize content and author presentation materials meeting layout best practices.

7-12. *Substance Abuse*. Knows the Policy Manual contents on substance abuse. Can refer individuals to the proper resource.

7-13. *Styles Analysis*. Knows the four-style tendencies model. Knows personal style and can mediate tendencies as indicated. Can change response to others based upon their style.

7-14. *Time Management*. Can manage to-do lists to meet deadlines and service goals. Can set priorities to perform most important tasks first. Can identify and eliminate unnecessary or unimportant tasks.

7-15. *Writing*. Can write business and technical content following organizational style guidelines. Can adapt the writing style to the readers' needs.

8. *Quality*

8-1. *Total Quality Management.* Knows the five basics of TQM. Can relate TQM concepts to the goals of the organization, workgroup, and position.

8-2. *ISO 9000.* Knows the contents of the ISO 9000 Quality Manual. Knows the processes required by ISO 9000 specifications. Can determine when a process meets standards.

8-3. *Customer Service.* Can identify internal and external customers for processes. Can execute excellent service in the five service areas.

8-4. *Facilitation.* Can perform as a facilitator for a process improvement team. Can intervene using first or second person approaches. Can coach and counsel members in each of the team roles.

8-5. *Team Building.* Knows the four stages of team development. Knows rules for effective team performance. Can assist teams in performing.

8-6. *Process Improvement.* Can identify the SIPOC process chain. Knows the two types of data. Can collect and analyze data using process tools. Can utilize data to improve processes.

8-7. *Reengineering.* Knows the principles of reengineering and the characteristics of reengineered processes. Can identify processes with potential for improvement with reengineering. Can perform as a reengineering team member.

8-8. *Core Competencies/Outsourcing.* Knows the characteristics of an outsourcing opportunity. Can assist in the selection and management of outsourcing vendors.

These competencies are already entered into the Competency Coach software on the CD-ROM included with this book and will be used as the basis for the working model standards and the assessment presented in Chapters 5 and 6.

Learning Points

1. Go for volume in creating competencies lists for a position.
2. Write a definition to clarify which qualifications the competency addresses.
3. Utilize as many sources as possible, to the extent time and resources allow. The variety of viewpoints will help ensure a complete model.
4. Published competency models are available but usually do not follow the definitions of Chapter 1 or are not in the proper format. Significant editing is often required.
5. The step of building a competency model is finished when the design team is not uncovering any additional competencies.

Notes

1. Elizabeth S. Kiesche, "CW-ISDI Survey: Customers Satisfied—Barely," *ChemicalWeek*, 6 April 1994, 68–72.
2. Kenneth Friedenreich and Donald J. Moine, "Winning Sales Strategies for the 1990s," *Insurance Review*, January 1990, 26–29.
3. National Council of Examiners for Engineering and Surveying, "Principles and Practice Exam—Interns," http://www.ncees.org/interns/pp_industrial.html (accessed 8 August 1999).

Establishing Job Standards

U p until now, the CMAR process has been one of decision and discovery. Once possible competency-model line items are identified, the next task is to consolidate the model into a practical number of competencies and set standards for them. This is where a considerable amount of thought and expertise comes to bear on the task, because standards decisions set performance levels for an organization. Standards that are too low, create a sense of complacency versus competitors or current performance. Standards that are too high generate an impractical amount of development requirements.

The design team must also decide how to differentiate levels of competency as they relate to standards. This can range from simple yes/no systems to multilevel gradations of competencies. Again, there are no right or wrong answers, only pros and cons based upon the goals and philosophy of the design team. But the first order of business is to decide who will determine required competencies.

Who Sets the Standards?

There rarely is total agreement among the three major participants in a process to determine what should be done. Customers are always demanding more service. Management wants to increase productivity and control costs. Front-line workers are in the middle trying to meet increasing service levels with diminishing resources. If competency standards are set too low, then performance levels will not be competitive. If standards are set too high, development needs will not be realistic and competency levels will not be attainable.

So who sets standards? This is a decision that should ideally be made at the beginning of a project along with the other actions discussed in Chapter 2. Instead, it usually comes up at the standard-setting stage when the lists of competencies have been assembled. There are four possible approaches to the decision.

Employee-Centered

In this approach, the deciding factor is what seems to work well in practice at the frontline level. Workers in essence set their own competency requirements. The design team can bring employee focus groups together to determine what makes employees successful at their positions. This is useful when there has been a recent reorganization or when little position documentation exists. Indirect worker input, such as time logs, expert modeling, contact mapping, and job task analysis information, can be utilized to establish standards.

Customer-Centered

This approach lets customer requirements set competency levels. Input comes in the form of direct customer feedback, needs analyses, satisfaction surveys, vendor research, and competitive analyses. Some managers may object to "customers running the company," but a customer-focused organization may decide that competency standards must totally support customer preferences.

Process-Centered

This is the easiest way to set standards. Here processes drive competency requirements. There is typically a wealth of supporting information, such as job descriptions, operations manuals, process charts, regulations, labor contracts, training manuals, vendor specifications, department plans, performance plans and appraisals, and quality documentation.

Management-Centered

As discussed in Chapter 3, sometimes standards are set by management fiat. They are considered elements of organizational values and strategies. Management should always be setting overall performance goals. It does not matter what observations, documentation, or customer feedback indicate if employees are not performing at competitive levels high enough to meet management directives.

The best solution may be to use a combination of the above approaches. Regardless, some approach and some individual (or team) has to have the authority to ultimately specify levels of performance for every position to be modeled.

Consolidating the Model

After utilizing a variety of sources, the design team may literally have thousands of individual competencies that apply to positions in a single workgroup. The next task is to consolidate them into a manageable list. This is a "successive approximation" process that requires multiple iterations to complete. The easiest way to manage this process is to use a simple spreadsheet model.

Each assessment requires its own spreadsheet. If the instrument covers only one position, then there will be one spreadsheet per position. If the instrument covers multiple positions within a workgroup (so that employees can be mapped to positions they do not currently hold), then there will be one spreadsheet per workgroup.

Figure 5-1 shows the simple spreadsheet used to manage the working model's raw competency data. Competencies can be organized by simply sorting in the proper column. Sort by Job Title for a position analysis. Sort by Category and then Competency to group competencies for consolidation. This is how more than two thousand sales department competencies at Anheuser-Busch were reduced to seventy-four line items.

The ultimate model size can be determined based upon preference or judgment. (See "Size of a Competency Model" in Chapter 4.) Factors include preferences on the level of detail required, how many positions are to be covered, and how lengthy an assessment instrument the respondents will tolerate.

Once a sample assessment has been completed, usually in a trial run, there are computational methods of statistical item selection such as item-total correlation, group differences, and factor analysis.[1] These can be used to group related items and consolidate redundant items. These are advanced mathematical analyses that can be completed by an organization's statistical process control experts.

Making the "Importance" Decision

A very difficult standards decision is that of ranking competencies for importance. Some design teams choose to ignore the issue altogether, figuring that a simple report of competency gaps is better than no report at all. Other designers recognize that some competencies in the model are more important than others and that gaps in these should be addressed first.

The most straightforward method of handling importance data is simply to use personal judgment to assign a relative value to each competency. Assessment reports of competency gaps can then list items in descending order of importance. A sample importance ranking might be:

3–Critical
2–Important

Figure 5-1. Consolidating competencies.

	A	B	C	
1	**Job Title**	**Category**	**Competency**	**Activity**
2	Salesperson	Sales	Sales call	Conduct sales call
3	Team Leader	Sales	Sales call	Coach reps on accompanied call
4	Manager	Management	Interviewing	Interview candidates for team positions
5	Salesperson	Leadership	Interviewing	Interview candidates for team positions
6	Administrator	Personal	Writing	Author memos and team reports
7	Administrator	Personal	Time management	Keep team records as to whereabouts
8	Administrator	Quality	ISO 9000	Be able to explain quality and vision
9	Administrator	Quality	ISO 9000	Be able to document processes for job
10	Tech Support	Personal	Creativity	Figure out ways to make our products solve cust
11	Manager	Administrative	Expense reporting	Fill out expense reports for travel, entertaining
12	Team Leader	Personal	Conflict management	Resolve problems between team members
13	Team Leader	Personal	Conflict management	Resolve problems that have escalated with custo

1–Useful

0–Not applicable to this position

(Competency Coach allows this form of ranking, although the working model on the CD-ROM does not utilize this feature.)

Another alternative for importance ranking is to derive it at the assessment stage. The easiest way to accomplish this is to rank competency gaps from largest to smallest. So a line item that requires a level five competence and is assessed at a level two (5 − 2 = 3 gap) would be ranked ahead of a line item that requires a level four and is assessed at a level three (4 − 3 = 1 gap) regardless of the competency. (This is how Competency Coach orders competencies on gap reports when no importance data is entered.)

A final alternative, and one of the most valid, is to statistically derive importance data. Assigning an importance number to individual competencies is a subjective process. Psychological research on surveys suggests that people are often poor judges about what information they think they use in deciding importance.[2] Instead, relative importance can be statistically determined.

The most common method of statistically deriving importance relationships is correlation analysis. In addition to assessment questions on individual competencies, the employee is also given an overall competence score. This can be derived from a separate assessment question for the employee, determined from 360 assessments or supervisor validity checks, or computed from competency or category averages. All that is needed is an overall number.

The sets of assessment responses across the entire workgroup (for a multiple-title assessment) or across all position holders (for a single-title assessment) can then be correlated with the set of overall competence scores. Correlation reflects the importance of each individual competency in predicting the overall competency score. The higher the correlation, the more important the competency is in measuring position competence.

This computational logic can be programmed into batch or online CMAR systems or can be done manually with a spreadsheet using built-in capabilities like Excel's CORREL function. Figure 5-2 shows a spreadsheet containing competency assessment results for a group of managers. Column A contains the overall assessments, and all columns to the right of Column A contain results for individual competencies. The summary line at the bottom shows the correlation coefficient (importance ranking) for the individual competencies.

In this sample, Interviewing shows the highest correlation with overall scores. This indicates that skill in evaluating applicants is an important factor. Ethics rates nearly as high. This is an important leadership trait and ranks higher in importance than the stand-alone Leadership competence. Performance Planning has a very low correlation and does not contribute much to the prediction of overall competence. In this organization, Performance Planning may be seen as time-wasting paperwork with little value.

There are additional statistical tools that are beyond the scope of this book.[3] Multiple regression analysis is a more sophisticated method for comput-

Figure 5-2. Importance ranking spreadsheet.

	H51	▼	=	=CORREL($A$2:$A$50,H2:H50)	

	A	H	I	J	K
1	**Overall**	**Leadership**	**Ethics**	**Interviewing**	**Perf Planning**
42	2	3	3	2	4
43	1	2	3	1	3
44	3	3	4	2	3
45	5	3	5	3	4
46	2	2	4	2	3
47	3	3	5	2	2
48	2	3	3	1	3
49	3	2	4	2	2
50	5	4	5	3	3
51		0.66	0.85	0.91	0.13
52					

ing relationships between sets of numbers. Response data can be analyzed using control charts to determine whether the process is in statistical control or whether there are special causes of variation. Again, this is something for an organization's statistical process control expert to explore.

The entire discussion of importance can also be helpful in consolidating lists of competencies for a position. Competencies can be grouped or ranked, and then items lower on the list can be evaluated for whether they measure qualifications that are truly critical to success on the job.

Choosing a Competency Continuum

Once individual competencies have been selected, the next task is to select a competency continuum. This is the basis for the words that will be used to describe levels of competency. The continuum must be able to differentiate levels of competence and be suitable for establishing requirements for a wide range of competency categories. The first step is to understand the basics of building standards continuums.

In surveying, there are two types of continuums, relative and absolute. Relative continuums are comparative measures—one item versus another. They are *rankings*. For example, any "average" sequence like the one below is a relative measure:

Below average–Average–Above average

These terms provide a comparison to some average sample. An individual could be ranked above average, yet still not be qualified to do the job. It just might be that everyone else is worse. And statistically, half the respondents are below average and half must be above average.

Absolute continuums measure to standards. They are *ratings*. These sequences illustrate absolute measures:

Does not meet–Sometimes does not meet–Meets–

Sometimes exceeds–Consistently exceeds

Bad–Poor–Fair–Good–Great

Very poor–Poor–Neither good nor poor–Good–Very good

These continuums provide a comparison to some specific measure. All employees could be rated in the "exceeds" range or none could be. Employee competence is either "good" or "bad" based upon some preset value.

Two words can be taken both ways, and might therefore cause some confusion. Based upon their primary dictionary definitions, "excellent" and "superior" are relative words. They connote that something excels or is superior to another. In normal conversation, these words are often used as absolutes. "Excellent" equates to "great" and "superior" relates to "good." Design teams should make certain that everyone understands how these words are to be used in an assessment.

One common design mistake is to mix absolute and relative terms in a standards continuum. This confuses respondents and reduces the validity of the assessment instrument. It is common to see continuums such as:

Poor–Below average–Average–Good–Excellent

These should be changed to either an "average" or a "poor/good" continuum.

Another concern is mixing in satisfaction terms in a competency standard. These series are examples:

Strongly disagree–Disagree–Neither agree nor disagree–Agree–Strongly agree

Very dissatisfied–Dissatisfied–Neither satisfied or dissatisfied–

Satisfied–Very satisfied

These continuums are better suited for capturing opinions than for assessing qualifications.

A final mistake is to include terms that are subject to varying interpretations. Words such as "strongly," "very," or "sometimes" mean different things to different people, and their use can lower the reliability of an assessment instrument.

Choosing a Scoring Scale

An issue closely related to the selection of a standards continuum is deciding upon a scoring scale. The simplest scale is a yes/no checklist:

I can [insert competency here]:   Yes   No

The benefit is that this is easy to use and fast to complete. The limitation is that it provides only a binary on/off look at competencies. An employee either possesses a competency or does not. There is no way to provide an evaluation of skill level.

The ideal number of response options in a scoring scale has been well studied. Statistically, scoring scales with only two responses have less reliability than scales with five responses. Reliability tends to level off after five points, which suggests that there is little advantage to using more than five response options.[4] So the use of seven or ten response options, which is common, is not statistically justified.

A Useful 5-Point Scale

One of the challenges in establishing standards for workplace competencies is in determining gradients of expertise. Line items such as Negotiations or Communications Skills do not readily lend themselves to a clear, objective, multilevel definition. In his 1979 book, *Quality Is Free*, Philip Crosby defined a five-point model for a "quality management maturity grid" that has proven useful in developing competency standards.[5] Crosby rates an organization's status in adopting quality using these categories:

1. *Uncertainty.* Confused and uncommitted. Management has no knowledge of quality as an improvement tool. Quality is seen as an enforcement or after-the-fact inspection function.
2. *Awakening.* Management is realizing quality can help, but is not yet willing to commit the necessary resources.
3. *Enlightenment.* Management "gets it" and decides to commit to a quality focus.
4. *Wisdom.* Management has the opportunity to make the changes permanent. This is the most critical stage of adoption.
5. *Certainty.* Management considers quality is a permanent part of the organization's focus and is being properly managed.

In 1986, the U.S. Air Force asked the Software Engineering Institute (SEI) at Carnegie Mellon University to develop a method for evaluating the capabilities of software contractors. Crosby's model, along with other classic TQM principles, provided the conceptual basis for the development of a Capability Maturity Model (CMM) for Software. The success of CMM for Software created interest in applying the concepts to other organizational development tasks. The result has been the Systems Engineering Capability Maturity Model and the Department of Defense's System Acquisition Capability Maturity Model.[6]

In the mid-1990s, the SEI extended CMM concepts to create the People Capability Maturity Model (P-CMM) for developing the workforce. The P-CMM defines these five levels:

1. *Initial.* Processes are not standardized. Performance is based upon previous experience and personal skills. There is little or no effort to measure and improve competencies.

2. *Repeatable.* The focus is on eliminating problems. Employees take personal responsibility for making certain tasks are completed correctly. Processes may be standardized within workgroups, but often not across departments.
3. *Defined.* Organizations know their core competencies. Employees' competency development and career growth are systematically managed.
4. *Managed.* Organizations measure competency levels and set quantitative growth targets. High performance teams are formed and utilized. Performance is standardized across the organization.
5. *Optimizing.* There is a continuous focus on continuously improving competencies. The organization has a culture of performance excellence.

These levels can be further refined for use in establishing individual competence standards and in authoring assessment questions. A general continuum of individual competence can be:

1. *None.* Employee has no knowledge or skills in this area.
2. *Personal.* Employee uses personal knowledge and experience to perform.
3. *Process.* Employee can perform to process requirements.
4. *Advanced.* Employee possesses advanced competence levels.
5. *Developing.* Employee can improve processes and/or develop competencies in others.

While not every standard exactly fits this approach, it will accommodate most competencies. This five-level model is used throughout the working model featured in Chapters 4 through 6 and has been entered in the Competency Coach program on the CD-ROM included with this book.

Yes/No Examples: Teaching Skills

The softer the skills, the more difficult it can be to build the competency model and to establish standards. This is especially true in one of the largest industries in the United States, public and private education. Teacher assessment is a leading issue in elementary and secondary education as school districts and state agencies are working to systematize the measurement and development of teachers. Some leading-edge work has been done in Connecticut in creating a program for beginning teachers, and in establishing standards for teachers by specialty.

Connecticut Competency Instrument

In the late 1980s, a team of researchers and teachers, coordinated by the Bureau of Research and Teacher Assessment in the Connecticut State Department of Education, developed the Connecticut Competency Instrument (CCI).[7] The initial version of the CCI was used to assess teachers during the 1989–1990 school year. This led to further refinement of the CCI, and minor modifications were made in the early 1990s. The instrument is used in the Beginning Educator Support and Training (BEST) Program that provides support and assessment for new teachers in Connecticut.[8]

There are five philosophical assumptions behind the CCI process:

1. Effective teaching can take many forms. The goal of competent teaching is student learning, not adherence to a single model of instruction. The CCI focuses on teacher behaviors and classroom learning processes that research has shown to promote learning.
2. Critical dimensions of teacher performance that promote learning can be defined across diverse educational contexts. These dimensions are independent of grade level, subject matter, locale, or special populations.
3. Competence of beginning teachers as decision makers can be differentiated from that of experienced teachers. The levels of competencies important for beginning teachers are different from the levels that might define more experienced teaching.
4. Effective teaching must be judged in the context of the teacher's objectives. The effectiveness of teaching behaviors can only be assessed with reference to the teacher's goals.
5. Professional judgment is vital to teacher assessment. Experienced educators are specially trained to use the CCI criteria in an assessment.

The assessment is based upon observations of actual performance. Assessors formally observe a beginning teacher on six occasions during the teacher's first year and rate the teacher's skill level as "acceptable" or "unacceptable" on each of what the CCI calls "indicators"—what this text calls standards. A teacher's provisional certification recommendation is then made based upon the combined scores.

This is an excellent example of a yes/no model of assessment. The standards are well developed, defined, and described. The acceptable/unacceptable criteria are not as rigidly defined, but this is addressed through specific assessor qualifications and training to ensure consistency and reliability.

Following is a summary of the CCI Indicators assessment guidelines for new teachers. The general format is indicator, rationale, defining attributes. (The decision rules will be covered in Chapter 6.) Numerous examples are provided in the training sessions to help assessors understand the defining attributes and apply the standards consistently. The complete text of the CCI can be found on the State of Connecticut Department of Education Web site (http:// www.state.ct.us/sde/brta/cciindic.htm).

I. Management of the Classroom Environment

Indicator IA: The Teacher Promotes a Positive Learning Environment

The teacher is responsible for the nature and quality of teacher-student interactions in her or his classroom. The teacher's perception of students and their abilities directly affects students' responses, motivation, and achievement. The teacher's interactions with students should be positive and designed to enhance the learning environment. The beginning teacher, therefore, establishes and maintains a positive learning environment by creating a physical environment conducive to learning and maintaining both positive teacher-student and student-student interactions.

Defining Attributes

There are three defining attributes of promoting a positive learning environment. They reflect the use of a variety of techniques for promoting positive teacher-student interactions and a physical environment that is conducive to learning:

1. Rapport: The teacher establishes rapport with all students by demonstrating patience, acceptance, empathy and/or interest in students through positive verbal and non-verbal exchanges. The teacher avoids sarcasm, disparaging remarks, sexist and racial comments, scapegoating and physical abuse. The teacher also exhibits her or his own enthusiasm for the content and for learning and maintains a positive social and emotional atmosphere in the learning environment.

2. Communication of expectations for academic achievement: The teacher creates a climate that encourages all students to achieve. Expectations for success may be explicitly verbalized or communicated through the teacher's approach to assigning tasks, rewarding student effort and providing help and encouragement to all students.

3. Physical environment: To the extent it is under her or his control, the teacher establishes a physical environment that is safe and conducive to learning.

IB. The Teacher Maintains Appropriate Standards of Behavior

Research shows that effective teachers use management practices that include concrete, functional and explicit rules and standards that are established early in the school year and maintained throughout the year. Fitting consequences should be applied to both appropriate and inappropriate behaviors. Teachers' standards or rules may vary, but their use in the management of behavior should assist in effectively facilitating the teaching-learning process in the classroom. The beginning teacher will maintain these standards through clear and consistent expectations for appropriate student behavior.

Defining Attribute

1. Rules and standards of behavior are maintained: Either through explicit statements of rules or through responses to student behavior, the teacher communicates and reinforces appropriate standards of behavior for the students. The teacher applies fitting consequences when student behavior is either appropriate (i.e., consistent with the standards) or inappropriate. Even though a teacher's standards may vary, they should have the effect of facilitating student learning. A pattern of appropriate behavior indicates that rules and standards have been previously communicated to the students. A pattern of inappropriate behavior indicates that rules and standards of behavior are not being maintained.

IC. The Teacher Engages the Students in the Activities of the Lesson

The amount of time students spend on the tasks of the lesson is important because it is a reflection and outcome of the teacher's management and instructional skills. Research consistently shows that the amount of time students spend successfully engaged in activities relevant to the lesson objectives is positively related to student achievement. Conversely, time spent disengaged or off-task is associated with low achievement gains. This indicator assesses the engagement of students in the activities of the lesson.

Defining Attributes

1. Student engagement: The beginning teacher engages a clear majority (at least 80 percent) of the students in the activities of the lesson. Engagement is defined as students' involvement in lesson activities consistent with the teacher's expectations or directions. Although a high rate of engagement is expected, it is acceptable for students to be momentarily off-task from time to time during a lesson.

2. Re-engagement: When any student is persistently off-task, the teacher must attempt to bring her/him back on task. A variety of strategies may be used. A teacher's attempt to re-engage a student need not be successful; however, when unsuccessful, the teacher must make additional attempts to re-engage the student.

ID. The Teacher Effectively Manages Routines and Transitions

How teachers allocate and manage the administrative and organizational activities of the classroom has a direct bearing on the amount of time that is available for instruction, and the quality of that instruction. Whereas Indicator IC is concerned with the amount of instructional time in which students are actually engaged in learning activities, Indicator ID deals with how the teacher manages the non-instructional time. It is expected that the beginning teacher will effectively use the time allocated for instruction by managing routines and transitions to support the purposes of instruction.

Classroom routines are non-instructional, organizational, administrative, or repetitive activities such as roll-taking, pencil-sharpening, or the distribution of materials and equipment, although the latter may be in preparation for subsequent instruction. Transitions are non-instructional organizational or administrative moves from one classroom activity or context to another. Transitions may occur between instructional activities as well as between an instructional and a non-instructional activity.

Defining Attributes

1. Effectiveness: The teacher should provide effective routines and transitions that reflect planning, established norms and a sense of structure. When appropriate, resources and materials should be organized and available. In addition, the amount of time spent on routines and transitions should be appropriate for their purpose and the makeup of the class. Depending upon the nature and purpose of a routine or transition, proceeding too quickly may be as detrimental as taking too much time with the noninstructional activities.

II. Instruction

Assessor judgment about the acceptability of teacher performance on the instruction indicators rests heavily on the clarity of the teacher's objectives. Beginning teachers must have clear and specific objectives for their lessons or for all learning activities. (Indicators IIA, IIB, IIC, and IID relate directly to the lesson objective.) It is important, therefore, for beginning teachers to fully understand what the students are expected to learn and clearly convey that understanding to assessors through the Pre-Assessment Information Form and Pre-Observation Interview. The Post-Observation Interview gives teachers an opportunity to indicate any changes made in their objectives or activities during the course of the lesson, or any unexpected classroom occurrences that could impact the observation.

There are frequent references to lesson elements within the indicators of the instruction cluster. These are discrete parts of a lesson, the beginnings or endings of which may be indicated by a change in activity, topic, or instructional arrangement.

IIA. The Teacher Presents Appropriate Lesson Content

Research shows that teaching is most effective when content is both accurate and at a level of difficulty or complexity appropriate for the learners. The competent beginning teacher should demonstrate mastery of the subject matter through the representation and delivery of accurate content. The content of the lesson should also be aligned with the objectives of the lesson. Content includes, but is not limited to, lesson materials, student discussion, activities, practice, modeling, demonstrations, teacher presentation, and teacher questioning.

Defining Attributes

1. Choice of content: The content must be aligned with the lesson objectives. Teachers should not significantly deviate from the lesson content as specified in the objectives, unless the objectives or activities are modified during the lesson.

2. Level of difficulty: The lesson content must be at a level of difficulty (neither too easy nor too hard) that is suitable for the level of students' cognitive development. Content should also be at an appropriate level for the students' social, emotional, and/or physical development. The teacher will use vocabulary and language appropriate to the learners. The appropriate level of difficulty may differ among students, and often the appropriateness may be judged by student responses and behavior.

3. Accuracy: The lesson content must be accurate. Infrequent, minor inaccuracies not significantly related to the content should not be considered in the rating of this defining attribute.

IIB. The Teacher Creates a Structure for Learning

The beginning teacher is responsible for providing the structure in which learning occurs. A consistent research finding is that when teachers appropriately structure instructional information, student achievement is increased. Research shows that initiations facilitate student understanding. Research suggests that closures assist students in integrating and processing information, and practitioners and education specialists believe it is an important part of lesson structure. Lesson elements are discrete parts of a lesson, the beginnings or endings of which may be indicated by a change of activity, topic or instructional arrangement.

Defining Attributes

1. Initiations: Initiations must relate to lesson objectives and help students anticipate or focus on the lesson content. The beginning teacher will provide initiations at the beginning of the lesson or between significant instructional elements throughout the lesson. Fre-

quently, initiations preview what is to be learned, why it is to be learned, or how it relates to past or future learning. Initiations have a role in motivating students. Initiations may be explicit statements or may occur through established instructional activities or teacher modeling tied to the lesson objectives. Simply stating the activities in which the students will engage is not sufficient for initiation.

2. Closures: Closures must relate to lesson objectives and help students understand the purpose of the lesson content. The beginning teacher is responsible for closure at the end of the lesson or between significant instructional elements throughout the lesson. Simply restating lesson objectives is not sufficient for closure.

IIC. The Teacher Develops the Lesson to Promote Achievement of the Lesson Objectives

Development is the heart of the lesson and the key to establishing meaning for students and achieving lesson objectives. It is in developing the lesson that the teacher organizes instructional activities and materials to enhance students' learning of lesson content. Effective development motivates and moves students toward the lesson objectives. In an effectively developed lesson, related elements are manifestly linked to each other, and the materials and instructional arrangements contribute to the lesson's momentum. Lesson elements are discrete parts of a lesson, the beginnings or endings of which may be indicated by a change of activity, topic or instructional arrangement.

Defining Attributes

1. Lesson development: Effective lesson development:
a. provides an underlying order within and among lesson elements,
b. manifests a link between related lesson elements, and
c. leads students to learn the content of each element.

Effective lesson development integrates these three components into a conceptual whole which establishes meaning for students and moves them toward achieving the lesson objective(s). The content of the lesson element(s) must be related to the lesson objective(s).

2. Use of instructional arrangements and materials: Materials and instructional arrangements must purposefully support the development of the lesson. They should be used to promote student interest and involvement in the lesson.

IID. The Teacher Uses Appropriate Questioning Strategies

Questioning is an important aspect of instruction which stimulates and develops students' thinking and helps communicate what is to be learned. Questioning strategies also involve students, encourage the exchange of ideas or information between and among students and assist students in meeting the lesson objectives. Questioning may be explicit and verbal or may be implicitly embedded in lesson materials or activities. When using explicit questioning, the competent beginning teacher waits for and listens to student answers, effectively responds and incorporates those answers into the lesson. Questioning may be explicit and verbal or may be implicitly embedded in lesson materials or activities. Questioning includes any activity the teacher uses to obtain student oral, written or nonverbal responses to the content of the lesson.

Defining Attributes

1. Cognitive level: The level of questioning must be appropriate to the lesson objectives. If the teacher is seeking recall of basic facts or concepts, then questions of a lower cognitive level are appropriate. If the teacher's purpose is to stimulate higher-level thinking, such as analysis and evaluation, then questions of a higher cognitive level are appropriate. In many lessons, a variety of questioning levels will be appropriate.

2. Responding to students: The teacher should respond to student replies, failures to answer, questions and/or comments. Where appropriate, the teacher builds upon student contributions to work toward the lesson objectives. Responses may include waiting, clarifying, refocusing, acknowledging correct responses, providing corrective feedback, extending or prompting.

3. Opportunities for student involvement: Opportunities for student involvement must be provided by allowing all students an opportunity to answer the question(s) and seeking answers from a variety of students. Opportunities may include student-initiated questions and tasks as well as teacher-initiated questions. Appropriate use of wait time allows all students an opportunity to become involved in questioning activity.

IIE. The Teacher Communicates Clearly, Using Precise Language and Acceptable Oral Expressions

The quality of teacher communication is important for student learning. Teachers should provide clear presentations and explanations of the lesson content. Precise communication and clear speech should serve to enhance student understanding. Teachers are expected to model acceptable oral expressions.

Defining Attributes

1. Precision of communication: Precision of communication refers to the communication of meaning. The teacher must communicate in a coherent manner, avoiding vagueness and ambiguity that interfere with student understanding. Precision of communication includes giving directions.

2. Clarity of speech: Clarity of speech refers to the technical quality of communication. This consists of the teacher's articulation, volume and rate of delivery, which must not interfere with student understanding.

3. Oral expressions: A pattern of unacceptable oral expressions must be avoided. Incorrect grammar and slang should be avoided; however, it is acceptable for teachers selectively to use current popular phrases or slang to make a point, establish rapport or enhance the learning. Vulgarity should be avoided.

III. Assessment

Assessor judgement about the acceptability of teacher performance on the assessment indicator rests heavily on the clarity of the teacher's objectives. Consequently beginning teachers must have clear and specific objectives for their lessons for all learning activities. It is important, therefore, for beginning teachers to fully understand what the students are expected to learn and to clearly convey that understanding to assessors through the Pre-Assessment Information Form and Pre-Observation Interview. The Post-Observation Interview gives teachers an opportunity to indicate any changes in planned objectives or activities made as a result of monitoring.

IIIA. The Teacher Monitors Student Understanding of the Lesson and Adjusts Instruction When Necessary

The importance of monitoring and adjusting is underscored by research on teaching. More learning will occur when teachers regularly monitor their students' understanding and adjust instruction when appropriate. The two components support one another in promoting student understanding; appropriate adjustment is contingent upon sufficient monitoring and should not be viewed separately. The beginning teacher should monitor students' understanding at appropriate points in the lesson and adjust her or his teaching when the resulting information indicates it is necessary to do so.

Lesson elements are discrete parts of a lesson, the beginnings or endings of which may be indicated by a change of activity, topic or instructional arrangement. ·

Defining Attributes

1. Monitoring for understanding: The purpose of monitoring is to see that students are understanding the lesson content and moving toward the lesson objectives. Toward this end, the teacher must check the level of understanding of a variety of students at appropriate points during the lesson. These points include (but are not limited to) the completion of a lesson element and after an adjustment resulting from monitoring.

2. Adjusting when necessary: The teacher must use appropriate strategies to adjust his or her teaching when monitoring or spontaneous student response indicates that students are misunderstanding or failing to learn. Strategies for adjustment may include re-presenting information, re-explaining a concept, asking different types of questions, and/or slowing the pace of instruction. The teacher will also use appropriate strategies to adjust when monitoring indicates that students have mastered the concepts being taught. Such strategies may include accelerating the pace of instruction, providing enrichment activities, and/or moving on to new material. When monitoring indicates that adjustment is necessary but not possible within the lesson, the teacher must acknowledge to the students the need for adjustment at a later time.*

The first reaction to this CCI assessment is that teaching school is more complicated than a parent or student might assume. The second is that many business presenters would be hard pressed to pass a new teacher assessment in Connecticut. The third is that this is an instrument that teaches as well as documents. The fourth is that this is a far more comprehensive evaluation and development program than what is typically in place for new hires in business and government.

A concern is that, upon initial inspection, the CCI can seem like a performance evaluation. Some of its language supports that view, with its focus on teacher behaviors rather than skills, knowledge, and attitudes. But there is an implicit, and justifiable, assumption in the CCI that observable and repeatable demonstrations of required behaviors and processes indicate that a new teacher possesses the competencies for preliminary certification.

The process also generates high reliability. Skills and knowledge are evaluated by examining the educator's equivalent of "business results"—classroom

*Bureau of Research and Teacher Assessment, *Beginning Educator Support and Training (BEST) Program* (Hartford: Connecticut State Department of Education, 1999), http://www.state.ct.us/sde/brta/index.htm Used with permission.

teacher and student behaviors and performance. This provides a high level of measurement as an assessment of teacher competence.

What keeps the CCI from being an appraisal is its periodic nature. An appraisal is the result of an evaluation of continuous performance over time. The CCI is used six times throughout a school year to determine what the teacher *can* do when under observation. What the teacher *does* do is best determined by local school personnel.

Subject Area Standards

In addition to the CCI for new teachers, Connecticut also provides professional standards for teaching specialties, such as art, elementary, English, math, music, physical education, school leaders, science, social studies, and special education.[9] This two-level approach is an interesting model for business and government to consider. In essence, the CCI represents core classroom competencies that all new teachers should possess, while professional standards address requirements by specialty.

Following is an example of standards by subject area, the Connecticut Professional Music Teaching Standards:

   I. Teacher as Musician
      1. Effective music teachers understand, perform, create, conduct, and communicate about music accurately and artistically.
      2. Effective music teachers are knowledgeable of a variety of music from diverse cultural and historical traditions.
      3. Effective music teachers understand the nature and significance of music and its relationship to other arts and disciplines outside the arts.
  II. Teacher as Educator
      1. Effective music teachers plan developmentally appropriate curriculum and instruction that empower students to carry out the artistic processes with skill, knowledge, and expressiveness in music.
      2. Effective music teachers plan instruction that reflects a knowledge of students.
      3. Effective music teachers utilize appropriate literature, technology, and other resources to plan and deliver instruction.
      4. Effective music teachers use a variety of developmentally appropriate teaching methods and strategies to involve students actively in the learning process and promote a high level of music achievement.
      5. Effective music teachers create a safe, positive learning environment that enhances student motivation, participation, and risk-taking.
      6. Effective music teachers incorporate assessment and evaluation to promote student learning.

III. Teacher as Professional
 1. Effective music teachers pursue lifelong learning and improvement through reflective practice, musical and professional development, and participation in music making.
 2. Effective music teachers articulate and enhance the role of the arts in the school and community.
 3. Effective music teachers demonstrate organizational and administrative skills in program management.*

While this is written to describe what music teachers do, these standards would fit into the writing approach used in this text with the simple addition of the word "can," as in, "Effective music teachers *can* . . . ." Again, when assessment is done by observation, the implicit assumption is that a demonstration of skill equates to the possession of the competency.

The music standard has content similar to the new teachers' CCI; for example, see items II.4, on teaching methods, or II.5, describing a safe and positive learning environment. But it also includes advanced competencies, including I.3, on understanding music's relationship to other arts and disciplines outside the arts, and III.2, enhancing the role of arts in the community.

The Connecticut approach is an excellent benchmark for a yes/no, soft-skills standards program, whether in education or in business. It is based on research on educational effectiveness, is well defined, has been tested and validated for nearly a decade, measures actual results, and is executed by experienced and specially trained assessors. The result is a CMAR process with very high accuracy, validity, and reliability.

The education industry has been heavily criticized in the last few years. It is under increasing pressure to deliver high-quality learning experiences and measurable increases in student performance. The State of Connecticut responded by focusing on new teacher development, and then expanding into more advanced standards with a sophisticated process. In an era of tight educational budget, this is a significant expenditure of resources on competencies.

Perhaps the typical business would not want to spend that much time and money on an assessment process, yet the needs for validity, reliability, and accuracy are the same. A yes/no standards system can be an excellent starting point.

Five-Point Example: Working Model

The next step in the development of the competency working model introduced in Chapter 4 is to establish standards. A yes/no system, where the description of the competency is nearly the standard itself, is ideal for assessing basic competencies. It is not as powerful in assessing levels of competency among experienced employees. The working model uses the five-point "none–developing"

*Bureau of Research and Teacher Assessment, *Connecticut Professional Music Teaching Standards* (Hartford: Connecticut State Department of Education, 1997), http://www.state.ct.us/sde/brta/music.htm. Used with permission.

dimension inspired by the P-CMM model to differentiate varying skills, knowledge, and attitudes within a single competency.

This can be created and reported using a simple spreadsheet format, as shown in Figure 5-3. Since the working model represents a multiple-title workgroup, an array of competencies by title was created. This can be very helpful visually in deciding what level of competency will be required for one position compared with another.

One question that arises concerns the difference between a blank cell and a competency standard of "1." A blank entry means that the competency is not relevant for a position. A "1" entry means that the position requires no competency in this area. This is a minor distinction that could be eliminated by putting a "1" in every empty cell. Some organizations, particularly those not using importance ranking, prefer to keep the distinction. They use the "1" standard to mean that this is a relevant competency, but that it is relatively unimportant. This way, an organization can measure a competency and have the results in its database, but not generate any gap reporting or develop needs related to that competency.

Here are examples of some of the thinking that goes into developing multi-level standards by position:

Some competencies are clear in their applicability. For Interviewing, only the manager and team leader are assumed to conduct hiring interviews. The financial exposure for mistakes is high, and frontline employees do not have the legal or procedural training for interviewing. The numbers are relatively low in this case because the operational leadership interviews only for the candidate's suitability to work on the team. In this case, HR takes care of other interviewing requirements. If managers and team leaders did all of their own hiring, then they would likely need to be a level "4" for this competency.

A competency that is less clear is Questioning. Every person who communicates needs to be able to ask questions. Yet this line item appears in a Sales/ Marketing category listing. This is an important sales skill, one that the team leader must be able to coach for others, and one in which the salesperson should be advanced. The competency is not listed for the manager; although the manager might make executive sales calls, managers are usually not involved in the prospecting or needs development phase. If they were, then this would likely be a "3" or higher-level competency for them.

A competency such as Conflict Management clearly applies to all positions. First, it is an essential internal team skill. Everyone should be at least a "2" in this area. Administrators need basic skills, because they may be the first contact point, but they can probably forward any complaints to someone who can resolve the issue. Remaining team members need to be a "3" to deal with customers. Team leaders are required to be a "4" because they are the likely contact for customer problems that escalate beyond frontline personnel.

This is the manner in which a design team can work through the competency model. The process of establishing numerical standards is somewhat iterative with the development of an assessment instrument. The five-point

Figure 5-3. Sample competency model.

Sample Competency Model			Team		
© CooperComm, Inc. 1999.					
http://www.coopercomm.com					
Competency	*Mgr*	*Admin*	*Leader*	*Sales*	*Tech*
General					
Organizational Information	4	3	4	3	3
Basic Industry Knowledge	3		5	4	2
Policies & Procedures	3	5	3	2	2
Legal Review & Approval	5	4	3	2	2
Diversity	5	3	4	3	3
Sexual Harassment	5	3	4	3	3
Management/Leadership					
Planning	2	2	2	2	2
Leadership	4		3	2	
Ethics	4	2	3	3	3
Interviewing	3		2		
Performance Planning	5		3		
Performance Reviews	5		3		
Salary Administration	4				
Coaching	3		4		
Counseling	3		3	2	
Open Book Management	3	2	3	3	2
Sales/Marketing					
Account Planning			4	3	
Complex Account Selling			4	3	
Product Strategies	2		2	5	2
Sales Call	2		5	3	4
Questioning			5	4	3
Competitive Activities	2		3	5	3
Negotiating	3		5	3	
Territory Administration	3		3	4	3
Trade Shows			4	3	2
Technical					
Product Knowledge	2		2	3	4
Services Knowledge	2		2	3	4
Contracting & Consulting	2		2	2	4
Project Management	2		3	2	4
Training	2		3		
Administration					
Personnel Policies	4	3	3		
Budgeting	3	4	2		
Expense Reporting	2	4	2	2	2
Order Entry		5	2	2	
Financial Justification		3		2	4
Statistics	3	4	2		

(continues)

Figure 5-3. *(continued).*

Personal Computing					
Operating System	3	4	3	3	3
Word Processing	3	4	3	3	3
Spreadsheets	2	5	2	2	4
Presentation Software		4	2	3	3
Database Management Software	1	3	1	1	3
E-Mail Software	3	4	3	3	3
LAN Access	3	5	3	3	3
Mainframe Access		5	4	2	2
Internet Access		4			
Personal					
Assertiveness	2	2	2	2	2
Nonverbal Communications	3	2	4	4	3
Conflict Management	3	2	4	3	3
Creativity			4	2	2
Change Management	4		3	2	2
Decision Making	2		2		
Effective Meetings	4		5		
Humor				3	
Listening	3		3	4	4
Memory			2	2	2
Presentation Skills	2		2	3	2
Substance Abuse	3		2		
Styles Analysis	5		5	5	4
Time Management	3	5	3	4	4
Writing	3	2	3	4	2
Quality					
TQM	3	2	3	2	2
ISO 9000	5	2	3	2	2
Customer Service	2	3	4	3	3
Facilitation	4		4		
Team Building	4		3		
Process Improvement	2	4	3	2	2
Reengineering	3	4			
Core Competencies/Outsourcing	2				

"none–developing" dimension provides a starting point that may well be adjusted as the design team begins actually writing assessment responses. A "3" can suddenly become a "4" in light of the final wording. Some designers want to start immediately with the assessment text, but experience shows that this is more difficult when there are no general competency levels to use as starting points.

Regardless of the dimension, once yes/no or numeric standards are established, the related assessment instrument can be created. This is the topic of Chapter 6.

Learning Points

1. Management should be setting organizational performance goals and should have strong input about standards as "what will be." This

should then be supported by a cross-functional decision team working out the details of individual competency standards.

2. There is no specific method for consolidating a long competency item list. Pick a target competency model size, then start sorting and combining like items.

3. Importance data is very useful in consolidating lists of competencies and in setting standards. Statistically derived importance is the most reliable.

4. A competency dimension can be absolute or relative, but not both.

5. A competency dimension can be a simple two-level, yes/no system or a multilevel continuum. The most reliable dimension is five items long.

6. Well-written competency descriptions make it much easier to create standards (and later to write assessment instruments.)

7. The better the standards, the more valid the CMAR process (as was shown in the CCI example).

8. There are generally three classes of competencies in a multiposition, multilevel standards, workgroup model: targeting by position, general competencies with specific uses, and generic competencies everyone needs. Competency requirements should be established accordingly.

Notes

1. Bob E. Hayes, *Measuring Customer Satisfaction: Development and Use of Questionnaires* (Milwaukee: ASQC Quality Press, 1992), 63–67.
2. Hayes, *Measuring Customer Satisfaction*, 82–85.
3. Ibid.
4. Ibid., 59.
5. Philip B. Crosby, *Quality is Free: The Art of Making Quality Certain* (New York: Mentor, 1979), 21–34.
6. Bill Curtis, William E. Hefley, and Sally Miller, *Overview of the People Capability Maturity Model* (Pittsburgh: Carnegie Mellon University, 1995), CMU/SEI-95-MM-01.
7. Bureau of Research and Teacher Assessment, *CCI Indicators* (Hartford: Connecticut State Department of Education, 1999), http://www.state.ct.us/sde/brta/cciindic.htm
8. Bureau of Research and Teacher Assessment, *Beginning Educator Support and Training (BEST) Program* (Hartford: Connecticut State Department of Education, 1999), http://www.state.ct.us/sde/brta/index.htm
9. Ibid.

6

Developing the Assessment

Assessing competencies is the most critical step in a CMAR process. No matter how exacting the model is, no matter how carefully the standards are set, if the measurement process is not effective, the results can be worthless.

This is where many organizations run into trouble. Lacking survey-writing and test-writing skills, HR professionals are often not comfortable writing feedback instruments. In addition, creating competency measurement instruments is very difficult. Putting the overwhelming amount of competency and standards data into a succinct measurement system is a complex task for a first-project design team.

The good news is that if the preliminary steps have been done correctly—design decisions made ahead of time, competencies properly identified and defined, and appropriate standards set—then much of the work required to build the assessment instrument has been completed. All that is required is to choose a measurement system and to execute it.

Getting Started

It is important to review the goals of an assessment system before beginning design activities. A CMAR project must possess three characteristics: validity, accuracy, and reliability. *Validity* refers to competencies and the model. To be worthy of measure, they must be the ones that drive organizational goals. Friendliness may be a helpful competency, but it is not necessarily valid for a maintenance technician who repairs diesel engines on earthmovers. *Accuracy* refers to the ability of the assessment to measure actual competencies. For example, for a diesel mechanic, a true-false test is likely to be less accurate than a hands-on repair test. *Reliability* refers to consistency. Employees in the same position with equal competencies must generate equivalent assessment results, no matter when the assessment is completed or who does the assessing.

Design teams must keep these three factors in mind in creating assessment processes and instruments. The factors arise in the form of questions during the authoring process:

"Does this accurately measure the competency?"
"Is there any way for employees to 'game the system' or bias the result for whatever reason?"
"Will this give us consistent results?"
"Is there more than one way to interpret this?"
"Have we inadvertently inserted any assumptions or hidden bias?"

Writing assessment instruments is an iterative process. Design teams should start with a simple approach and build in sophistication and complexity over time. The authoring process is also very collaborative. The more stakeholders that can be involved in the authoring process, the better. Everyone brings a different viewpoint and experience level.

What the design team must do is get something started. Going from blank sheet of paper to first draft is the most difficult step. The challenge is to get something, anything created, even if it is poor. Stakeholders are typically not able to create assessment line items, questions, or activities. But in a classic continuous improvement application, they can readily feed back what they like or don't like about existing entries. This helps the process and/or instrument evolve into a process with high validity, accuracy, and reliability.

A Closer Look at Assessment Methodologies

There are many possible approaches to assessment. Each has its pros and cons in accurately measuring competencies and in maintaining consistency across individuals. The challenge for the CMAR design team is to convert the competency model and standards data into an instrument that reliably measures qualifications of employees.

Opinion Survey Assessments

Surveying in all its forms—direct, third-party, and 360°—is the most common method of competency assessment. Surveying makes a good starting point. It is a familiar process in a quality-focused organization where internal and external customer satisfaction is regularly measured. Surveys, even competency assessments, are relatively simple to write and tabulate and straightforward to administer. Respondents are experts on their own opinions and can readily provide input.

The concern with survey assessments is reliability. As was discussed in Chapter 2, respondents may not be qualified to rate their own competencies and those of their coworkers. A survey captures opinions that may not be based upon established standards and measures. The result is a chorus of "I think . . ." feedback that may or may not have much to say about individuals' actual competencies.

If surveying is to be used at all, it should be considered a transition methodology on the way to a more reliable form of competency assessment. Some organizations prefer to ease into competency-based HR applications in order to minimize the trauma of organizational change and the fears and levels of discomfort of the participants.

Test Assessments

Another popular approach to assessing competencies is testing. This has a high comfort factor with design teams due to the pervasive use of tests, both standardized and by course, in K–12 and higher education. Design team members have all taken thousands of tests throughout their lives. Testing has the advantage of providing an objective result that is generated in a consistent fashion. Everyone takes the same test. Testing is also easily automated using standardized programming tools and can be delivered remotely using Web-based technology.

The main disadvantage of testing is that there are justified concerns as to whether tests are accurate measures of competence. A second problem is that tests emphasize knowledge over skills. It is difficult to create a test that measures the competence to repair a diesel engine. Writing tests can require great skill. There are many question formats, each with their own pros and cons.

✧ *True/false*. These are the easiest to write, and also the easiest to write poorly. They often provide the least reliable results. A guesser will average 50 percent correct. Someone who overanalyzes or takes questions containing words like "always" or "never" literally can rate very low. In general, true/false questions are not good candidates for competency assessments.

✧ *Multiple choice*. This format reduces the success rate of guessers, but still rewards the good test-taker. Multiple-choice questions are harder to write, but still focus on knowledge rather than skills. Some experienced test-authoring consultants offer to come in and pass any test used in the organization sight unseen and with no special topic preparation. They can do this because most multiple-choice tests have hidden tip-offs and patterns built into the questions that allow respondents to score higher without actually possessing the knowledge. Multiple-choice tests are little better than true/false for reliability.

✧ *Fill-in-the-blanks*. This type of question rewards respondents with good factual recall. (This is generally thought to be about three times harder than the recognition memory required by true/false or multiple-choice tests.) It reduces the ability of good test-takers to guess their way through the assessment. It also puts a heavy emphasis on memorization rather than capability to perform.

✧ *Short answer*. These suffer many of the same problems of fill-in-the-blank questions, and have the same reliability concerns of essay questions. However, short-answer test items do allow the respondent to explain an answer, which can help the scorer determine if the respondent really does have the knowledge being queried.

❖ *Essay*. This format allows a respondent to provide a more detailed answer to a specific question. It also makes it harder to score the response objectively because responses are likely to vary greatly based upon the interpretation and writing skills of the respondent. Bias can result from giving a high score to a respondent who writes well but gives a relatively weak answer, and giving a low score to someone with a good answer that is poorly expressed. Consistency is also an issue, because different scorers grade the same essay at different levels. Essay questions often work best in a pass/fail assessment situation and are ideal for testing what they require—writing competence. For example, colleges request a short essay be submitted with an application in order to evaluate whether a student has the skills necessary to complete college-level written assignments.

❖ *Simulation*. This is a very powerful testing tool in determining competencies. Here the respondent is put into a realistic situation and asked to perform to standards. This may consist of handling an angry customer to test conflict management skills or taking a typing test to measure keyboard speed. The challenge is to make the simulation as real as possible by minimizing the "pretend" nature of the exercise. Concerns include how to make the simulation broad enough to measure a range of skills and knowledge and how to evaluate the results of the simulation consistently.

For example, a common simulation assessment in the computer industry is to give a technician a hardware or software system that has been purposely disabled. The technician is than asked to correct the problems and bring the system up and running. The time required and approach used to do this are documented and evaluated.

❖ *Adaptive testing*. A special mention should be made concerning this relatively new technique, currently used in many technology tests. In computer applications, the amount of potential information and skills to be assessed is so vast that only a small portion can be evaluated at any one sitting—even when the material is broken up into a series of tests. Adaptive testing is a "smart" approach that varies the sequence of test questions based upon the respondent's progress through the test.

Adaptive testing is similar to a high-level executive who, sensing uncertainty in a subordinate, begins to ask that person more probing questions. First, questions indicative of general subject knowledge are asked. If the respondent misses one, the test begins to take a more detailed look at the respondent's knowledge in that area. If succeeding questions are answered correctly, the test moves on to the next general subject. If further mistakes are made, then the respondent is ultimately rated low in that area and, potentially, fails the entire test. The total number of questions becomes a key factor. The fewer the questions, the more right answers were given. The longer the test, the more wrong answers were given, lowering the likelihood of passing.

Surveys and tests make up the majority of current competency assessment solutions. They focus primarily on knowledge and have a harder time measuring skills or attitudes. These two types of competencies require different methods.

Experiential Assessments

A simple form of assessment is to document experience. The assumption is that certain competencies have been mastered by successfully working in a position. In essence, a series of successful appraisals is one form of assessing competencies. For example, in baseball, umpires are assumed to have seen every possible play that could ever happen in a game over the course of about ten years of umpiring. This is why major league baseball likes its umpires to have lengthy minor league experience before coming to the big leagues. Pilots are rated by how many hours of flying they have. Certifications require a minimum duration of professional experience. Union positions are assigned by seniority, and so on.

The fundamental assumption is that experience equals competence. Experience criteria assure that every respondent has completed the "school of hard knocks." The concern with this approach is obvious when looking at the number of workers who currently are not competent in their positions. Time on the job does not ensure that employees automatically learn how to meet competency standards. Also, experiential development may not be the proper goal for workers. There's no room for trial-and-error learning in a nuclear plant control room, a missile silo, an operating room, or a cockpit.

At best, experiential assessment can be one of several measurements used to determine competence. The real advantage of including an experience requirement may not be so much the measure of what has been learned but the indication of a significant opportunity to understand it, apply it, and master it.

Interview Assessments

This is the dominant method used to assess competencies in hiring situations, yet it is rarely used in assessing competencies for current employees. A trained interviewer, knowledgeable about position requirements, can determine a significant amount of information in a relatively short time. Questioning techniques are well established in the HR profession, and they include obtaining data through open/closed questions, asking situational "What would you do?" questions, conducting role playing, and talking through simulations.

There are still significant concerns with interviewing. Employees who are quick thinkers and good communicators may be able to "talk the talk" without actually possessing the competencies. The interview may not uncover all the competency information required to evaluate every element in a complex model. And the process is highly interviewer dependent. There is often little consistency between interviews—even with the most structured process.

Observation Assessments

Most performance-based competencies require firsthand information. No written test or conversation can measure competency in juggling three balls or in adjusting for a last-minute crosswind while landing a jetliner. Respondents can "ace the test," "talk a good story" for an interview, or have all the experience, yet not be able to perform on the job. Confirming these performance skills requires direct observation.

Many common applications require an observation assessment. Professional football prospects attend tryout camps. Competitive figure skaters, gymnasts, and divers are evaluated by certified judges according to published guidelines for grading difficulty and style. Pilots complete check flights. Obtaining a driver's license requires a written exam, an eye exam, and an evaluated test drive. Salespeople complete ride-along days with their supervisors. Certified ISO 9000 lead auditors perform on-site organizational assessments.

What is common to all these examples is that trained assessors evaluate individuals or organizations consistently based upon established standards. There is a standardized evaluation process for observing performance and rating competency levels. In the best of these systems, results are then repeatable and reliable.

Measurement of Results

Many organizations are trying to move to using actual business results to measure competencies. The thinking is that if employees are truly competent in their positions, then business results should reflect it. If results are below goal, then something must be wrong. Everyone cannot be competent when the company is losing money.

Certainly, competencies and business results are related, or organizations would not be interested in CMAR processes. But saying that salespeople or plant worker competencies are inadequate because revenue is down may not be accurate. Blacksmiths and buggy makers were highly skilled at their jobs when automobiles came into fashion. In their cases, other factors were driving business results.

Rating competence based upon business results works best only for leadership positions at the very highest level. Competencies for positions lower in the organization tend to focus on being able to do the things that are known to drive business results rather than to control them. It is similar to rating a basketball player on the ability to pass, shoot, and handle the ball rather than on the ability to win. Business results are better indicators of overall organizational competencies and may be difficult to include into an individual position CMAR system.

The best approach to assessment is ultimately to combine methods in a complementary fashion in order to fill in shortcomings of individual approaches. For example, the initial Connecticut Competency Instrument new teacher assessment process used pre- and post-interviews along with the series of teacher observations. The CCI assessment now includes a numeric rating that replaces the original yes/no standards approach. Professional sports teams observe an athlete's on-the-field performance, conduct interviews and personality analyses, and physically test the athlete's health, sports-related skills, and physical capabilities before making a contract offer. Combining these approaches provides a far greater reliability and consistency in the assessment process.

Rules for Writing Assessment Line Items

Once one or more assessment approaches have been selected, the next step is to begin writing assessment response statements. On the hard/easy scale, writing statements is very hard, so the goal is to make this as simple as possible. Soft-skill responses are almost always the most difficult to create. (As the TQM gurus say, "Soft is hard, hard is easy.") To illustrate the challenges, following is an example using a particularly difficult soft skill—Conflict Management.

Line Item Criteria

The first step is to recognize the weaknesses of the most common assessment approaches. This is especially critical when the design team is hoping to use or adapt competencies obtained from a third-party source. These instruments, particularly survey-based assessments, often contain constructs such as:

Rate yourself on:	Argumentative				Calming
Conflict Management	1	2	3	4	5

The strength of this approach is that it is relatively easy to write and score. As a starting point, it is better than capturing no information whatsoever, and it can provide a gentle transition for the organization into competency-based HR applications. Its weakness is that it delivers relatively low reliability, if any at all.

A proper line item should meet these five criteria:

✦ *Specific:* It should deal with a single competency.
✦ *Relevant:* It should be applicable to success in the position being considered.
✦ *Positive:* It should focus on what an employee should do in the position, not attempt to enumerate all the things the employee should not do.
✦ *Measurable:* It should be as objective as possible, providing specifics to explain when the standard has been met or not met.
✦ *Verifiable:* It should be able to be validated, duplicated, or checked.

The Conflict Management self-rating scale example meets only two of the five criteria:

✧ *Specific:* Yes; it does deal with a single competency.
✧ *Relevant:* Yes; the assumption here is that it is an accurate competency for the position under consideration.
✧ *Positive:* Not applicable; it does not specify any standard of knowledge or skill.
✧ *Measurable:* No; this is a self-rating that is not based upon any standards or evaluation criteria.
✧ *Verifiable:* No; different evaluators are likely to generate different results.

The problem is that the response indicates nothing of real use since there is no consistent reference for what the numbers mean. There is too much room for varying interpretations.

Establishing a "Referent"

A concept first introduced in junior-high English class provides great value in writing assessments. During the section on categorizing parts of speech, students learn that nouns have *referents*—they refer to something. Tell someone, "You'll find the report on the table." Will they be able to find it? "Table" is a solid noun, but with an indistinct referent. Out of the millions of tables in this world, which table holds the report? "Table in my office" is better. But is that the desk, credenza, computer table, or conference table? "The conference table in my office" has an exact referent. Tell three different people to look there and all should search in the same location.

Similarly, assessment line-item words must have specific *referents*. Everyone who reads a line item should be clear on exactly what the statement means. The ultimate goal is always that different respondents with the same level of skill for a competency should reply with the same assessment level choice.

A Knowledge Continuum Example

Here is a version included in a customer service assessment that has been incrementally improved from the previous example. It attempts to measure the level of knowledge in dealing with conflict. Since the assessment needs to clearly indicate what the numbers mean, it defines each response level with a statement:

1–I have no knowledge of conflict management.
2–I have a basic knowledge of conflict management.
3–I have a working knowledge of conflict management.

4–I have a thorough knowledge of conflict management
5–I have a complete knowledge of conflict management.

This is another common response approach. It follows a basic "know nothing/know everything" continuum. Here is how this set of statements rates according to the criteria for writing assessments:

⟡ *Specific:* Yes; they deal with a single competency
⟡ *Relevant:* Yes; this is a customer service position that deals with conflict.
⟡ *Positive:* Not applicable; they don't say what you should or shouldn't do.
⟡ *Measurable:* No; the key words such as *basic, working, thorough,* and *complete* have uncertain definitions.
⟡ *Verifiable:* No; since there are no referents for the words, there is nothing to verify.

This style of question will show up even in generally well-written assessment instruments. It happens on competencies for which the author is stuck as to what the standards for performance are. The problem is usually not with the author. The root cause of the poor statement is most often a weak standards definition. In this example, the solution is to go back and get more information on what skills and knowledge are required to properly handle conflict according to the needs of the various internal and external customer sets.

A Skill Continuum Example

Properly written response statements need another round of editing to pass the five-point test. Here is the Conflict Management example from the working model:

1–I have no knowledge of conflict management.
2–I can empathize with people involved in conflicts but rely on my personal ability to resolve issues.
3–I can use the 5-Step Conflict Management Process: empathize, qualified agreement, negative inquiry, resolution, and confirmation.
4–I can adapt my communications approach to minimize conflict using Multi-Form Tendency analysis.
5–I can anticipate areas of conflict and develop communications that minimize discord.

There are several response design decisions illustrated in this example. First, this set of responses follows a cumulative format. Each item within the competency builds upon the previous statement. Respondents completing the assessment are to read competency line items until they reach an item for which the answer is "no." They then circle the previous number. For example, responding with a "4" assumes that there is also mastery of response levels 1–3.

Second, in writing individual line items, the general flow of the competency continuum is as follows: no knowledge, personally developed competency with no formal process, some process used, advanced skills applied, and complete mastery. This provides a framework for constructing any competency response set that focuses on a continuum of skills or knowledge.

Third, the response set makes use of the learning points and content of established training resources. The "5-Step Conflict Management Process" referenced in response #3 is a specific module in an existing internal customer service training course. The statement reminds the respondent of the five steps in case there are any questions. This is an acceptable practice for middle-level competencies.

Response #4 references another conceptual tool, the Multi-Form Tendency analysis. This is a Marston-based, four-type personality tendencies model, which is taught in a number of management, supervision, sales, and frontline training courses. A common theme is that employees should adapt any soft-skill process according to an assessment of their own tendency/style and the tendency/style of the person with whom they are dealing. In this example, a response of "4" means that the respondent can apply the 5-Step Conflict Management model and can adapt the model according to Multi-Form personality principles.

Response #5 does not reference specific training content. Instead, it focuses on the TQM concept of prevention. The ultimate goal of a quality organization is to prevent defects (conflict) rather than handle or manage them. Since this item is not as specific as the previous four, it is somewhat more difficult to verify.

There are other key issues in evaluating and verifying the five Conflict Management responses.

✧ *1–I have no knowledge of conflict management.* Some authors have a problem with this "no knowledge" form of statement for a soft competency. Concerns are: "Have we really hired someone who doesn't have a clue how to handle conflict management? What respondent would be foolish enough to select response #1 and look like an idiot with no people skills?"

A "no knowledge" response makes better sense for a hard skill: "I have no knowledge of the marketing applications of chaos theory." Employees can still be functional without this particular competency. Some job titles being assessed, such as an administrator, may not require any knowledge of chaos theory. There are reasonable situations where an organization needs to know when no knowledge exists. Still, for consistency—even with soft competencies—response #1 usually indicates "no knowledge."

✧ *2–I can empathize with people involved in conflicts, but I rely on my personal ability to resolve issues.* In an assessment, particularly for soft skills, there needs to be recognition for individualized learning. Response #2 provides a choice for someone who has developed competencies through experience and personal development. While this is better than no competency at all, using a personalized process suggests that there will be little consistency between employees in dealing with conflict. TQM labels this "tampering," a prime cause of variation resulting from employees each freelancing instead of following established processes.

This response can be validated in an interview by asking, "How do you empathize with someone in a conflict situation? Give an example of when that happened recently. What is your approach to resolving conflict situations? Can you give an example of how you resolved a recent conflict?"

✧ *3–I can use the 5-Step Conflict Management Process: empathize, qualified agreement, negative inquiry, resolution, and confirmation.* The #3 response establishes a minimum competency by specifying a process. It is easy to verify this by asking, "I am calling you and I am furious. My complaint is that a delivery showed up late and damaged at our warehouse. What would you say to me? Walk me through the five steps."

✧ *4–I can adapt my communications approach to minimize conflict using Multi-Form Tendency analysis.* Response #4 is similarly easy to verify. This organization's standards require customer service personnel to modify the 5-Step Approach for the styles of others. You can ask, "You call me to follow up on a complaint about a damaged shipment. I answer the phone with, 'Cooper, what can I do for you?' What TIPC style am I likely to be, and how would you adapt the Empathize and Resolution steps in the Conflict Management Process to deal with me?"

✧ *5–I can anticipate areas of conflict and develop communications that minimize discord.* Response #5 is less specific. The author chose to define mastery of Conflict Management as having strategies for preventing conflict in the first place. But it does have clear indicators for validation. "What are some areas of anticipated conflict in your job? What processes are in place to minimize potential conflict? What has been the effect of those processes?"

The final and most powerful test of a properly written response statement is this: Authors should be able to immediately think of questions to verify an employee's response for each statement in the assessment.

Note that a well-written response statement is closely tied to specific skills, knowledge, and processes from the competency model. The statements should contain references to procedures, course learning points, and business practices, i.e., all the information sources discussed in Chapter 3. This is essential for validation and verification.

A People-Capability Maturity Model Example

Writing response statements for "hard" competencies is far easier. Here are the Spreadsheet competency responses from the working model that begins to adopt a P-CMM approach:

1–I have no knowledge of spreadsheets.

2–I can enter data into a spreadsheet created by someone else.

3–I can create a basic spreadsheet using labels and formulas.

4–I can add advanced formulas, formatting, and charts to a basic spreadsheet.

5–I can create a spreadsheet for novice users that includes macros and data protection, or create a spreadsheet that includes data tables, what-if calculations, macros for redundant tasks, and all types of charts and graphs.

It can be very difficult to break a complex process down to four or five significant measures. A spreadsheet has hundreds of functional capabilities. Here the author chose a representative sample of operations at each complexity level. Common functions such as printing were not included. The author also separated the response statements so that they would map effectively to the multiple position titles in the working model. The standards are:

Manager	2
Administrator	5
Team Leader	2
Salesperson	2
Technical Support	4

The Administrator is expected to be the workgroup's expert, creating a variety of spreadsheets for use by the team. The Technical Support specialist must be able to modify existing spreadsheets and create visually attractive specialized spreadsheets if needed. The Manager, Team Leader, and Salesperson should be able to utilize spreadsheets created by others and to make up their own simple spreadsheets, if necessary.

The working model Negotiating competency series takes the P-CMM concepts even further, combining a knowledge/skills continuum with aspects of organizational competency management and personal competency development:

1–I have no knowledge of negotiating.

2–I use negotiating skills developed through personal and work experience as both a supplier and customer.

3–I can negotiate based upon the six-step negotiations process: analyze, develop power/leverage, prepare, apply/counter, agree, and follow up.

4–I can develop a negotiations strategy, select specific tactics to be used, develop offer/counteroffer scenarios, and execute the concessions cycle using structured negotiations processes.

5–I can coach others in their negotiations situations and can recognize when negotiating principles could be effectively applied in the Multi-Form selling process.

This series introduces the issue of strategic skills and individual coaching. A series based completely on the P-CMM would also have to include a last line item addressing continuous workforce development.

Writing response statements is an iterative process. Each pass through the response sets usually identifies additional wording clarifications or content additions. Allow time for multiple edits. As is true for writing reports, there is great benefit to a continuous-improvement editing process.

Allow for elapsed time between edits so that statements become a bit "cold." Familiarity breeds off-target statements. Put the current draft in a drawer for a few days, then get it out and review it. This will allow an author to read response statements more as an outsider rather than as a contributor. Things that seemed clear when first written will often be somewhat obscure upon later review. (A common reaction is, "What in the world was I thinking of when I wrote this?")

Designers must keep asking, "Does everyone understand what we're getting at here? Are we making sure there are referents for as many ambiguous words in the statement as possible? Is the statement specific? Is it linked to a specific competency? Does it focus on a business result? Does it point to a specific resource for remediation? Does it describe a positive business activity rather than proscribe a negative action? Can we measure it, and therefore verify it?" If so, the assessment will deliver the most reliability possible from the set of line items.

Validating the Results

Validation of assessment results is impossible for line items that are written using the "rate yourself" approach. There are no standards and no common referents. It is merely one person's opinion against another's.

If assessment line items are written properly, skill levels are readily verified by asking a few simple questions. For the Spreadsheet competency series, questions might include: "What are the different ways to navigate from cell to cell in the spreadsheet? What are the arithmetic operators in a cell formula? What is the formula to sum up a row or column of data? How would you set up a macro to automate the printing of a spreadsheet? How do you lock or hide information on a spreadsheet?" and so on. Skills can easily be verified using testing, interviewing, simulation, or observation.

Automating the Process

Administering and scoring assessments have never been easier. There are dedicated survey programs that simplify the creation and scoring of nearly any type of survey or test. Most handle distribution in either paper, e-mail, or Internet format.

For example, the LIBRIX Open Learning System (http://www.librix.com) has a built-in Web-based question and scoring capability that automatically produces the question formats shown in Table 6-1. (The corresponding screen dialog box is shown in Figure 9-7.)

Most computer-based training programs also have extensive testing/feedback capabilities. One of the simplest to use is Asymetrix Learning Systems' ToolBook Assistant (http://www.asymetrix.com). This program is designed to allow content experts to quickly develop interactive courseware and multimedia applications using predesigned templates and built-in capabilities. Courses can then be delivered either locally on a PC, on CD-ROM, or over the Internet using a single course source file. Figure 6-1 shows the options for multiple-choice question layouts in ToolBook Assistant 7.

Figure 6-2 shows the alternatives available for true-false questions. Note from the menu system on the left of the screen that there are also capabilities to handle fill-in-the-blank question formats. Scoring is similarly easy to set up. Figure 6-3 shows how built-in buttons and fields can be inserted where needed in an interactive assessment application.

Chapters 9 and 10 provide further information on the range of survey and online feedback tools that are currently available. It is very helpful that most are reasonably priced, are easy to use, generate professional results quickly, provide flexibility in instrument delivery options, and are highly functional.

Assessment Examples

Following are three actual assessment instruments illustrating different levels of complexity. The first is the evaluation criteria for the yes/no model used in

Table 6-1. LIBRIX ActiveBuilder question formats.

	All That Apply	Multiple Choice	Text Essay	True-False
Text or graphics questions			x	
Text or WMP questions			x	
Text answers, horizontal	x	x		x
Graphic answers, horizontal	x	x		
Text or graphic answers	x	x		x
Text or graphic answers, horizontal	x	x		x
Text or WMP answers	x	x		
Columns	x	x		
Combo box		x		
Graphic question, text answer(s)	x	x		x
Graphic question, text or graphic answers, horizontal		x		
WMP question, text answer(s)	x	x		x
Text only	x	x		x
Text essay			x	
Text short response			x	

WMP = Windows Media Player

Figure 6-1. ToolBook Assistant multiple-choice options.

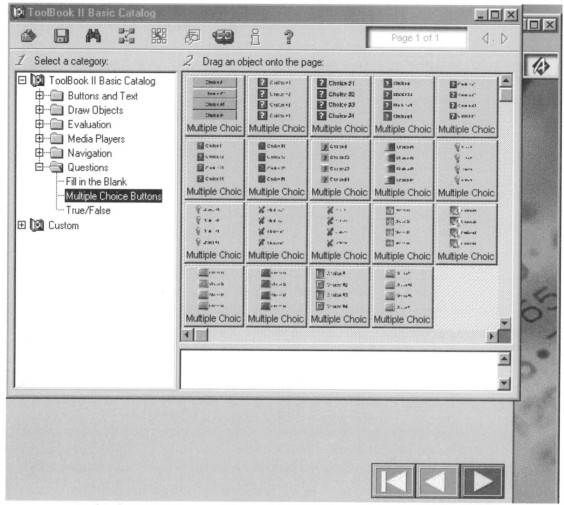

ToolBook Assistant II screen shots copyright © 1998 Asymetrix Learning Systems Inc.

the Connecticut Competency Instrument. The second is an organization-wide employee survey assessment used to assess training needs for small and inter-mediate-size organizations. The third is a complete skill-based assessment used with the working model. These provide design teams with a range of live examples to evaluate when designing their own assessment approaches.

Yes/No Teacher Assessment

Not all good competency-based application examples come from industry, nor do they need to be heavily automated. The Connecticut Competency Instrument introduced in Chapter 5 utilizes a "preponderance of positive evidence" approach to making the acceptable/unacceptable decision. The CCI includes this assessment language for its ten indicators:

Figure 6-2. ToolBook Assistant true/false options.

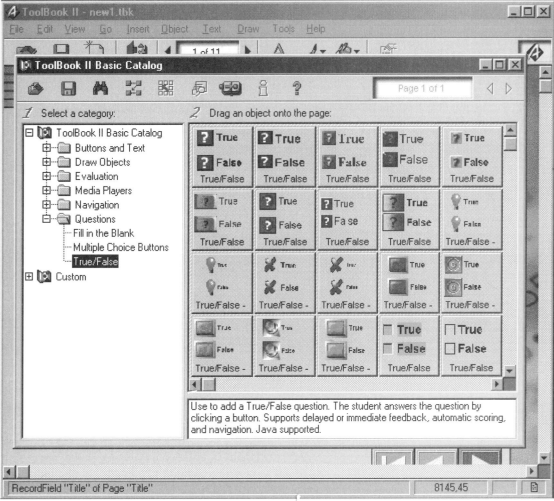

ToolBook Assistant II screen shots copyright © 1998 Asymetrix Learning Systems Inc.

I. Management of the Classroom Environment

IA. The Teacher Promotes a Positive Learning Environment (rapport, communication of expectations for academic achievement, physical environment). For this indicator to be rated ACCEPTABLE, there must be:

✧ positive evidence for each of the three defining attributes;
✧ a preponderance of positive evidence for rapport;
✧ no physical abuse; and
✧ a physical environment that is safe.

IB. The Teacher Maintains Appropriate Standards of Behavior (rules and standards of behavior are maintained). The indi-

Figure 6-3. ToolBook Assistant assessment option.

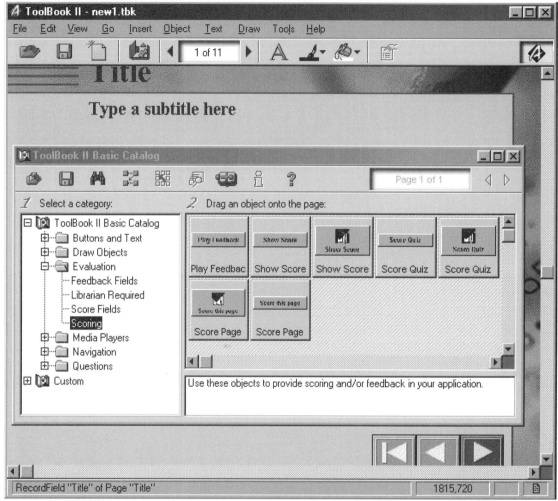

ToolBook Assistant II screen shots copyright © 1998 Asymetrix Learning Systems Inc.

cator must be rated UNACCEPTABLE if a *pattern* of inappropriate student behavior interferes with other students' opportunities to learn.

IC. The Teacher Engages the Students in the Activities of the Lesson (student engagement, reengagement). For this indicator to be rated ACCEPTABLE, on the average, 80 percent of the students must be engaged in activities of the lesson, and the teacher must demonstrate efforts to reengage students who are persistently off-task.

ID. The Teacher Effectively Manages Routines and Transitions (effectiveness). The indicator must be rated UNACCEPTABLE if, overall, the management of routines and transitions significantly detracts from instruction.

II. Instruction

IIA. The Teacher Presents Appropriate Learning Content (choice of content, level of difficulty, accuracy). For this indicator to be rated ACCEPTABLE, there must be a preponderance of positive evidence for each of the three defining attributes.

IIB. The Teacher Creates a Structure for Learning (initiations, closures). For this indicator to be rated ACCEPTABLE, there must be a preponderance of positive evidence for each of the two defining attributes.

IIC. The Teacher Develops the Lesson to Promote Achievement of the Lesson Objectives (lesson development, use of instructional arrangements and materials). For this indicator to be rated ACCEPTABLE, there must be:

✧ a preponderance of positive evidence for lesson development; and

✧ positive evidence for use of instructional arrangements and materials.

This indicator must be rated UNACCEPTABLE if:
The lesson objectives (from pre-assessment information form and pre- and post-assessment observation interviews) are unclear, so that effectiveness of the lesson development cannot be judged.

IID. The Teacher Uses Appropriate Questioning Strategies (cognitive level, responding to students, opportunities for student involvement). For this indicator to be rated ACCEPTABLE, there must be a preponderance of positive evidence for each of the three defining attributes. If there are no questions during the lesson, this indicator must be rated UNACCEPTABLE.

IIE. The Teacher Communicates Clearly, Using Precise Language and Acceptable Oral Expressions (precision of communication, clarity of speech, oral expression). For this indicator to be rated ACCEPTABLE, there must be a preponderance of positive evidence for each of the three defining attributes.

III. Assessment

IIIA. The Teacher Monitors Student Understanding of the Lesson and Adjusts Instruction When Necessary (monitoring for understanding, adjusting when necessary). For this indicator to be rated ACCEPTABLE, there must be a preponderance of positive evidence for:

    ✧ monitoring; and

    ✧ adjusting, or acknowledging to students the need for adjustment, when necessary.*

Note that the CCI includes both positive and negative definitions. Certain requirement are must-haves, such as the absence of abuse, controlling student behavior, effective transitions, questions from students, and clear lesson goals for the evaluator to use. Other competencies require a general "preponderance of positive evidence." This is similar to the ISO 9000 definition of "objective evidence"—qualitative or quantitative information or statements of fact that are based upon observation, measurement, or test, and that can be verified.

This yes/no approach provides a clear set of standards and a singular decision suitable for assessing how new teachers compare to minimum standards. What it cannot do is differentiate among the competency levels of experienced teachers or help with integrating an overall evaluation that includes all ten factors. This requires providing gradation in the scoring system.

Scaled Organizational Assessment

The Business Training Library (BTL) provides a unique approach to training and development for small and intermediate-size organizations (http://www. bizlibrary.com). Instead of buying training and personal development programs, organizations can join the BTL service and borrow from an extensive inventory of video, CBT, and CD-ROM training programs at a fraction of the cost of purchase.

As a service to members, BTL offers an Internet-based assessment survey that can be completed by every employee and tabulated to determine organizational development needs.[1] The competencies measured are linked to BTL offerings so that member organizations can build customized development plans tailored to competencies identified by employees. The format is a standard five-point "strongly agree/strongly disagree" continuum and includes the statements in the following competency areas as shown in Table 6-2.

Again, this is a high-level opinion survey, not an actual assessment of competencies. As such it provides an excellent first step in shifting to a data-driven development philosophy. Employees provide their view of the organization's competencies and needs. The summarized responses to this survey, viewable on screen in real time, allow BTL member organizations to identify areas in need of development.

Top management typically needs to do further analysis to understand exactly what the issues are and how they should be addressed. Management can then utilize automatic links to the library's inventory of materials. This helps leaders provide just-in-time, just-as-needed training to employees. It also helps

---

*Bureau of Research and Teacher Assessment, *CCI Indicators* (Hartford: Connecticut State Department of Education, 1989), http://www.state.ct.us/sde/brta/cciindic.htm. Used with permission.

Table 6-2. Business Training Library organizational development assessment.

Scale:

    5–Strongly agree
    4–Agree
    3–Neither agree nor disagree
    2–Disagree
    1–Strongly disagree

Leadership:

1. Our leaders coach us in understanding the goals of the organization.
2. Our leaders' actions support our organizational values.
3. Top management supports quality improvement, not just talks about it.
4. Top management delegates authority for completing a job.
5. Top management delegates responsibility for completing a job.
6. Top management gives us regular feedback on our performance.
7. Our leaders provide opportunities for us to grow professionally.

Management/Supervision:

8. Supervisors give us regular feedback on our performance.
9. The appraisal process accurately measures our performance.
10. Supervisors review processes and procedures to improve performance.
11. Supervisors can coach to develop our skills.

Sales/Marketing:

12. We have built good sales relationships with our customers.
13. Our salespeople conduct effective in-person sales calls.
14. Our salespeople sell effectively over the phone.
15. We make effective sales presentations.
16. We negotiate favorable price and terms and conditions.
17. Salespeople manage their territory to maximize sales.
18. Sales managers coach salespeople to increase sales.

Customer Service:

19. Satisfying customers is a top priority.
20. We are organized so that we can service customers.
21. We treat every customer with respect.
22. We listen to what our customers tell us about their changing needs.
23. We use information from our customers to improve our service.

Communications:

24. Communication and information flow freely throughout the organization.
25. All employees possess adequate skills in the "three R's" (reading, writing, arithmetic).
26. We use appropriate telephone conversational skills.
27. We handle voicemail for good caller service.
28. We practice proper e-mail etiquette.

(continues)

Table 6-2. *(continued)*

Teamwork:

29. Top management encourages everyone to work as a united team.
30. All departments welcome ideas and feedback from other departments.
31. Team members trust each other.
32. Team members are open and candid with each other.
33. Team members from different departments work together to solve common problems.

Motivation/Personal:

34. Supervisors clearly explain what is expected of employees.
35. All employees are treated with respect.
36. Employees maintain a positive work attitude.
37. All employees are rewarded for their performance.
38. The right training is provided so we can continuously learn how to do our jobs better.
39. We receive coaching to help us improve our skills.

Quality:

40. Everyone is committed to giving customers quality products and services.
41. Everyone is accountable for the quality of their work.
42. We continuously improve the quality of our products and services.
43. We learn from our mistakes and correct them.

Productivity:

44. Our interviewing and hiring process selects the best candidates.
45. The new-hire orientation process is effective.
46. We manage our work time well.
47. Meetings are efficiently run.
48. We accept change as a normal part of everyone's job.

Personal Computing:

49. We can perform all word processing functions required in our jobs.
50. We can perform all spreadsheet functions required in our jobs.
51. We can perform all presentation functions required in our jobs.
52. We can perform all database functions required in our jobs.
53. We can perform all desktop publishing functions required in our jobs.
54. We can perform all multimedia functions required in our jobs.
55. We can perform all Internet functions required in our jobs.
56. We can perform all e-mail/groupware functions required in our jobs.

Organization:

57. The work environment is physically safe.
58. The workplace is free of ethnic or cultural bias.
59. The workplace is free of sexual harassment.
60. The workplace is drug-free.
61. The average level of workplace stress is manageable.
62. Overall, our company performs effectively.

the Library in understanding which materials need to be acquired for members, and in what volume.

Skill-Based Working Model Assessment

The Competency Response Form for the working model shows a fully developed assessment instrument using the associated standards matrix from Chapter 5 and a generalized P-CMM approach in building the response sets. The line items refer to specific concepts from CooperComm training materials and can easily be adapted to learning content of other organizations. Each line item, whenever possible, is a skills-based response that can be verified through simple questioning or testing. Note the emphasis on "I can . . ." wording that focuses on skills rather than on mere knowledge.

The full text of the assessment is shown in Figure 6-4. A rich text format (RTF) version that can be read and edited by Microsoft Word or most other popular word processors is located in the "Working Model" folder on the CD-ROM included with this text.

This completes the discussion of how to build competency modeling and assessment systems. At this point in the project, position models are in existence, standards have been set, and a method exists to measure competencies. Now concerns shift from design to utilization. Where can this process be utilized? How should data be tabulated and reported? What are the administration and delivery options? How should the data be leveraged? What are the next steps in improving the process? The answers to these questions are in the forthcoming chapters, which examine application areas and fully functional CMAR systems.

Learning Points

1. An assessment must reflect a CMAR process that is valid, accurate, and reliable.
2. The best assessment approaches utilize more than one assessment methodology in order to gain the most accurate measure of employees' competencies.
3. This typically requires more advanced methods, such as observation, testing, and simulation.
4. Assessment line items must be specific, relevant, positive, measurable, and verifiable.
5. Assessment line items must have clear "referents," i.e., words in the line item have standard meanings for all employees.
6. Assessment sets should be built on knowledge or skill continuums.
7. The P-CMM makes a good starter model for building line item assessment sets.

(text continues on page 185)

Figure 6-4. Competency response form.

Competency Response Form

Name: _____ Security Number: _____ - ___ - _____
Mailing Address: _____
City: _____ State: _____ Zip: _____ - _____
Current Position: _____ Manager's Name: _____

Instructions:

Quality standards require us to document the qualifications and competencies of our employees to do their work tasks. You and your manager will fill out similar forms detailing your competency levels. Following is a self-rated form which will help us determine your development needs for the coming year.

Read each statement carefully. Circle the response number which best describes you at this time. Be sure to circle a single statement number for each competency. (The results will *not* be used for performance appraisal or merit increase purposes—only for development planning and scheduling.)

---

1. General Information

1-1. Organizational Information

1. I have no knowledge of basic organizational information.
2. I have attended the new employee orientation program and have read all provided employee literature.
3. I know basic organizational information and can use my knowledge of the organization to find the answers to most of my questions.
4. I have a wide network of contacts and keep up to date on organizational goals, objectives and issues.
5. I can use my extensive knowledge of organizational goals, objectives, issues and resources to help others learn more about the organization.

1-2. Basic Industry Knowledge

1. I have no knowledge of industry information.
2. I have some basic knowledge of industry information sources.
3. I can access industry information sources for basic data and trends.
4. I can access industry information sources, analyze the contents and make practical application to everyday operations.
5. I can access industry information sources, and can analyze and interpolate data in order to make practical application of the data to everyday operations.

1-3. Policies & Procedures

1. I have no knowledge of organizational policies and procedures.
2. I have some basic knowledge of organizational policies and procedures.
3. I know when I can make decisions on my own and when I should consult with someone else.
4. I am the person others consult with to determine the proper application of existing policies and procedures.
5. I can use my thorough knowledge of policies and procedures to determine the proper course of action in unique situations.

1-4. Legal Review & Approval

1. I have no knowledge of legal requirements.
2. I am familiar with the areas where legal review and approval is required.
3. I know when legal review and approval are required.
4. I have a thorough working knowledge of the legal review and approval for invoices, promotional authorizations, personnel documentation and services contracting and can recognize when policy has not been followed.
5. I know the policies for legal review and approval and can identify and implement corrective actions.

1-5. Diversity

1. I have no knowledge of diversity issues.
2. I have attended diversity training and am familiar with the sensitivities required in organization locations.
3. I can modify my behavior to work effectively without bias and with sensitivity to diversity.
4. I can recognize when specific behaviors of myself and others do not properly address diversity requirements.
5. I can identify behaviors which should be modified, recommend improved behaviors and counsel others on more effective behaviors concerning diversity issues.

1-6. Sexual Harassment

1. I have no knowledge of sexual harassment.
2. I have read the organization's policy on sexual harassment.
3. I have attended sexual harassment training and am familiar with the requirements of the Civil Rights Act of 1964, resulting case precedents, and organizational sexual harassment policies.
4. I can apply the Six Levels of Harassment and Offender Stereotypes to insure that I participate in no harassment in the workplace.
5. I can lead a harassment complaint investigation and determine appropriate action steps.

2. Management/Leadership

2-1. Planning

1. I have no knowledge of planning.
2. I can create plans for completing my longer term work projects.
3. I can execute a complete planning process from needs determination and SWOT analysis through activity monitoring and project reporting.
4. I can apply critical path, bottleneck, flow simulation and other analysis methods to shorten project cycle time and improve the quality of results.
5. I can create a planning process, manage it and conduct a post-plan review of effectiveness.

2-2. Leadership

1. I have no knowledge of leadership.
2. I provide direction and decisions for my followers.
3. I have empowered my followers to take responsibility and make decisions.
4. I have unified my followers with a common vision, values and mission.
5. I have created a learning environment which develops my followers.

(continues)

Figure 6-4. *(continued)*

2-3. Ethics

1. I behave according to my personal and professional ethics.
2. I have read the employee Code of Conduct for organizational ethics.
3. I can apply the Code of Conduct in everyday business situations.
4. I can extrapolate the Code of Conduct to borderline/gray area situations.
5. I can coach others in applying the Code of Conduct to their situations.

2-4. Interviewing

1. I have no knowledge of interviewing.
2. I am familiar with legal interviewing techniques and know what questions are improper.
3. I can develop a structured interview process with varied interviewers, position needs, standardized questions and objective selection techniques.
4. I can develop competency testing and measurement approaches for open positions.
5. I can perform post-selection interview effectiveness studies.

2-5. Performance Planning

1. I have no knowledge of performance planning.
2. I can create a performance plan based upon job descriptions.
3. I can create a performance plan based upon job descriptions and needs of the workgroup.
4. I can create a performance plan which directly relates to the performance goals of the workgroup.
5. I can create a performance plan which helps develop and grow individuals.

2-6. Performance Reviews

1. I have no knowledge of performance reviews.
2. I can follow organizational guidelines in reviewing a subordinate on an established performance plan.
3. I can use the performance plan criteria to provide an assessment of employee strengths and weaknesses.
4. I can use the performance review results to identify areas for personal and professional development of the employee.
5. I can use the performance review results to facilitate a discussion of career planning.

2-7. Salary Administration

1. I have no knowledge of salary administration.
2. I can explain the salary administration guidelines.
3. I can apply the salary administration guidelines to an individual situation.
4. I can apply the salary administration guidelines to a workgroup.
5. I can justify and obtain salary administration guideline exceptions where needed.

2-8. Coaching

1. I have no knowledge of coaching.
2. I can show an employee how to do a task.
3. I can observe an employee doing a task and provide feedback.
4. I can follow the tell–show–try–feedback cycle of coaching.
5. I can create a winning reinforcement experience for the employee.

2-9. Counseling

1. I have no knowledge of counseling.
2. I can discuss employee's work related attitude concerns based on my knowledge and experience.
3. I can use the Counseling Statement to guide an employee through the five steps of counseling.
4. I can use directed questioning to help an employee discover attitude concerns and be open for feedback.
5. I can design an unfreezing experience to change attitudes.

2-10. Open Book Management

1. I have no knowledge of open book management.
2. I can read and interpret a basic balance sheet and income statement.
3. I know the "key measures" of the organization/department and can determine, analyze and interpret them.
4. I can identify additional financial measures which will assist in improving organizational performance.
5. I can create an open book management rollout, training and development program.

3. Sales/Marketing

3-1. Account Planning

1. I have no knowledge of account planning.
2. I can identify, segment and prioritize accounts according to the current sales relationship and future sales potential.
3. I can develop coverage plans to allocate my time to the necessary account segments.
4. I can utilize the "sales funnel" process to determine territory status, create accurate sales forecasts, and determine likelihood of meeting established sales goals.
5. I can identify potential performance gaps, identify resources required, and create action plans to meet established sales goals.

3-2. Complex Account Selling

1. I have no knowledge of complex account selling.
2. I can identify the four (to six) buying influences in my complex accounts.
3. I can create a tailored sales message for each buying influence which continually moves the account forward towards an order.
4. I can create a calling plan which fits the political and functional "sales decision cycle" of my prospects.
5. I can provide a greater value add by assisting clients in developing their needs and ordering criteria for purchase before the sales process begins.

3-3. Product Strategies

1. I have no knowledge of product strategies.
2. I know the product strategy message for all of our products.
3. I can determine which products are best for each of my prospects/clients.
4. I can develop a sales plan for meeting all established product sales goals.
5. I can identify new opportunities for our products in existing and new accounts.

3-4. Sales Call

1. I have no knowledge of structured sales calls.
2. I can follow the multi-form six-step sales call process: rapport, initial benefit statement, questioning to determine needs, feature/advantage/for instance/reaction, close, and handling objections.

(continues)

Figure 6-4. *(continued)*

---

3. I can determine sales call goals as part of an overall complex account sales effort.
4. I can identify customer concerns before the call and build a sales call message and support tools which effectively meets needs and minimize objections before they occur.
5. I can perform as a senior sales representative in coaching a new sales representative on the call.

3-5. Questioning

1. I have no knowledge of questioning techniques.
2. I can ask simple open and closed questions which assist in determining needs.
3. I can develop a line of questioning leading from facts to explicit needs: What? So what? Then what? Now what?
4. I can use a questioning process to help customers define their needs.
5. I can use a questioning process to help set a customer needs agenda which is best addressed by our products.

3-6. Competitive Activities

1. I have no knowledge of competitive activities.
2. I can generally summarize our competitors' strategies.
3. I can detail the competitive activity in my territory.
4. I have plans in place to counter current competitive activity.
5. I have plans in place to minimize competitive activity before it begins.

3-7. Negotiating

1. I have no knowledge of negotiating.
2. I use negotiating skills developed through personal and work experience as both a supplier and customer.
3. I can negotiate based upon the six-step negotiations process: analyze, develop power/ leverage, prepare, apply/counter, agree, and follow-up.
4. I can develop a negotiating strategy, select specific tactics to be used, develop offer/ counter-offer scenarios, and execute the concessions cycle using structured negotiations principles.
5. I can coach them on their negotiations situations and can recognize when negotiating principles could be effectively applied in the multi-form selling process.

3-8. Territory Administration

1. I have no knowledge of territory administration.
2. I can complete my weekly Call Report and monthly Market Activity Report.
3. I have a structured method for tracking to-do's, deadlines, and appointments.
4. I have records of daily internal and external interactions so that the records can be referenced as needed.
5. I have a complete database of key contacts and information for all accounts.

3-9. Trade Shows

1. I have no knowledge of trade shows.
2. I can set up and work trade show exhibits to maximize exposure of our products and services.
3. I can use a structured trade show specific multi-form sales call process.
4. I can develop a trade show strategy, message, contract for the best location for cost/ delivery, organize an optimal setup for visibility and flow, and work the booth.
5. I can evaluate the effectiveness of the trade show effort, identify recommended changes and determine whether or not to participate in future shows.

4. Technical

4-1. Product Knowledge

1. I have no knowledge of our products.
2. I can explain each product's areas of application, features and general advantages.
3. I can identify and explain each product's "feature differential" over competition.
4. I can answer detailed questions about our products' features, installation, operation and maintenance.
5. I can install/operate/maintain our products in the workplace.

4-2. Services Knowledge

1. I have no knowledge of our services.
2. I can explain each service's areas of application, features and general advantages.
3. I can identify and explain each service's "feature differential" over competition.
4. I can answer detailed questions about our services' features and operation.
5. I can perform our services in the workplace.

4-3. Contracting & Consulting

1. I have no knowledge of internal contracting/consulting.
2. I can identify areas for internal and external contracting/consulting.
3. I can contract for a Scope of Effort or a "Phase 0" scoping study.
4. I can lead contracting, data collection, diagnosis and feedback meetings.
5. I can anticipate contracting/consulting problems and determine activities to eliminate them.

4-4. Project Management

1. I have no knowledge of project management.
2. I can create plans for completing complex, multi-departmental work projects.
3. I can track responsibilities and deadlines for project activities and take appropriate action to stay on schedule.
4. I can utilize PC software to perform project tracking, resource allocation and cost budgeting.
5. I can apply critical path, bottleneck, flow simulation and other analysis methods to shorten project cycle time and improve the quality of results.

4-5. Training

1. I have no knowledge of training.
2. I can determine training needs and learning goals.
3. I can evaluate existing training resources for their suitability to needs and goals.
4. I can create a training program curriculum design which meets needs and goals.
5. I can perform training effectiveness studies measuring information seen, knowledge gained, competencies developed and results generated.

5. Administration

5-1. Personnel Policies

1. I have no knowledge of personnel policies.
2. I have read the personnel policies manual.
3. I can apply the guidelines as described in the personnel policies manual.

(continues)

Figure 6-4. *(continued)*

4. I can make recommendations on the appropriate action to take for incidents which are not specifically covered in the personnel policies manual.
5. I can author sections of the personnel policies manual.

5-2. Budgeting

1. I have no knowledge in budgeting.
2. I can monitor/track my expenses against my budget.
3. I can monitor/track actual vs. anticipated expenses and calculate a PYE.
4. I can use the on-line budget system to track expenses and calculate a PYE.
5. I can create budgets and train others to do the same.

5-3. Expense Reporting

1. I have no knowledge of expense reporting.
2. I can post my personal and departmental weekly expenses onto the appropriate forms.
3. I can allocate expenses according to the proper expense code category.
4. I can post allocated expenses into the on-line expense reporting system.
5. I can train others to do complete expense reporting and allocation.

5-4. Order Entry

1. I have no knowledge of order entry.
2. I can fill out the order form for products and for services.
3. I can add office specific data and check order forms for accuracy and completeness.
4. I can enter orders into the on-line order entry system.
5. I can utilize the on-line order entry system to expedite or modify active orders.

5-5. Financial Justification

1. I have no knowledge of financial justification.
2. I can determine the relevant cash flows and perform simple breakeven and payback analysis.
3. I can perform discounted cash flow analysis to determine project NPV, ROI, IRR.
4. I can create thorough product and services life cycle cost/benefit models and estimate appropriate cash flows.
5. I can customize financial justification models to show the benefits of our products and services to specific prospects/customers.

5-6. Statistics

1. I have no knowledge of statistics.
2. I can calculate basic central measures, variance/standard deviation, business ratios, and then graph the results.
3. I can discuss, compute, and analyze horizontal and vertical ratio analysis and use the results to identify opportunities for marketing/sales improvement.
4. I can use data to statistically identify distributions, compute measures of variance, forecast future sales and expense trends, and compute correlation and line fits.
5. I can perform Design of Experiments (DOE) and Multivariate Testing (MVT) to create statistically valid studies of sales needs and operational processes.

6. Personal Computing

6-1. Operating System

1. I have no knowledge of the operating system.
2. I can turn on the personal computer and run programs.
3. I can arrange the desktop, manipulate files, create folders and move data files on the internal hard disk or to external portable disks.
4. I can perform configuration modifications to tailor the operating environment to my preferences.
5. I can modify the operating system to recognize the installation of new hardware or software.

6-2. Word Processing

1. I have no knowledge of word processing.
2. I am a hunt-and-peck typist and know I don't have to press the Enter key at the end of the line.
3. I can create simple text documents and can cut and paste words and paragraphs.
4. I can do basic formatting, including changing fonts and point sizes, create and modify a simple table, apply character styles and know how to center or justify text.
5. I can create near desktop published documents including custom layout, embedded graphics and live data from other applications.

6-3. Spreadsheets

1. I have no knowledge of spreadsheets.
2. I can enter data into a spreadsheet created by someone else.
3. I can create a basic spreadsheet including labels and formulas.
4. I can add advanced formulas, formatting and charts to a basic spreadsheet.
5. I can create a spreadsheet for novice users which includes macros and data protection, or create a sophisticated spreadsheet which includes data tables, what-if calculations, macros for redundant tasks, and all types of charts and graphs.

6-4. Presentation Software

1. I have no knowledge of presentation software.
2. I can create a text presentation with multiple levels of bullets and a slide master.
3. I can create a presentation which integrates text, clip art, graphics, charts and graphs.
4. I can create from scratch a presentation which integrates the above data types with an effective visual design and layout.
5. I can create a multimedia presentation which integrates the above data types with animation, sound, video and digital pictures.

6-5. Database Management Software

1. I can enter data into a simple database created by someone else.
2. I can create a flat file database.
3. I can create a multi-file database used by myself.
4. I can create a relational database.
5. I can create a multi-user, large scale relational database system.

(continues)

Figure 6-4. *(continued)*

6-6. E-Mail

1. I have no knowledge of e-mail.
2. I can create simple text messages and send them.
3. I can attach files to text e-mail and send them both.
4. I can use group names, broadcast and forwarding capabilities to target multiple addressees.
5. I can set up an e-mail mailbox for single access to sending and receiving messages from various organizational systems.

6-7. LAN Access

1. I have no knowledge of LAN access.
2. I understand that computers can be connected together to share resources and data.
3. I can work with another user on the network to create/update a single document or file.
4. I can navigate across the organization's network to locate individuals, data and equipment resources.
5. I can add users to the LAN and can change the security access for existing users.

6-8. Mainframe Access

1. I have no knowledge of mainframe access.
2. I can complete batch reports and send them to the mainframe.
3. I can update the order entry and pricing system either locally or through remote dial-up.
4. I can retrieve mainframe sales data, port it into a spreadsheet, and create custom sales reports.
5. I can create business models using mainframe sales data.

6-9. Internet Access

1. I have no knowledge of the Internet.
2. I can access and navigate the Internet through a service such as America Online or CompuServe.
3. I can access and navigate the Internet through an Independent Service Provider using a stand-alone Internet browser.
4. I can download files, expand them and send/receive e-mail across the Internet.
5. I can set up agent software to perform repetitive tasks such as browsing for specified information or retrieving e-mail.

7. Personal

7-1. Assertiveness

1. I have no knowledge of assertive verbal skills.
2. I can state my thoughts and feelings without aggression or defensiveness.
3. I can recognize when I am encountering one of the eight levels of manipulation, any verbal games or any psychological pastimes.
4. I can respond to manipulation or games/pastimes using "adult" verbal skills.
5. I can communicate with others using the ten "assertive rights."

7-2. Nonverbal communications

1. I have no knowledge of nonverbal communications (vocal expression and body language).
2. I can identify nonverbal negatives and develop a feedback system to eliminate them.
3. I can utilize the position scan and the movements scan to better read others.
4. I can utilize nonverbal principles to better present myself in formal and informal situations.
5. I can coach others in more effective nonverbal communications.

7-3. Conflict Management

1. I have no knowledge of conflict management.
2. I can empathize with people involved in conflicts but rely on my personal ability to resolve issues.
3. I can use the five step conflict management process: empathize, qualified agreement, negative inquiry, resolution, confirmation.
4. I can adapt my communications approach to minimize conflict using multi-form tendency analysis.
5. I can anticipate areas of conflict and develop communications which minimize discord.

7-4. Creativity

1. I have no knowledge of creativity.
2. I can act as a participant in brainstorming sessions.
3. I can use creative techniques such as fractionation, reversal, analogies, random stimulation, point of view shift, etc., to generate additional ideas.
4. I can lead a creative ideas session.
5. I can develop a creative culture in the workplace through personal actions and leadership.

7-5. Change Management

1. I have no knowledge of change management.
2. I facilitate change using existing processes such as the suggestion program, customer surveys, and team suggestions.
3. I create a climate tolerant and supportive of change and experimentation.
4. I set performance goals which require continuous improvement/change.
5. I anticipate change by proactively identifying opportunities and investigating them.

7-6. Decision Making

1. I make decisions based upon my knowledge and work experience.
2. I can use simple team decision making skills such as consensus, voting and multi-voting.
3. I can use simple analytical decision making skills such as factor analysis and ranking.
4. I can use analytical decision making skills such as risk and matrix analysis.
5. I can simulate decision results and make decisions based upon projected outcomes.

7-7. Effective Meetings

1. I have no knowledge of effective meetings.
2. I can distribute an agenda with meeting topics and goals prior to the meeting.

(continues)

Figure 6-4. *(continued)*

3. I can utilize team roles in the meeting by having a leader, recorder, facilitator, timekeeper, and so on.
4. I can insure that the meeting results in SMART action goals accepted by specific individuals.
5. I can lead a debrief at the close of the meeting to determine meeting effectiveness and make recommendations for future sessions.

7-8. Humor

1. I have no knowledge of organizational humor.
2. I can recognize what and when humor is appropriate and applicable for the workplace.
3. I can utilize humor from other sources such as quotes or cartoons.
4. I can adapt humor from other sources for use in the workplace.
5. I can create humor for use in the workplace.

7-9. Listening

1. I have no knowledge of listening.
2. I can focus attention and actively listen.
3. I can utilize concentration techniques to minimize distractions and increase retention.
4. I can use note taking techniques such as concept mapping to capture and organize thoughts and conversations.
5. I have a system for storing, indexing and recalling information.

7-10. Memory

1. I have no knowledge of memory techniques.
2. I can use imagining techniques to remember names and faces.
3. I can use imagining techniques to remember items in lists.
4. I can use assorted techniques for general study learning such as imaging, chunking, acronyms, rhyming number lists, phonetic number lists, and so on.
5. I can teach others to use memory techniques.

7-11. Presentation Skills

1. I have no knowledge of effective presentations.
2. I can effectively present information to a small group.
3. I can effectively present complex topics to departmental groups.
4. I can speak to a large audience/auditorium integrating content, humor and effective platform nonverbals.
5. I can act as an organization media spokesperson for print, radio and TV.

7-12. Substance Abuse

1. I have no knowledge of substance abuse.
2. I can deal with substance abuse concerns using the guidelines in the personnel policies manual.

3. I know to involve Personnel on any issues or instances of substance abuse.
4. I can counsel someone admitting to a substance abuse problem.
5. I know the legal and illegal substances currently available and their early warning signs.

7-13. Styles Analysis

1. I have no knowledge of styles analysis.
2. I know the four individual multi-form style tendencies: transform, inform, perform and conform.
3. I can analyze the styles of others as measured by the TIPC Questionnaire.
4. I can identify the styles of others by observing their typical behaviors.
5. I can modify my interaction with others to reflect their preferences based upon TIPC styles.

7-14. Time Management

1. I manage my time in order to meet deadlines.
2. I use time management for a tactical things-to-do list on a daily basis.
3. I understand the components of my job and manage my daily tasks on a priority basis.
4. I spend time on a periodic basis determining what is required of me, planning my time and activities, and regularly send plans to my team.
5. I understand the three value-added hallmarks of an activity and strive to identify and eliminate non-value-added tasks whenever possible.

7-15. Writing

1. I rely on the writing skills of others to put my communication in readable form.
2. I can write informal, internal communications.
3. I can write business and technical communication in a clear, concise, readable style.
4. I can adapt the style of my writing for different audiences and for different purposes using specific organization and expression techniques.
5. I can write lengthy proposals, reports and white papers for wide reproduction and readership.

8. Quality

8-1. TQM

1. I have no knowledge of TQM.
2. I can explain why TQM is essential.
3. I can explain how TQM is related to the organization's vision, values and mission.
4. I can describe the five basics of TQM.
5. I can give examples of how TQM, vision/values/mission statements or the five basics have modified my behavior.

8-2. ISO 9000

1. I have no knowledge of ISO 9000.
2. I am familiar with the organization's Quality Manual.
3. I can identify some of my processes which are addressed in the ISO standards.
4. I can explain a quality process which is designed to meet the appropriate ISO standard.
5. I can identify processes which do not currently meet ISO standards.

(continues)

Figure 6-4. *(continued)*

8-3. Customer Service

1. I have no knowledge of customer service.
2. I can identify internal and external customers for my processes.
3. I can execute exceptional customer service in the five service areas: reliability, empathy, responsiveness, assurance, and tangibles.
4. I can determine customer needs through activities such as surveys, focus groups, interviews, response cards and visits.
5. I can perform statistical or behavioral Customer Map importance/satisfaction analysis to identify customer service improvement priorities and next steps.

8-4. Facilitation

1. I have no knowledge of facilitation.
2. I can follow accepted team productivity standards to develop team roles and tasks.
3. I can execute first and second person facilitator interventions during a meeting to improve productivity and quality of results.
4. I can coach and counsel team leaders and members to conduct more effective team meetings.
5. I can train and develop other Lead Facilitators to assist teams in their workgroups.

8-5. Team Building

1. I have no knowledge of team building.
2. I can assist teams through the formation stage in identifying members and in developing a mission.
3. I can assist teams through the storming and norming stages in developing the ability to be candid, agreeing upon behavioral rules, and establishing mutually agreed upon goals.
4. I can assist teams to reach the performing stage where team roles are being properly executed and measurable results have been generated.
5. I can train and develop others to assist in the creation and maturation of teams.

8-6. Process Improvement

1. I have no knowledge of process improvement.
2. I can identify the process owner, determine the process SIPOC chain, and write an object-defect statement.
3. I can identify defects, collect variable and attribute data with checksheets and spreadsheets, performance root cause analysis, and analyze data statistically with control charts and other graphs.
4. I can document current processes with value-added flow, workflow and flowchart diagrams, and identify potential areas for improved customer satisfaction, decreased cycle time and reduced error rates.
5. I can perform all steps of the PDCA Cycle to redesign current processes to improve customer satisfaction, decrease cycle time and reduce error rates.

8-7. Reengineering

1. I have no knowledge of reengineering.
2. I can analyze a process from the viewpoint of the things going through the process and calculate their "value time/elapsed time" in-use vs. idle time quotients.
3. I can identify opportunities for a case worker/case worker team approach to consolidate and simplify existing processes.

4. I can identify opportunities for technology solutions to consolidate and simplify existing processes.
5. I can perform as a member of a reengineering team to redesign major organizational processes.

8-8. Core Competencies/Outsourcing

1. I have no knowledge of core competencies/outsourcing.
2. I can identify opportunities for non-core competencies to be outsourced for greater value to the internal and external customer.
3. I can assist in the selection of outsourcing patterns.
4. I can manage outsourced relationships.
5. I can measure the results of outsourced relationships.

8. Administering the assessment is the easy step. There are a wide range of high-power, easy-to-use tools.
9. It can be helpful to start with a simple assessment for a first competency-based HR application and then build in sophistication over time.

Notes

1. Dan Shasserre, *Organizational Climate Assessment* (St. Louis: Business Training Library, 1999), 1–4.

7

Expanding the Model to Other HR Applications

At this stage in the CMAR process, the team has a common terminology, an accurate competency model has been developed, position standards exist, and an assessment instrument has been written. So the design work has been completed. All that is left is to administer the tools, after which individuals' competencies can be measured and gap analysis and reporting can be completed. (Chapters 8 and 9 show several approaches for implementing a complete CMAR process focusing on personnel development.)

If an organization stops here, it will likely still achieve major benefits in employee productivity and satisfaction, and it will be in a position to improve business results. But this would be a significant waste of intellectual capital. The difficult tasks, building models and assessments, are completed. Once these have been written, it requires a relatively small marginal effort to leverage them into other HR processes.

This effort demands no skills that have not already been discussed. What is required are management commitment and design team motivation to utilize them outside of employee development processes. Consequently, this is a chapter short on content but long on exhortation.

The Employee Cycle

Competency-based projects typically start with assessing and developing incumbent employees. This is all the quality standards require, and it is an effort that fits comfortably within the classic training department. Questions that typically lead to a competency research and development effort include:

"Are we using our training dollars most effectively?"
"How do we know that training is delivering on its promises?"
"Are we training on the right things?"
"Are we training the right people?"

The result is that many organizations are locked into competency-based applications as enhancements to the training function rather than using them in an organizational strategy.

Improving the skills of incumbent employees is just one competency-based HR application and, for some organizations, may not be the most important one. Figure 7-1 shows how employees cycle through a position. This is an employee-oriented view of the major HR activities illustrated in Figure 1-1.

Note the division between "discover" and "develop." The employer is often a passive information seeker at the first three positions. Job seekers bring a set of skills with them to the organization. It is the duty of the personnel acquisition process to uncover those skills but not to modify them. Once a person is hired, the employer shifts into an active development mode, taking on the responsibility for providing appropriate performance enhancement resources. Now an individual's skills are considered a variable that can be improved by the individual and the organization.

In many industries, particularly those facing labor shortages, this distinc-

Figure 7-1. The employee cycle.

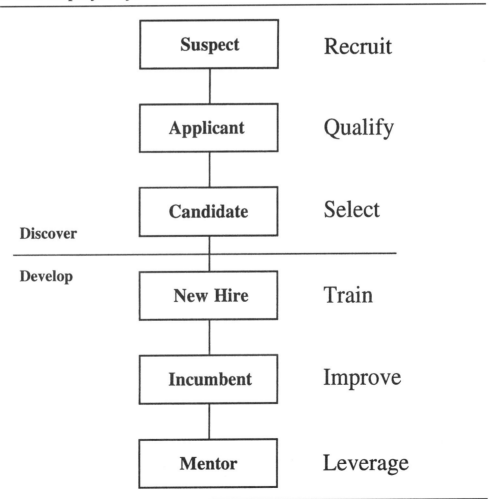

tion is breaking down. The classic methods of acquisition and development are failing to provide qualified employees for all positions. One solution is to push competency concepts backward and forward from skills management in the employee cycle (see Figure 1-1). Another is to shift the discover/develop line to a position earlier in the cycle, using competency concepts.

Expanding to Other HR Applications

Organizations today are applying competency concepts all along the employee cycle. Employers can no longer afford to evaluate individuals at the various stages of the cycle based upon subjective criteria that are measured through weak processes. CMAR concepts can be into utilized at the very beginning of the cycle.

Suspects

Suspects are individuals from the population that organizations have reason to believe might make suitable employees. Sometimes this is not much of a distinction. A classified ad effectively defines a suspect as anyone capable of reading the weekend newspaper and writing a response. Other qualified suspects are people who know headhunters, who walk in off the street, or who know the headquarters address for sending mail. Any of these individuals can generate an application that will be at least minimally reviewed and evaluated.

Some organizations are moving competency assessment right up front. One major hardware chain requires that all job aspirants sit down at a personal computer on-site and complete a skills test before filling out an application. Another large organization uses a Web-based approach. Candidates indicate the positions they are interested in from a list on the company's site, then are required to pass a test before they receive authorization to e-mail their resume to the appropriate contact. In essence, this company does not process an application until the individual has met minimum standards for an applicant.

While Web-based solutions allow the possibility of applicant cheating, there is a strong statement of intent from the employer to the suspect. These organizations are clearly fact based and are likely to continue this approach throughout the hiring process. Deception will likely be discovered later in the cycle.

Applicants

In a competency-based organization, an applicant becomes someone who has demonstrated enough skills to move from being a suspect to a prospect. Think of this as a yes/no assessment of minimum competence. The employer is now justified in spending resources in examining an individual's suitability for an open position. At this stage, most organizations use a single assessment method to determine qualifications—the interview.

Employers have spent enormous sums of money to make the interview process more effective. There are a myriad of training seminars, video programs, worksheets, interview scripts, and other tools. There is also a wide range of variants, such as team interviewing, stress interviews, outsider/expert interviewing, or 360-degree interviews—all designed to improve the evaluation process. The results are still often hit-and-miss.

As one technology industry contributor wrote on an *InfoWorld* magazine Web forum, "[At our company,] a headhunter pushes people. My boss/brother does a corporate overview—'HR, warm and fuzzy.' If the person passes, then I get to grill them. I've cut interviews after 60 seconds, or I've let them go two hours. And I still only got one really good person after three really bad hires."[1]

The answer lies in competency assessment techniques. Interviewing is just one of the tools—and a not very powerful one—that can be used for measuring qualifications. Chapter 6 covered an entire range of approaches for developing a valid and reliable assessment of competence.

Candidates

Candidates are those applicants who have proven themselves qualified for an open position. These are equivalent to the three to five "finalists" who are under consideration for being hired. All appear suitable. The goal is to hire the "best" candidate. Think of this as an assessment with a dimension that measures levels of competence.

Again, organizations utilize a range of tools to better evaluate and select from the pool of candidates. Typical activities include an additional round of interviews, physical examinations, psychological testing, psychological evaluation, ethics testing, reference checking—mostly soft measurement activities. Many organizations with the most extensive and costly candidate evaluation procedures actually do no formal evaluation of competence. Upon hiring an individual, management finds that they merely accepted a candidate's verbal assurances that he or she could do the job.

Formal competency measurement establishes a candidate's true skills, knowledge, and attitudes relevant to the position under consideration. Properly constructed, it can fill in the gaps in understanding what candidates truly bring to the organization, and it can help differentiate competency levels among candidates.

Moving the Discover/Develop Line

A note is needed here on the issue of labor shortages. At the bottom end of the job spectrum, competency concepts may be of little help. Low wages and undesirable jobs make poor inducements for recruiting employees. The fast-food industry lives and dies based upon the available pool of youthful workers. Yet even some good positions are difficult to fill, particularly in the technology industry, where hundreds of thousands of jobs remain open. People with necessary competencies simply do not exist.

This is where the discover/develop line has to move up. Facing severe labor shortages, organizations are taking fledgling steps to develop their own candidates *before* they become employees. This is very different from the low-pay "management training program" of years past. Today, workers with potential are identified and trained on the required skills. The entire paradigm is reversed. Instead of "hire them and train them," it becomes "train them and then hire them." Some firms are even going into high schools and colleges and providing incentives for students to take technical courses in return for a promise to accept a position there after graduation, much like the military does with ROTC.

In the computing industry and others, development must extend beyond the employed workforce, or else organizations will fail through lack of people. In the not-too-distant future, as Internet-based training delivery costs continue to fall, people will be able to take Web-based courses that prepare them for specific positions in a sponsoring organization. Instead of being offered for thousands of dollars by training vendors, these professional development courses may be free of charge or may even provide a bonus payment upon successful completion and being hired by the sponsoring organization. A thoroughly implemented competency modeling and assessment program will be required to accomplish this.

New Hires

A new hire is a person in the initial period of employment. Traditionally, this means that employees are going through some sort of "orientation" in which they are prepared to be a member of the company. What this orientation consists of depends upon a key philosophical decision that was described in Chapter 2.

Employers must decide whether people are required to be ready to perform in a position before they are hired, or whether they are put in a position in order to learn until they reach required levels of competence. Most organizations do the latter. New hires are put into a job and then begin the process of learning it. The result is a workforce in which a significant percentage of employees are not qualified to do their job. For them, orientation consists of both employer-related assimilation information and position training.

There are many analogies that show why this causes problems:

"Here's your bus and route, now learn to drive the bus."
"We need the side of that hill blasted out for the on-ramp. Here's the dynamite you'll need. Let's see how you do on your first shot."

"It's time you learned how to do knee reconstructions. Your first surgery is scheduled for 7:00 A.M. tomorrow."

It is unthinkable in many industries that unqualified workers are put into live processes and expected to perform. The only result that can be guaranteed is that there will be what quality analysts call "defects." Yet, thirty years after *The Peter Principle* was written, many organizations still promote on competency, but competency in the old job, not the new one.[2] As Laurence Peter and Raymond Hull point out, permanent problems ensue when employees are put into situations beyond their capability to master.

There is only one way to keep employees from rising to their level of incompetence, even temporary incompetence. Competency-based organizations must work to develop and identify people who are already qualified for a position and place them where they can be immediately productive. Orientation then means teaching new hires what they need to know about the employer—its vision, values, mission, organizational structure, ethics, personnel processes, benefits, expense accounting procedures, and so on.

Incumbents

An incumbent is an employee who is qualified for a position and is performing to standards. This is where the bulk of CMAR efforts are typically focused. The goal is one of continuous improvement to raise position standards and employee qualifications.

Mentors

A mentor is an incumbent employee who can help raise the competency levels of others. In the situational leadership model, this is similar to an "M4" high-maturity follower who is able and willing to take on responsibility.[3] In the P-CMM model, these individuals are present in a Managed Level (4) or Optimizing Level (5) organization, where mentors and coaches are provided to support the continuing development of individual or workgroup competencies.[4]

With mentors, the focus is on improving competencies in an objective, quantifiable manner. These individuals are capable of bringing others up to their high standards of performance and can help create other mentors. The organization needs to leverage their skills to create the maximum benefit.

This employee progression truly is a cycle. One position's incumbent is a suspect for a possible promotion. If development and qualification for a job are going to happen before someone is promoted, then competency assessment, gap analysis, and personnel development must take place prior to the hiring decision.

The Future: A Range of Standards

Another ramification of expanding competency-based functions into the employee cycle should be coming into focus. There is now an additional level of complexity necessary for CMAR programs. So far the discussion has centered on single-position standards. Ultimately, instead of a universal position standard, the cycle suggests that there will need to be a standard adapted *for the individual's location in the employee cycle.* If employee development is an organization-wide function, then the standards for a candidate cannot be the same as for an incumbent or mentor. These additional variants will require their own models, assessment instruments, and development resources.

This fragmentation of position standards appears to impose a daunting administrative burden on an organization. CMAR efforts are suddenly increased by a factor of six. In the old world of paper-based systems and manual tabulation, this would be impractical. In the new world of relational databases, e-mail, and Web-based interactive delivery, this is a natural progression with a very low marginal cost beyond the effort of modifying existing models and assessments.

Moving competency measurement into all levels of the employee cycle provides many benefits to organizations. Less personnel time is wasted evaluating candidates who are not qualified for the job. Better candidates are selected from the pool of applicants, and better new hires are selected from the group of candidates. New hires are productive more quickly. Incumbents receive just-in-time, just-as-needed development. Mentors help to develop the competencies of those around them and help to create additional mentors before moving on to another position. All it takes is to put the necessary systems in place.

Learning Points

1. Organizations are going to have to make a hard decision concerning what is "good enough." Is it going to be "hire and learn" or "assess and hire?" Employing capable people without the required competencies means filling the organization with "talented amateurs."
2. Much of the hard work has been done with the development of models and assessments. For a small marginal investment, organizations can leverage this intellectual capital into HR functions beyond the development of current employees.
3. Traditional measures of applicant or candidate qualifications are largely ineffective. Objective assessment of competencies is a requirement in a hiring process.
4. Organizations need to change the mind-set that says personnel development is only for employees. Competency development for outsiders,

which can be done over the Internet at a marginal cost, may be required to fill positions with qualified new hires.

5. Expanding competency models to other levels of the employee cycle complicates the CMAR process. Systems need to be in place to facilitate the growth of competency-based HR applications.

Notes

1. "Can HR Handle IT Hiring Headaches?" *InfoWorld*, 6 September 1999, 56.
2. Laurence J. Peter and Raymond Hull, *The Peter Principle: Why Things Always Go Wrong* (New York: Bantam, 1969), 7.
3. Paul Hersey and Ken Blanchard, *Management of Organizational Behavior: Utilizing Human Resources*, 4th ed. (Englewood Cliffs, N.J.: Prentice Hall, 1982), 152–155.
4. Bill Curtis, William E. Hefley, and Sally Miller, *Overview of the People Capability Maturity Model* (Pittsburgh: Carnegie Mellon University, 1995), CMU/SEI-95-MM-01, 18–20.

Automating Competency Modeling, Assessment, and Reporting

Until the 1990s, it was not unusual to find organizations, even enterprise-sized, attempting to manage competencies with paper-based systems. Any computerized record keeping that did exist usually handled only the administrative processes related to training, such as enrollment, scheduling, and billing. As Chapter 1 discussed, concerns about productivity, competitive pressures, and demands of quality programs for documenting employee qualifications led to the need for more comprehensive competency applications that could be deployed across an organization. This meant understanding and systematizing informal practices and simple administrative systems.

A Pilot Implementation

In late 1994, the Anheuser-Busch sales department asked CooperComm to assist with the development of an automated solution to provide annual assessments of sales staff and to report on individual and departmental competency gaps and resource needs. The anticipated business results of the project were:

1. Make learning more relevant by adjusting content and offerings to fit specific competency needs.
2. Facilitate the transfer of learning to immediate use on the job.
3. Reduce personnel development costs by providing resources only to individuals that need them and by eliminating resources not addressing competency gap needs.
4. Provide planning information to the Busch Learning Center (BLC) for resources needed in the coming year. Generate potential attendee/participant lists.

5. Identify new competency development needs for input into the BLC Research and Development (R&D) effort.
6. Provide career development information to help employees prepare for future positions.

The Anheuser-Busch (A-B) goal was to have the development completed in time for the next planning period (in the fall of 1995). The BLC eventually assumed responsibility for the project, providing project management and subject matter expertise. CooperComm was retained to assist with creating models and assessments, to develop the software, and to perform the initial round of surveying, tabulating, and reporting.

The first step was to construct a logical model of the interrelationships among competency data sets. Figure 8-1 illustrates general competency modeling, assessment, and reporting (CMAR) information relationships.

The process to create this logical information system follows the model introduced in this text. The steps are:

1. Select the workgroups and titles that will be included in the CMAR project. This establishes the People and Title databases, which must then be linked.
2. Develop competency models and performance standards for the titles indicated. Link Competency Standards with the Title database.
3. Create assessment instruments by title or by workgroup. Individual

Figure 8-1. Competency data sets.

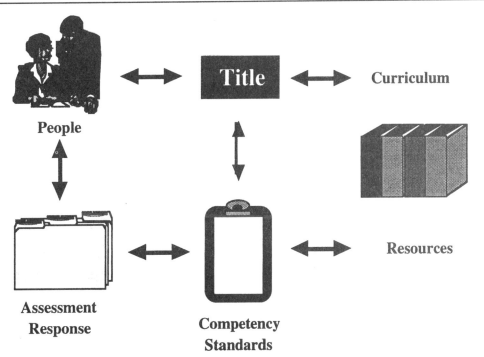

user Assessment Response must be linked to People and Competency Standards databases.

4. Identify development resources. Map resources to competency gaps and/or establish Curriculum standards by Title.

From a process viewpoint, each of the data sets must be entered, then all the linkages between sets must be specified. As a stand-alone batch system, this is an ideal database application. The result of the software development effort was Competency Coach, a general-purpose, PC-based CMAR relational database solution. (A sample version of this software is included on the CD-ROM accompanying this text and is described in the Appendix.)

The Competency Coach system, shown starting up in Figure 8-2, is similar to a blank spreadsheet, where all the formatting, formulas, printing, and cell relationships are embedded in the background. It allows nearly complete customization of content. All the user needs to do is enter the relevant data and print the desired reports. Competency Coach implements the database structures described in Figure 8-1 and can be used with almost any measurement approach that generates a numeric assessment response.

The software provides a standardized implementation of the design deci-

Figure 8-2. Competency Coach start-up screen.

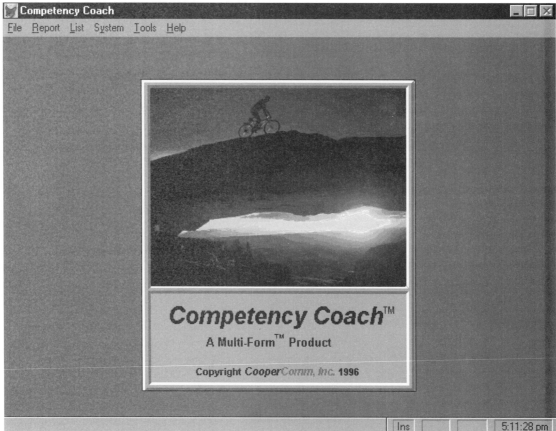

sions described in Chapter 2, and the competency-related development processes described in Chapters 3 through 6. The working model, standards, and assessment used in this text are already entered in this version of Competency Coach, and a list of example resources with all the appropriate linkages in place are also included. A sample group of employees has also been input so that the user can experiment with all the analysis and reporting capabilities of a representative CMAR program.

Competency Coach Implementation

This section illustrates a typical implementation project using Competency Coach. More detailed user information is available in the User Guide contained on the CD-ROM. This coverage offers an overview of the steps required to set up CMAR software and utilize its reporting capabilities. The descriptions and screen shots provide a sense of the scope of effort and time required and indicate the capabilities for reporting.

Stand-alone CMAR applications can require extensive setup for the initial run. Manual data-entry time can be compressed by writing translation code to mine the necessary information from existing databases and reformat it for Competency Coach. Subsequent reporting is usually much simpler, requiring only an update of the data sets.

Note: The following procedures use a menu designation convention indicating the selection of commands in sequence. "List/Workgroup/Workgroup" means to pull down the List menu from the horizontal bar at the top of the main Competency Coach window, select the Workgroup list item, then click on the Workgroup tab in the dialog box that opens up. All selection options designated in the chapter will be either menu items or folder tabs.

Personnel Data Entry

The best place to start in data entry is with personnel. This can begin early in the development process before the competency model and assessment information are ready. That can be entered later.

Step 1.

Workgroups are a major organizing and selection category for reports. Choose with care which workgroups will be used for personnel. This division usually follows a natural pattern, such as departments, regions, locations, or branches, but it can represent any desired grouping of people. Enter all of the workgroup data in the List/Workgroup/Workgroup window as shown in Figure 8-3.

Figure 8-3. Creating workgroups.

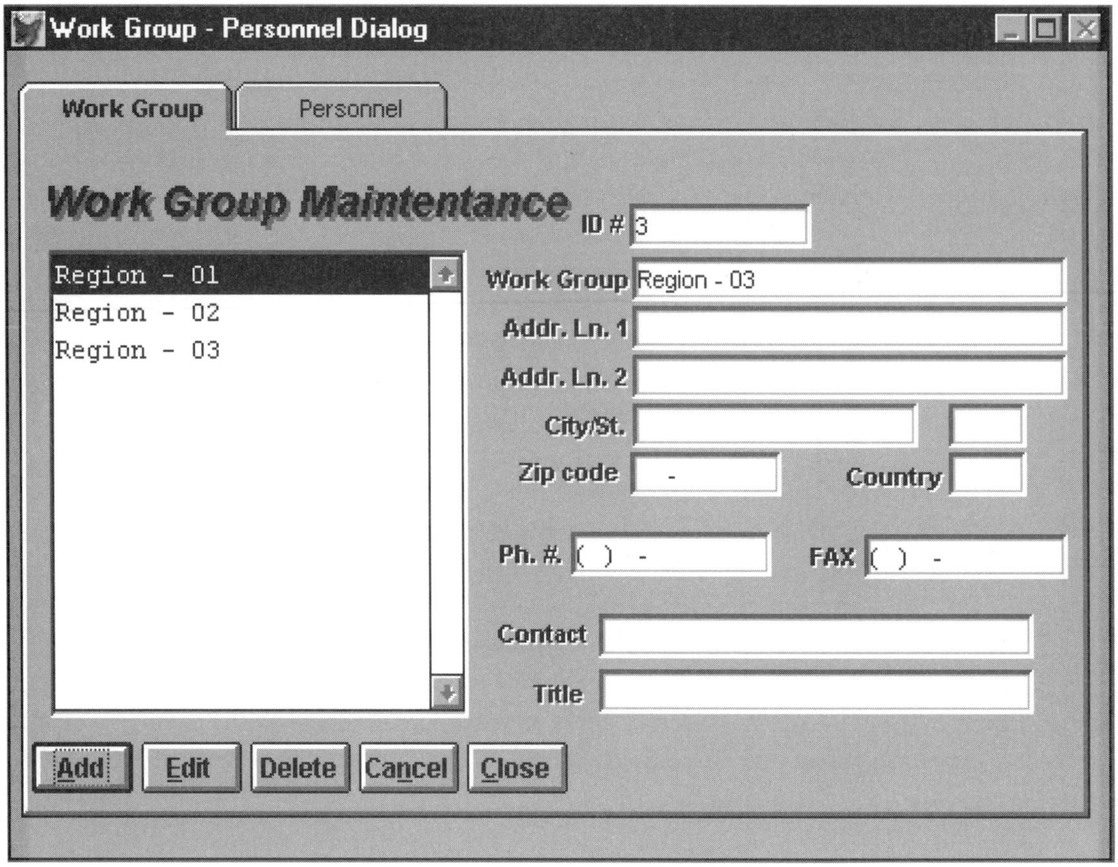

Step 2.

Enter the employees in each workgroup using the List/Workgroup/Personnel window, as shown in Figure 8-4. It is helpful to include all contact information for the workgroup, because there are often a myriad of questions that arise concerning titles that do not quite match positions included in the system or who is currently in which job.

Step 3.

Enter the complete list of titles in the List/Title/Title window shown in Figure 8-5 (on page 200). The title list should cover every employee entered in Step 2 above.

Step 4.

Now people and titles can be linked. If the source personnel list is alphabetical by person, use the List/Personnel/Title window shown in Figure 8-6 (on page 201). If the personnel list is organized by title, use the List/Title/Personnel

Figure 8-4. Entering employees.

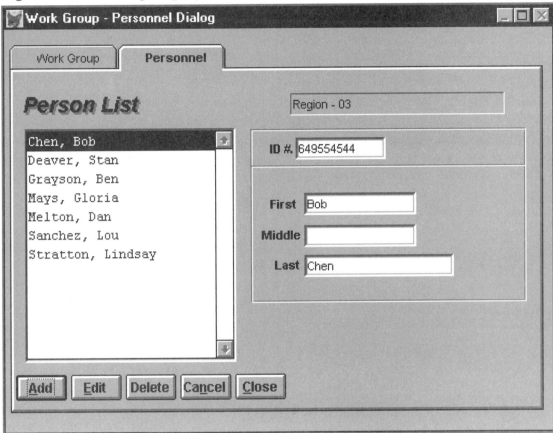

window shown in Figure 8-7 (on page 202). This dual entry mode is a common feature of Competency Coach. Because source data may not be organized the way a system requires it, for convenience it should be possible to link data starting from either side. Again, this manual data-entry process can be circumvented by extracting the appropriate personnel database information and formatting it for Competency Coach.

The personnel data-entry process is completed. People are linked to their workgroups and titles. The system is now ready for the entry of the competency model and assessment information when it becomes available.

Competency Data Entry

There are three levels of competency-related data: category, competency, and response. Categories are groups of individual competencies organized by subject. Each competency has a choice of possible assessment responses.

Designers must evaluate how the enterprise should have its competency models organized. A model can contain fifty or more individual competencies; dividing the list into categories makes the assessment instrument and summary reports easier to select, read, and understand. A category may typically contain up to ten individual competencies. Sample categories might be man-

Figure 8-5. Entering titles.

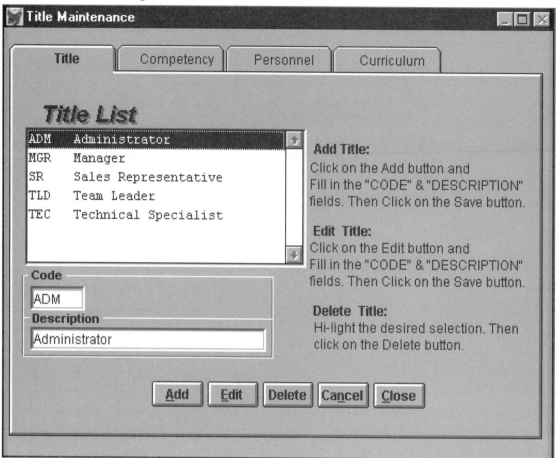

agement, personnel, organization policies, industry knowledge, computer skills, or community involvement.

Step 5.

Create the competency categories. Enter the competency categories that make up the model in the List/Competency/Category window as shown in Figure 8-8 (on page 203). Categories are normally listed on the printed questionnaire and on reports in the order in which they were entered, so time can be saved by inputting categories in the desired report sequence. (The order of the category listing can be changed by going into the System/Setup/Cat. Order window and modifying the sequence as required.) Also, it is worth investing the time to enter the code and description information because they are both useful later in labeling reports.

Step 6.

Enter the individual competencies in the List/Competency/Competency window as shown in Figure 8-9 (on page 204). A code can be used to reference

Figure 8-6. Linking people to titles.

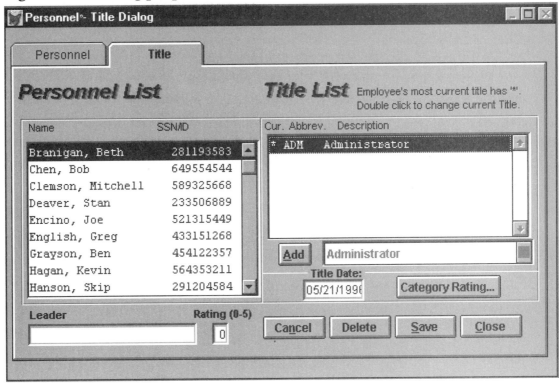

the competency; for example, "0501" could refer to the first competency of the fifth category. There is also room for descriptive text, which will be useful when printing out the assessment form. Note that it is possible to vary the number of choices allowed for responses. This is particularly useful in occasionally using a two "yes/no" response set. (In general, it is less confusing when a standard number of responses is used consistently throughout an assessment.)

Step 7.

Enter the possible response answers for each competency in the List/Competency/Response window as shown in Figure 8-10 (on page 205). These answers make up the assessment contents used to measure competencies and provide the detailed specifics of the competencies being measured.

Step 8.

Link competency standards to job titles using the List/Competency/Title window. Figure 8-11 (on page 206) illustrates that, based on the answers entered earlier, a manager may need to be a "2" in Spreadsheet competency, a technical specialist may need to be a "4," and an administrator may need to be a "5."

It is also possible to apply a "1 to N" weighting factor to each competency

Figure 8-7. Linking titles to people.

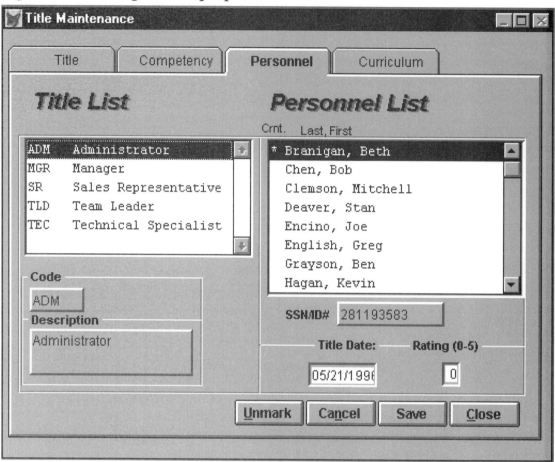

by title. This way competencies can be given different levels of importance in identifying and reporting gaps. For example, a personnel manager might have a "3" weight for the Personnel Policies competency, a line manager a "2," and a frontline worker a "1" weight. Safety, on the other hand, might be weighted a "3" in importance for all employees.

Weighting, although not used in the sample working model included in this text, helps to identify priority development needs by ranking competency gaps first by importance and then by size of gap. Otherwise, only gap differential is available for prioritizing competency improvement needs.

This completes the data-entry portion of the competency model. The systems portion of this effort is straightforward. It is critical that the content entered be of the highest quality. The system cannot discern whether a model is accurate or an assessment is valid. It only takes what is input and performs the "hard-wired" comparisons and reporting. The effectiveness of the CMAR process depends upon the quality of the design team's efforts.

Resource Data Entry

The final data to be input involves linking developmental resources to individual competencies. While gap identification and reporting can be done without

Figure 8-8. Creating competency categories.

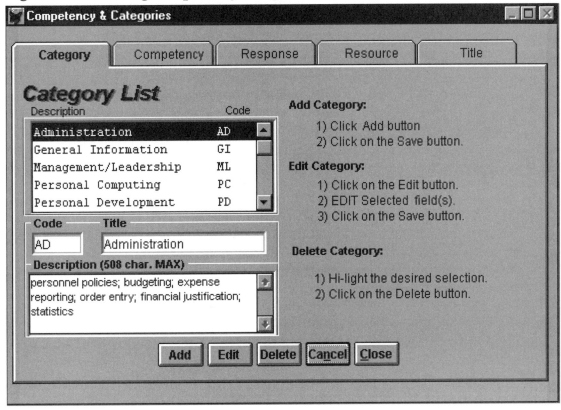

this data, no individualized development plans or overall training planning can be provided without resource data, so this is a very important step.

Step 9.

The entry and linking process used for personnel and competencies must now be done for resources. Enter the relevant resource types in the List/Resource/Type window as shown in Figure 8-12 (on page 207). For example, types might include seminars, workshops, books, videotape, audio tape, CBT, on-the-job training, work-beside, mentoring, and self-study. As before, the small amount of extra time taken here to complete the description boxes will help clarify reports later.

Step 10.

Enter all individual resources in the List/Resource/Resources window as shown in Figure 8-13 (on page 208). These resources support the development of individual competencies in the model.

Step 11.

Link individual resources to resource type in the same window. As explained in detail in the user manual and help system on the CD-ROM, links in

Figure 8-9. Entering individual competencies.

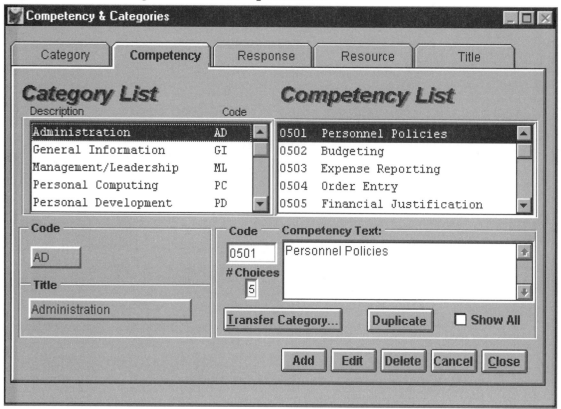

Competency Coach are created by highlighting the resource category on the left, then double-clicking on the appropriate resource(s) on the right. Linked items are marked with an asterisk.

Step 12.

Resources must now be linked to competencies. This is not a one-to-one relationship. An individual resource can support more than one competency, and individual competencies may be developed through using more than one resource. Competency Coach provides the ability to link from either direction. One way is to link individual resources to competencies using the List/Resource/Competency window shown in Figure 8-14 (on page 209).

An alternative method of linking resources to competencies is to use the List/Competency/Resource window as shown in Figure 8-15 (on page 210). This allows starting with individual competencies and identifying supporting resources. Use both approaches to make certain that all competencies are supported and that all resources are effectively used.

Step 13.

If this feature is being implemented in the competency model, create position curriculums that will be used in the individual development plan report.

Figure 8-10. Entering response answers.

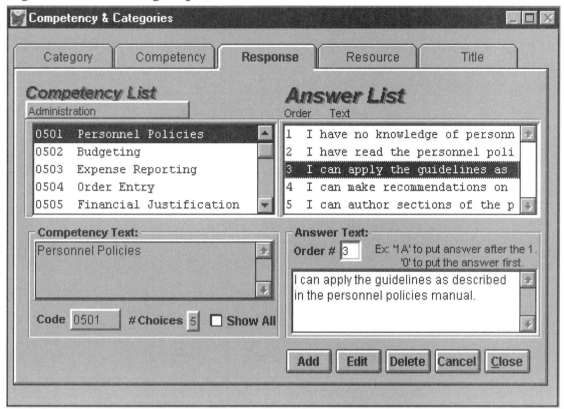

Link Title to Resources in the List/Title/Curriculum window as shown in Figure 8-16 (on page 211). Note that since Competency Coach is not a training administration system and does not have links to an outside package, no curriculum course tracking information can be provided. The curriculum reported in the individual development plan report must be manually compared with completion records to determine what remains to be done. This is a typical limitation of a stand-alone system.

This completes the resources data-entry and linking requirement. Competency Coach is now ready for assessment data entry.

Assessment

Competency Coach has no database link to an actual assessment form at the response answers level. Answer text is entered into the system solely for the convenience of the CMAR administrator.

Step 14.

Print and distribute the assessment. Figure 8-17 (on page 212) shows the command sequence to print out the assessment response form. This is not required by Competency Coach but is provided as a convenience to CMAR ad-

Figure 8-11. Linking competency standards to job titles.

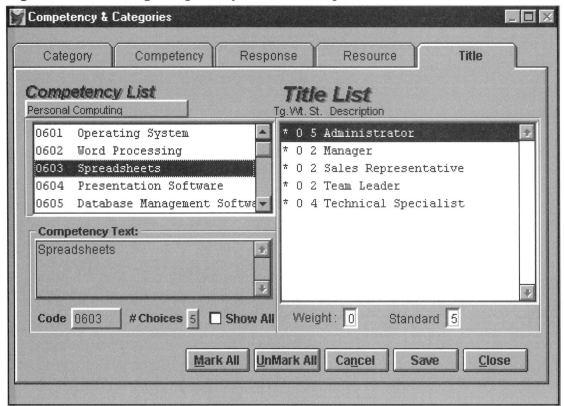

ministrators because the physical assessment process for employees is separate from the program. After the initial system setup, the actual assessment form can be given to employees on paper, as an electronic spreadsheet or word processing document, by e-mail, or through a stand-alone online surveying program. All Competency Coach requires are the sets of employee response numbers from the assessment.

Step 15.

Enter assessment responses. The assessment response numbers must be individually keyed into Competency Coach, as shown in Figure 8-18 (on page 212). The system has the capability of holding a user-defined number of assessments, keeping them separated by date. If an electronic data-entry approach is desired, similar to the option for Steps One through Four in loading personnel data electronically, custom database translation code can prepare an electronic record of assessment results in Competency Coach format.

Proofing Reports

Competency Coach provides the capability of generating customized reports without additional programming. The reports support complete individual de-

Figure 8-12. Creating resource types.

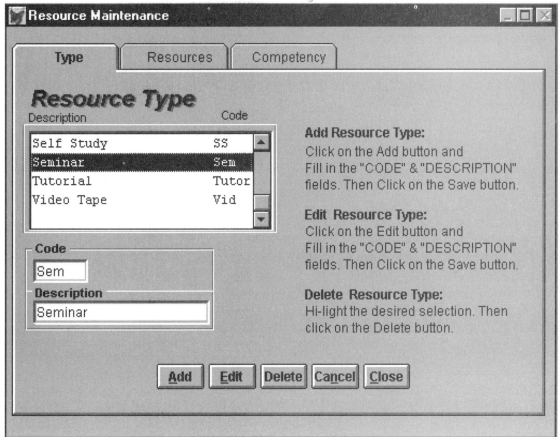

velopment planning and organizational resource planning processes. A standard feature of the reporting function is the ability to output reports to the screen, to a printer, or to a data file. In addition, some reports can be output to a spreadsheet file for further manipulation and analysis. This allows organizations to extract data from Competency Coach and add functionality without having to perform specialized programming.

Many of the reports, as well as Competency Coach program screens, take advantage of color capabilities, but none require color. This is important, since a small percentage of users, mostly males, are color-blind and may not be able to interpret color-coded information correctly. For this reason, Competency Coach provides text backup in reports and includes visual indicators such as solid versus striped bars in graphs.

Samples of the first page of each of the Competency Coach reports are included at the end of this chapter. Complete reports generated by the screens in this section are included on the CD-ROM in the Reports folder. For convenience, they are stored in Adobe Acrobat PDF format that can be read using the free Acrobat Reader application. Many Internet users already have this application, or it can be downloaded from Adobe's Web site (http://www. adobe.com).

Figure 8-13. Entering individual resources and linking to types.

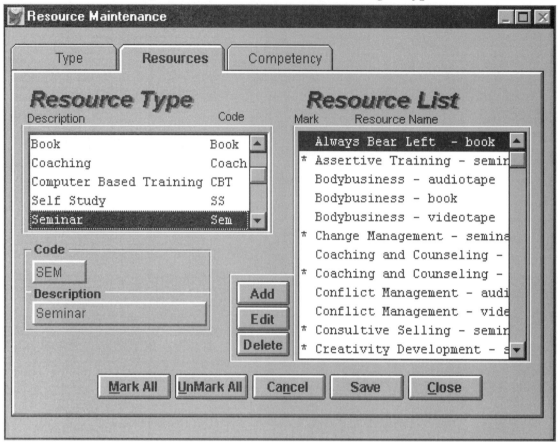

Step 16.

The first step is to verify the accuracy of data entry. The windowing architecture of Competency Coach can make it difficult to see the "big picture of people, competencies, answers, and resources. Therefore, proofing reports are available to check the accuracy of all key entry activities. These are available in the Report/Proofing/ . . . menu sequence as shown in Figure 8-19 (on page 213).

Specific proofing reports include the following:

⬦ *Title List.* This is a by-title, by-person listing of all individuals entered into the system. The report is reviewed for accuracy of people, dates that the current position was attained, and supervisor name.

⬦ *Title Competency List.* This is a listing by title, by competency category, by competency of all position standards and weighting priorities. This report assists in checking for the correct entry of position competency standards.

⬦ *Competency/Title Report.* This is a listing by competency category, by competency, by title of all position standards and weighting priorities. While it duplicates the information in the Title Competency List report

Figure 8-14. Linking resources to competencies.

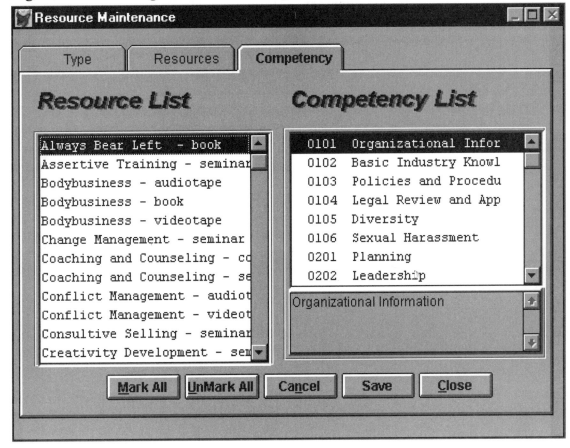

above, it is useful in looking at single competencies across multiple titles rather than all competencies by single position.

✧ *Competency/Resource Report.* This is a listing by competency, by resource of all resources that address specific competency gaps. It is useful for reviewing development resources that are indicated in gap reports given to users and their managers.

✧ *Resource/Competency Report.* This is a by-resource, by-competency category, and by-competency listing of all competencies that are addressed by a particular resource. It is useful in examining how single resources map to multiple competencies.

✧ *Resource/Seminar Report.* This is a listing by resource type, by resource. Despite the title, this report contains resources by all resource types depending upon the report selection criteria.

✧ *Person/Response Report.* This is a listing by person, by competency category, by competency of the assessment responses of an individual. It is used to verify the correct entry of assessment results for an individual.

✧ *Leader Response.* This is a ranking report by leader, by person from the leader of an employee. Competency Coach is programmed to offer employee assessment by leaders only at the competency category level,

Figure 8-15. Linking competencies to resources.

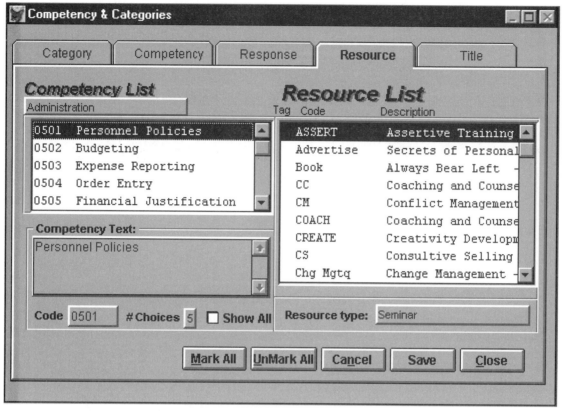

so this report does not list individual competencies. But this summary does include descriptive competency information, which is why it is important to have entered it earlier.

Individual and Supervisor Reports

Once the data entry has been proofed to the satisfaction of the CMAR administrator, individual reports can be produced. This is an ideal time to provide training to managers and supervisors whose subordinates are being assessed. The entire CMAR process is wasted if employees do not receive the proper counseling on development assignments.

Step 17.

Print out reports and distribute them to employees, managers, and HR or designated workgroup administrators. In a paper-based system, such as Competency Coach, this is an extensive process of creating batch reports, then collating them by individual, manager, and workgroup. Employee report packages can include:

Figure 8-16. Creating position curriculums.

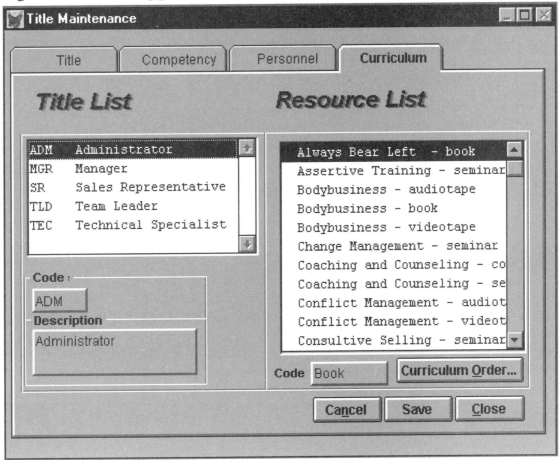

◇ *Response/Standard Comparison.* This report provides a complete visual summary of an employee's assessment and how it compares to specified standards. Variance by individual, by competency category, and by competency is indicated using bar charts and text.

Figure 8-20 (on page 213) shows the extensive set of printout options available for the important Response/Standard Comparison report. Administrators can select the following:

- ◇ All or some individuals
- ◇ All or some workgroups
- ◇ Report all assessment results compared to standards
- ◇ Report only competencies that were below standard (Priority Development Needs sub-report)
- ◇ Include applicable resources with below-standard competencies
- ◇ Print the response form with responses
- ◇ Print to screen for preview or printer for paper copy
- ◇ Print a graphical version or a text version of the report

Figure 8-17. Printing out a blank assessment response form.

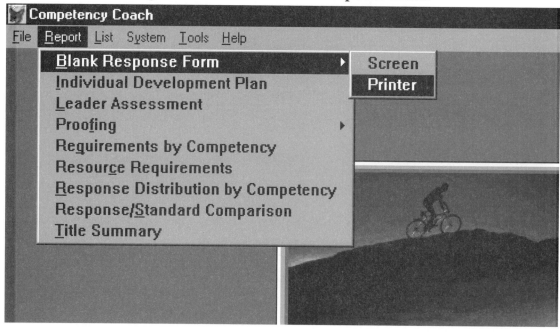

Figure 8-18. Entering assessment responses.

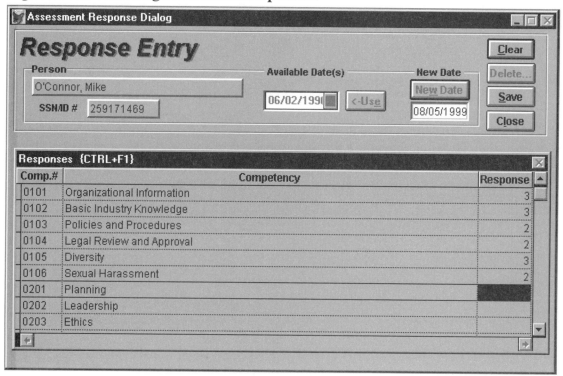

Figure 8-19. Proofing reports menu.

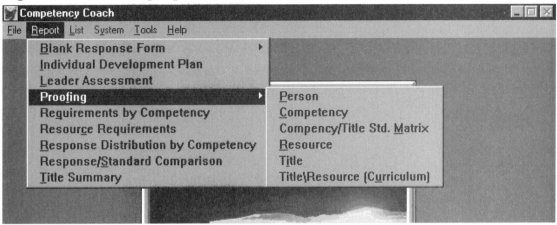

Figure 8-20. Response standard comparison print options.

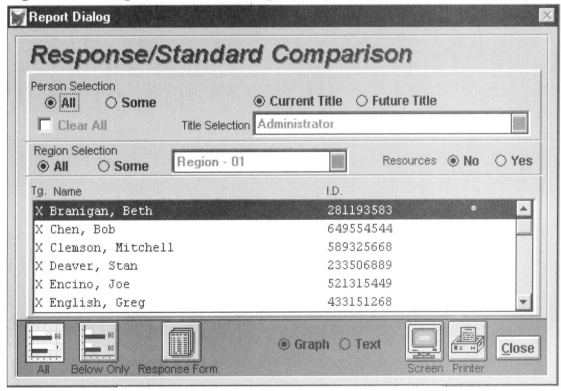

✧ Report on a current title or report based upon standards for a possible future position

✧ *Priority Development Needs*. This is an option of the Response/Standard Comparison report that includes only competencies that are below standard. Applicable resources can be included if desired.

✧ *Individual Development Plan*. This is a form that can be used to link business issues to competency development needs during the supervisor-employee development counseling session. It is very helpful in setting priorities for selecting resources to address competency gaps.

Managerial report packages can add the Leader Comparison printout. This compares the supervisor's competency category rating to a weighted category average computed from the employee's assessment report. Differences in self-assessment and leader assessment results can be discussed and resolved. Workgroup or HR administrators can receive a copy of the managerial package.

CMAR Administration Reports

Competency Coach provides several reports that are required by the organization to perform development research and planning. They provide the ability to analyze data at whatever level of detail is desired.

Step 18.

Print out the Response Distribution by Competency report. This is a competency report organized by title, by competency category that provides a summary view of the overall competency levels of participants. Data for individual competencies includes the number of respondents, the average response level, a distribution of responses by number, and a category response average.

The frequency distribution data provides an indication of the range of competencies determined in the assessment. A competency might have a narrow distribution, which indicates employees are mostly at the same level. If this is not at standard, then there is a widespread problem that requires nearly universal development activities. Another competency might have a wide distribution, which indicates that there are only spot problems and that a subset of employees should utilize the available resources.

Step 19.

Print out Resource Summary reports using the Report/Resource Requirements print selection window as shown in Figure 8-21. This report provides complete information on resource requirements.

The Resource Summary report selection screen shows the extensive set of printout options that are available. Administrators can select from the following:

◇ All or some resources
◇ All or some workgroups
◇ Print by competency or by weight

Also, note the third print option at the bottom of the screen. In all other print screens, a CMAR administrator can either preview reports on-screen or print

Figure 8-21. Resource summary print options.

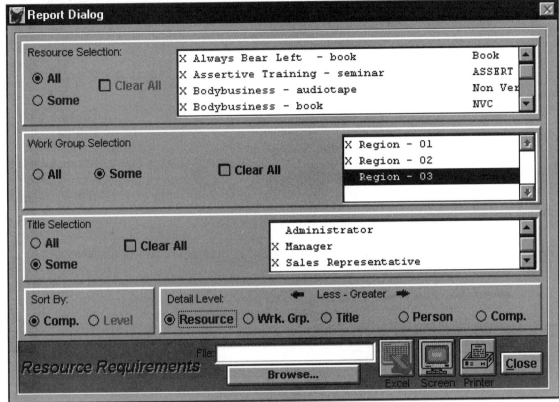

them out. This report, along with the Requirements by Competency report in Step 20, can also be exported as a Microsoft Excel spreadsheet file. The spreadsheet output option provides a method for enabling further analysis on these two critical management reports without having to do any custom database programming. (A sample from the working model is shown in Figure 8-50.)

Once the resource set is determined, the Resource Summary report can be printed in ever-increasing levels of detail, ranging from resource to workgroup, title, person, and competency. At the highest level of detail, the CMAR administrator has an invitation list of employees who need specific resources to address their competency gaps. This provides answers to planning questions, such as:

"How many managers from Regions One and Two should attend the Personnel Policy course?"

"If there aren't enough attendees from those two regions, how many would we get if we add Regions Three and Four?"

"How many sessions of a course should we schedule next year? Whom should we invite?"

"How many copies of this book are we going to need to buy? Who gets them?"

The Resource Summary report allows organizations to target their learning activities only to those individuals who require them. There is no more must-attend training by workgroup or by title when experienced employees do not need to participate. This can provide a significant and immediate cost savings to the organization.

Step 20.

Print out Requirements by Competency reports. This information helps identify the competencies that have the most individuals below standards. The report provides additional insight into the capabilities of participants and of specific areas of need.

As shown in Figure 8-22, administrators can choose from the following options:

⬦ All or some workgroups
⬦ All or some titles
⬦ All or some competencies

Figure 8-22. Requirements by competency print options.

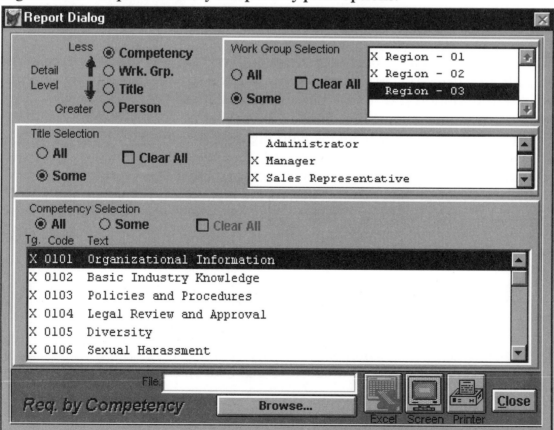

Once the competency set is determined, the Requirements by Competency report can be printed in ever-increasing levels of detail, ranging from competency to workgroup, title, and person. At the highest level of detail, the CMAR administrator has an invitation list of employees who need development to address specific competency gaps. This provides answers to R&D and planning questions, such as:

> "What new resources should we be developing? What competencies should they address?"
>
> "Region 2 has a meeting coming up in two months. There is a half-day slot open on the schedule. What competencies have the biggest gaps that we could address with a one-time development activity during the meeting?"

The Requirements by Competency report allows organizations to manage personnel development in a new manner. Rather than fitting attendees into existing resources, the CMAR administrator can start with competency needs and develop specific resources to address existing competency gaps. The result is just-as-needed development that is directly targeted to the competencies that drive business results.

Step 21.

Print out Response/Standard Comparison reports for future jobs on a request basis. As shown in Figure 8-20, one of the options in printing an employee's gap analysis report is to map the assessment to other positions using the Future Title feature. This only works when there is a workgroup-level competency model in which every employee completes the same assessment whether or not individual competencies apply to their current position.

The advantage is that employees can begin preparing for jobs they aspire to in addition to improving their current performance. This is often a very high-satisfaction item with employees because they now have a clear method of proving their readiness to be promoted.

Competency Coach Sample Reports

Figures 8-23 through 8-50 (on pages 218 through 276) are sample Competency Coach reports referenced in this section. In the case of the longer reports, only the first few pages are included. Complete versions of the reports can be found in the "Reports" folder on the CD-ROM included with this book.

This is a typical approach for implementing a stand-alone, automated CMAR process. The specifics of this program's operation are not important. There were many interface design and print layout decisions made during the development of the software that could easily have gone in another direction. The value of this chapter is in seeing what data relationships and procedures

(text continues on page 220)

Figure 8-23. Competency response form.

General Information

010 Organizational Information

1 I have no knowledge of basic organizational information.
2 I have attended the new employee orientation program and have read all employee literature.
3 I know basic organizational information and can use my knowledge of the organization to find answers to most of my questions.
4 I have a wide network of contacts and keep up-to-date on organizational goals, objectives, and issues.
5 I can use my extensive knowledge of organizational goals, objectives, issues, and resources to help others learn more about the organization.

010 Basic Industry Knowledge

1 I have no knowledge of industry information.
2 I have some basic knowledge of industry information sources.
3 I can access industry information sources for basic data and trends.
4 I can access industry information sources, analyze the contents, and make practical application to everyday operations.
5 I can access industry information sources, and can analyze and interpolate data in order to make practical application of the data to everyday operations.

010 Policies and Procedures

1 I have no knowledge of organizational policies and procedures.
2 I have some basic knowledge of organizational policies and procedures.
3 I know when I can make decisions on my own and when I should consult with someone else concerning any policy or procedure.
4 I am the person others consult with to determine the proper application of existing policies and procedures.
5 I can use my thorough knowledge of policies and procedures to determine the proper course of action in unique situations.

010 Legal Review and Approval

1 I have no knowledge of legal requirements.
2 I am familiar with the areas where legal review and approval are required.
3 I know when legal review and approval is required.
4 I have a thorough working knowledge of the legal review and approval for invoices, promotional authorizations, personnel documentation, and services contracting and can recognize when policy has not been followed.
5 I know the policies for legal review and approval and can identify and implement corrective actions.

010 Diversity

1 I have no knowledge of diversity issues.
2 I have attended diversity training and am familiar with the sensitivities required in organization locations.
3 I can modify my behavior to work effectively without bias and with sensitivity to diversity.
4 I can recognize when specific behaviors of myself and others do not properly address diversity requirements.

5   I can identify behaviors that should be modified, recommend improved behaviors, and counsel others on more effective behaviors concerning diversity issues.

010 Sexual Harassment

1   I have no knowledge of sexual harassment policies.
2   I have read the organization's policy on sexual harassment.
3   I have attended sexual harassment training and am familiar with the requirements of the Civil Rights Act of 1964, resulting case precedents, and organizational sexual harassment policies.
4   I can apply the Six Levels of Harassment and Offender Stereotypes to ensure that I participate in no sexual harassment in the workplace.
5   I can lead a sexual harassment complaint investigation and determine appropriate action steps.

Management/Leadership

020 Planning

1   I have no knowledge of planning.
2   I can create plans for completing my longer term work projects.
3   I can execute a complete planning process from needs determination and SWOT analysis through activity monitoring and project reporting.
4   I can apply critical path, bottleneck, flow simulation, and other analysis methods to shorten project cycle time and improve the quality of results.
5   I can create a planning process, manage the process, and conduct a post-plan review of effectiveness.

020 Leadership

1   I have no knowledge of leadership.
2   I provide direction and decisions for my followers.
3   I have empowered my followers to take responsibility and make decisions.
4   I have unified my followers with a common vision, values, and mission.
5   I have created a learning environment that develops my followers.

020 Ethics

1   I behave according to my personal and professional ethics.
2   I have read the employee Code of Conduct for organizational ethics.
3   I can apply the Code of Conduct in everyday business situations.
4   I can extrapolate the Code of Conduct to borderline/gray area situations.
5   I can coach others in applying the Code of Conduct to their situations.

020 Interviewing

1   I have no knowledge of interviewing.
2   I am familiar with legal interviewing techniques and know what questions are improper.
3   I can develop a structured interview process with varied interviewers, position needs, standardized questions, and objective selection techniques.
4   I can develop competency testing and measurement approaches for open positions.
5   I can perform post-selection interview effectiveness studies.

(continues)

Figure 8-23. *(continued)*

020 Performance Planning

   1   I have no knowledge of performance planning.
   2   I can create a performance plan based upon job descriptions.
   3   I can create a performance plan based upon job descriptions and needs of the workgroup.
   4   I can create a performance plan that directly relates to the performance goals of the workgroup.
   5   I can create a performance plan that helps develop and grow individuals.

020 Performance Reviews

   1   I have no knowledge of performance reviews.
   2   I can follow organizational guidelines in reviewing a subordinate on an established performance plan.
   3   I can use the performance plan criteria to provide an assessment of employee strengths and weaknesses.
   4   I can use the performance review results to identify areas for personal and professional development of the employee.
   5   I can use the performance review results to facilitate a discussion of career planning.

020 Salary Administration

   1   I have no knowledge of salary administration.
   2   I can explain the salary administration guidelines.
   3   I can apply the salary administration guidelines to an individual situation.
   4   I can apply the salary administration guidelines to a workgroup.
   5   I can justify and obtain salary administration guideline exceptions where needed.

have to be created in a CMAR application and in understanding the scope of the data management effort in creating and entering a model. Chapter 9 will show how many of the entry, distribution, and reporting shortcomings of a stand-alone CMAR application can be addressed by an online implementation using Internet technologies.

(text continues on page 276)

Figure 8-24. Title list.

Current Title

Person Name	Title Date	Supervisor	Overall Rate
Sales Representative			
Deaver, Stan	05/21/20XX		0
Hagan, Kevin	05/21/20XX		0
McGill, Steve	05/21/20XX		0
Meyerhoff, Jim	05/21/20XX		0
O'Connor, Mike	05/21/20XX	Wilson	3
Sakura, Lin	05/21/20XX		0
Sanchez, Lou	05/21/20XX		0
Stephenson, Bill	05/21/20XX		0
Stratton, Lindsay	05/21/20XX		0

Figure 8-25. Title competency list.

Current Title

Category Description

Code	Competency Short Text	Title Standard	Priority

Sales Representative

General Information

Code	Competency Short Text	Title Standard	Priority
0101	Organizational Information	3	0
0102	Basic Industry Knowledge	4	0
0103	Policies and Procedures	2	0
0104	Legal Review and Approval	2	0
0105	Diversity	3	0
0106	Sexual Harassment	3	0

Management/Leadership

Code	Competency Short Text	Title Standard	Priority
0201	Planning	2	0
0202	Leadership	2	0
0203	Ethics	3	0
0209	Counseling	2	0
0210	Open Book Management	3	0

Sales/Marketing

Code	Competency Short Text	Title Standard	Priority
0301	Account Planning	3	0
0302	Complex Account Selling	3	0
0303	Product Strategies	5	0
0304	Sales Call	3	0
0305	Questioning	4	0
0306	Competitive Activities	5	0
0307	Negotiating	3	0
0308	Territory Administration	4	0
0309	Trade Shows	3	0

Technical

Code	Competency Short Text	Title Standard	Priority
0401	Product Knowledge	3	0
0402	Services Knowledge	3	0
0403	Contracting and Consulting	2	0
0404	Project Management	2	0

Administration

Code	Competency Short Text	Title Standard	Priority
0503	Expense Reporting	2	0
0504	Order Entry	2	0
0505	Financial Justification	2	0

Personal Computing

Code	Competency Short Text	Title Standard	Priority
0601	Operating System	3	0
0602	Word Processing	3	0
0603	Spreadsheets	2	0
0604	Presentation Software	3	0
0605	Database Management Software	1	0
0606	E-Mail	3	0
0607	LAN Access	3	0
0608	Mainframe Access	2	0

(continues)

Figure 8-25. *(continued)*

Current Title

Category Description

Code	Competency Short Text	Title Standard	Priority
Personal Development			
0701	Assertiveness	2	0
0702	Nonverbal Communications	4	0
0703	Conflict Management	3	0
0704	Creativity	2	0
0705	Change Management	2	0
0708	Humor	3	0
0709	Listening	4	0
0710	Memory	2	0
0711	Presentation Skills	3	0
0713	Personal Styles Analysis	5	0
0714	Time Management	4	0
0715	Writing	4	0
Quality			
0801	TQM	2	0
0802	ISO 9000	2	0
0803	Customer Service	3	0
0806	Process Improvement	2	0

Figure 8-26. Competency/title standard matrix.

Category		
Competency		
Code	*Text*	*Sales Representative*

Code	Text	Sales Representative
General Information		
0101	Organizational Information	3
0102	Basic Industry Knowledge	4
0103	Policies and Procedures	2
0104	Legal Review and Approval	2
0105	Diversity	3
0106	Sexual Harassment	3
Management/Leadership		
0201	Planning	2
0202	Leadership	2
0203	Ethics	3
0209	Counseling	2
0210	Open Book Management	3
Sales/Marketing		
0301	Account Planning	3
0302	Complex Account Selling	3
0303	Product Strategies	5
0304	Sales Call	3
0305	Questioning	4
0306	Competitive Activities	5
0307	Negotiating	3
0308	Territory Administration	4
0309	Trade Shows	3
Technical		
0401	Product Knowledge	3
0402	Services Knowledge	3
0403	Contracting and Consulting	2
0404	Project Management	2
Administration		
0503	Expense Reporting	2
0504	Order Entry	2
0505	Financial Justification	2
Personal Computing		
0601	Operating System	3
0602	Word Processing	3
0603	Spreadsheets	2
0604	Presentation Software	3
0605	Database Management	1
0606	E-Mail	3
0607	LAN Access	3
0608	Mainframe Access	2

(continues)

Figure 8-26. *(continued)*

Category

  Competency

    Code *Text*   *Sales Representative*

Personal Development

Code	Text	Sales Representative
0701	Assertiveness	2
0702	Nonverbal Communications	4
0703	Conflict Management	3
0704	Creativity	2
0705	Change Management	2
0708	Humor	3
0709	Listening	4
0710	Memory	2
0711	Presentation Skills	3
0713	Personal Styles Analysis	5
0714	Time Management	4
0715	Writing	4

Quality

Code	Text	Sales Representative
0801	TQM	2
0802	ISO 9000	2
0803	Customer Service	3
0806	Process Improvement	2

Figure 8-27. Competency/title report.

Category

Code   Competency Short Text

Title Description   *Desired Competency Level*   *Priority*

General Information

0101 Organizational Information		
Administrator	3	0
Manager	4	0
Sales Representative	3	0
Team Leader	4	0
Technical Specialist	3	0
0102 Basic Industry Knowledge		
Manager	3	0
Sales Representative	4	0
Team Leader	5	0
Technical Specialist	2	0
0103 Policies and Procedures		
Administrator	5	0
Manager	3	0
Sales Representative	2	0
Team Leader	3	0
Technical Specialist	2	0
0104 Legal Review and Approval		
Administrator	4	0
Manager	5	0
Sales Representative	2	0
Team Leader	3	0
Technical Specialist	2	0
0105 Diversity		
Administrator	3	0
Manager	5	0
Sales Representative	3	0
Team Leader	4	0
Technical Specialist	3	0
0106 Sexual Harassment		
Administrator	3	0
Manager	5	0
Sales Representative	3	0
Team Leader	4	0
Technical Specialist	3	0

Management/Leadership

0201 Planning		
Administrator	2	0
Manager	2	0
Sales Representative	2	0
Team Leader	2	0
Technical Specialist	2	0

(continues)

Figure 8-27. *(continued)*

Category

Code   Competency Short text

Title Description	*Desired Competency Level*	*Priority*
0202 Leadership		
Manager	4	0
Sales Representative	2	0
Team Leader	3	0
0203 Ethics		
Administrator	2	0
Manager	4	0
Sales Representative	3	0
Team Leader	3	0
Technical Specialist	3	0
0204 Interviewing		
Manager	3	0
Team Leader	2	0
0205 Performance Planning		
Manager	5	0
Team Leader	3	0
0206 Performance Reviews		
Manager	5	0
Team Leader	3	0
0207 Salary Administration		
Manager	4	0
0208 Coaching		
Manager	3	0
Team Leader	4	0
0209 Counseling		
Manager	3	0
Sales Representative	2	0
Team Leader	3	0
0210 Open Book Management		
Administrator	2	0
Manager	3	0
Sales Representative	3	0
Team Leader	3	0
Technical Specialist	2	0

Sales/Marketing

Title Description	*Desired Competency Level*	*Priority*
0301 Account Planning		
Sales Representative	3	0
Team Leader	4	0
0302 Complex Account Selling		
Sales Representative	3	0
Team Leader	4	0
0303 Product Strategies		
Manager	2	0

Figure 8-28. Competency/resource report.

Category

Code   **Competency Short text**

    Code   *Resource Description*

Administration

0501 **Personnel Policies**
    INTER   Interviewing—seminar

0502 **Budgeting**
    OBM   Open Book Management—seminar

0505 **Financial Justification**
    CS   Consultive Selling—seminar
    DMR   Decision Making with Risk—seminar
    OBM   Open Book Management—seminar
    PI   Process Improvement—seminar

0506 **Statistics**
    DMR   Decision Making with Risk—seminar
    OBM   Open Book Management—seminar
    PI   Process Improvement—seminar

General Information

0102 **Basic Industry Knowledge**
    OBM   Open Book Management—seminar

0103 **Policies and Procedures**
    EW   Effective Writing Skills—seminar
    PI   Process Improvement—seminar
    RE   Reengineering—seminar

0104 **Legal Review and Approval**
    LEAD   Leadership Thru Excellence—seminar

0105 **Diversity**
    LISTEN   Effective Listening—seminar
    INTER   Interviewing—seminar
    LEAD   Leadership Thru Excellence—seminar
    QUEST   Questioning Skills—seminar
    SH   Stop It Now—audiotape
    Sex Harass   Stop It Now—book
    Sem   Stop It Now—seminar

0106 **Sexual Harassment**
    LISTEN   Effective Listening—seminar
    INTER   Interviewing—seminar
    LEAD   Leadership Thru Excellence—seminar
    QUEST   Questioning Skills—seminar
    SH   Stop It Now—audiotape
    Sex Harass   Stop It Now—book
    Sem   Stop It Now—seminar

(continues)

Figure 8-28. *(continued)*

Category

Code   Competency Short text

      Code   *Resource Description*

Management/Leadership

0201   Planning

Code	Resource Description
EM	Effective Meetings—seminar
EW	Effective Writing Skills—seminar
PERPLAN	Performance Planning—seminar
RE	Reengineering—seminar
SP	Strategic Planning—seminar

0202   Leadership

Code	Resource Description
DEC	Decision Making—seminar
Dev. Mgt.	Development Management—audio tape
EFFECT	Effectance Motivation—seminar
LISTEN	Effective Listening—seminar
EM	Effective Meetings—seminar
LEAD	Leadership Thru Excellence—seminar
OBM	Open Book Management—seminar
QUEST	Questioning Skills—seminar
TIPC	TIPC Personal Styles Analysis—seminar

0203   Ethics

Code	Resource Description
LEAD	Leadership Thru Excellence—seminar
SH	Stop It Now—audiotape
Sex Harass	Stop It Now—book
Sem	Stop It Now—seminar

0204   Interviewing

Code	Resource Description
LISTEN	Effective Listening—seminar
INTER	Interviewing—seminar
QUEST	Questioning Skills—seminar
TIPC	TIPC Personal Styles Analysis—seminar

0205   Performance Planning

Code	Resource Description
Dev. Mgt.	Development Management—audio tape
PERPLAN	Performance Planning—seminar
RE	Reengineering—seminar
S LEAD	Situational Leadership—seminar
SP	Strategic Planning—seminar

0206   Performance Reviews

Code	Resource Description
CM	Conflict Management—audiotape
Con. Mgt.	Conflict Management—videotape
Dev. Mgt.	Development Management—audio tape
LISTEN	Effective Listening—seminar
EW	Effective Writing Skills—seminar
INTER	Interviewing—seminar
PERREV	Performance Reviews—seminar
QUEST	Questioning Skills—seminar
S LEAD	Situational Leadership—seminar
TIPC	TIPC Personal Styles Analysis—seminar

0208   Coaching

Code	Resource Description
COACH	Coaching and Counseling—coaching
CC	Coaching and Counseling—seminar
S LEAD	Situational Leadership—seminar

Figure 8-29. Resource/competency report.

Seminar Description
Resource Description
Category Description
Comp. #   Competency Text (short)

Assertiveness Training—seminar
Seminar
Personal Development
0701   Assertiveness
0703   Conflict Management

Change Management—seminar
Seminar
Personal Development
0705   Change Management

Quality
0806   Process Improvement
0807   Reengineering

Coaching and Counseling—seminar
Seminar
Management/Leadership
0208   Coaching
0209   Counseling

Consultive Selling—seminar
Seminar
Administration
0505   Financial Justification

Personal Development
0711   Presentation Skills

Sales/Marketing
0301   Account Planning
0302   Complex Account Selling
0303   Product Strategies
0304   Sales Call
0305   Questioning
0309   Trade Shows

Creativity Development—seminar
Seminar
Personal Development
0704   Creativity

Customer Service—seminar
Seminar
Management/Leadership
0210   Open Book Management

(continues)

Figure 8-29. *(continued)*

Seminar Description

Resource Description

Category Description

Comp. #   Competency Text (short)

Personal Development
0703   Conflict Management

Quality
0803   Customer Service
0808   Core Competencies/Outsourcing

Sales/Marketing
0308   Territory Administration

Decision Making—seminar

Seminar

Management/Leadership
0202   Leadership

Personal Development
0706   Decision Making
0707   Effective Meetings

Quality
0804   Facilitation
0806   Process Improvement

Technical
0403   Contracting and Consulting
0404   Project Management

Decision Making with Risk—seminar

Seminar

Administration
0505   Financial Justification
0506   Statistics

Personal Development
0706   Decision Making

Sales/Marketing
0302   Complex Account Selling
0306   Competitive Activities
0307   Negotiating

Effectance Motivation—seminar

Seminar

Management/Leadership
0202   Leadership
0209   Counseling

Seminar Description
Resource Description
Category Description
Comp. #   Competency Text (short)

Effective Listening—seminar
Seminar
General Information
- 0105   Diversity
- 0106   Sexual Harassment

Management/Leadership
- 0202   Leadership
- 0204   Interviewing
- 0206   Performance Reviews
- 0209   Counseling

Personal Development
- 0703   Conflict Management
- 0707   Effective Meetings
- 0709   Listening
- 0710   Memory
- 0711   Presentation Skills

Quality
- 0804   Facilitation

Sales/Marketing
- 0304   Sales Call
- 0305   Questioning
- 0307   Negotiating

Technical
- 0405   Training

Effective Meetings—seminar
Seminar
Management/Leadership
- 0201   Planning
- 0202   Leadership

Personal Development
- 0707   Effective Meetings
- 0711   Presentation Skills

Quality
- 0804   Facilitation
- 0805   Team Building

Technical
- 0405   Training

Effective Presentations—seminar
Seminar
Personal Development
- 0702   Nonverbal Communications
- 0708   Humor
- 0711   Presentation Skills

Figure 8-29. *(continued)*

Seminar Description

Resource Description

Category Description

Comp. #   Competency Text (short)

Sales/Marketing
   0302   Complex Account Selling
   0304   Sales Call
   0309   Trade Shows

Technical
   0405   Training

Effective Writing Skills—seminar

Seminar

General Information
   0103   Policies and Procedures

Figure 8-30. Resource/seminar report.

Resource Description

Seminar Title

Seminar
 Assertive Training—seminar
 Change Management—seminar
 Coaching and Counseling—seminar
 Consultive Selling—seminar
 Creativity Development—seminar
 Customer Service—seminar
 Decision Making—seminar
 Decision Making with Risk—seminar
 Effectance Motivation—seminar
 Effective Listening—seminar
 Effective Meetings—seminar
 Effective Presentations—seminar
 Effective Writing Skills—seminar
 Facilitation Skills—seminar
 Humor in the Workplace—seminar
 ISO 9000—seminar
 Interviewing—seminar
 Leadership Thru Excellence—seminar
 Multi-form Negotiating—seminar
 Multi-form Sales Skills—seminar
 Multi-form Sales Strategies—seminar
 Open Book Management—seminar
 Performance Planning—seminar
 Performance Reviews—seminar
 Process Improvement—seminar
 Questioning Skills—seminar
 Reengineering—seminar
 Situational Leadership—seminar
 Stop It Now—seminar
 Strategic Planning—seminar
 Strategic Selling to Key Accounts—sem.
 Substance Abuse—seminar
 TIPC Personal Styles Analysis—seminar
 Team Building—seminar
 Time Management—seminar
 Total Quality Management—seminar
 Train the Trainer—seminar

Figure 8-31. Person/response report.

Person Name

Category Description

Comp. #	Competency	Current Title	Title Date	Response	Response Date
O'Connor, Mike		**Sales Representative**	**05/21/20XX**		**08/05/20XX**

General Information
0101	Organizational Information			3	
0102	Basic Industry Knowledge			3	
0103	Policies and Procedures			2	
0104	Legal Review and Approval			2	
0105	Diversity			2	
0106	Sexual Harassment			2	

Management/Leadership
0201	Planning			2	
0202	Leadership			2	
0203	Ethics			2	
0204	Interviewing			2	
0205	Performance Planning			2	
0206	Performance Reviews			2	
0207	Salary Administration			2	
0208	Coaching			4	
0209	Counseling			2	
0210	Open Book Management			3	

Sales/Marketing
0301	Account Planning			4	
0302	Complex Account Selling			4	
0303	Product Strategies			4	
0304	Sales Call			4	
0305	Questioning			4	
0306	Competitive Activities			4	
0307	Negotiating			2	
0308	Territory Administration			4	
0309	Trade Shows			2	

Technical
0401	Product Knowledge			4	
0402	Services Knowledge			4	
0403	Contracting and Consulting			4	
0404	Project Management			4	
0405	Training			1	

Administration
0501	Personnel Policies			1	
0502	Budgeting			1	
0503	Expense Reporting			3	
0504	Order Entry			2	
0505	Financial Justification			1	
0506	Statistics			1	

Person Name

Category Description

Comp. #	Competency	Current Title	Title Date	Response	Response Date
O'Connor, Mike		**Sales Representative**	**05/21/20XX**		**08/05/20XX**
Personal Computing					
0601	Operating System			4	
0602	Word Processing			4	
0603	Spreadsheets			4	
0604	Presentation Software			3	
0605	Database Management Software			2	
0606	E-Mail			4	
0607	LAN Access			3	
0608	Mainframe Access			2	
0609	Internet Access			4	
Personal Development					
0701	Assertiveness			3	
0702	Nonverbal Communications			3	
0703	Conflict Management			3	
0704	Creativity			3	
0705	Change Management			2	
0706	Decision Making			2	
0707	Effective Meetings			2	
0708	Humor			3	
0709	Listening			4	
0710	Memory			4	
0711	Presentation Skills			4	
0712	Substance Abuse			2	
0713	Personal Styles Analysis			2	
0714	Time Management			3	
0715	Writing			3	
Quality					
0801	TQM			3	
0802	ISO 9000			1	
0803	Customer Service			4	
0804	Facilitation			2	
0805	Team Building			2	
0806	Process Improvement			3	
0807	Reengineering			2	
0808	Core Competencies/Outsourcing			1	

Figure 8-32. Proofing report.

Name	Current Title	Title Date	Leader	Leader Rating
McDonnell, John	Manager	05/21/20XX		0
Category	**Rating**			
General Information	0			
McGill, Steve	Sales Representative	05/21/20XX		0
Category	**Rating**			
General Information	0			
Melton, Dan	Team Leader	05/21/20XX		0
Category	**Rating**			
General Information	0			
Meyerhoff, Jim	Sales Representative	05/21/20XX		0
Category	**Rating**			
General Information	0			
O'Connor, Mike	Sales Representative	05/21/20XX	Wilson	3
Category	**Rating**			
General Information	2			
Technical	4			
Personal Computing	3			
Sales/Marketing	3			
Management/Leadership	2			
Quality	1			
Personal Development	2			
Administration	3			
Phillips, Bryce	Technical Specialist	05/21/20XX		0
Category	**Rating**			
General Information	0			
Reed, Sylvia	Administrator	05/21/20XX		0
Category	**Rating**			
General Information	0			
Sakura, Lin	Sales Representative	05/21/20XX		0
Category	**Rating**			
General Information	0			
Sanchez, Lou	Sales Representative	05/21/20XX		0
Category	**Rating**			
General Information	0			
Stephenson, Bill	Sales Representative	05/21/20XX		0
Category	**Rating**			
General Information	0			
Stratton, Lindsay	Sales Representative	05/21/20XX		0
Category	**Rating**			
General Information	0			

Figure 8-33. Leader response.

Leader: **Wilson**
Person: **O'Connor, Mike**
Title: **Sales Representative**

This form is to be used in conjunction with the Field Assessment 95 Survey. Its sole purpose is to provide a general cross check indicator for the validity and accuracy of the self-assessments. It also provides a tool for managers and subordinates to discuss assessment areas and development tools.

This form is not to be used in any performance evaluation process. It is to be used only for providing employee feedback on current knowledge, skills, and possible areas for development.

Each section below corresponds to a topic area on the Assessment 95 survey. Individual assessment survey topics are listed. Generally assess the subordinate's knowledge and skills based on the following scale:

5—Consistently exceeds minimum requirements for the position.
4—Exceeds minimum requirements in some areas.
3—Meets minimum requirements for the position.
2—Does not meet minimum requirements in some areas.
1—Does not meet minimum requirements.

Category Rating
for Title

General Information
   Organization info.; industry knowledge; policies & procedures; legal review & approval; diversity; sexual harassment   **2**

Management/Leadership
   planning; leadership; ethics; interviewing; performance planning; performance review; salary admin.; coaching; counseling; open book mgmt.   **2**

Sales/Marketing
   account planning; complex account selling; product strategies; sales call; questioning; competitive activities; negotiating; territory administration; trade shows   **3**

Technical
   product knowledge; services knowledge; contracting & consulting; project mgmt.; training   **4**

Administration
   personnel policies; budgeting; expense reporting; order entry; financial justification; statistics   **3**

Personal Computing
   operating system; word processing; spreadsheets; presentation software; database mgmt. software; e-mail; LAN access; mainframe access; Internet access   **3**

Personal Development
   assertiveness; nonverbal communications; conflict mgmt.; creativity; change mgmt.; decision making; effective meetings; humor; listening; memory; presentation skills; substance abuse; personal styles analysis; time mgmt.; writing skills   **2**

Quality
   TQM; ISO 9000; customer service, facilitation; team building; process improvement; reengineering; core competencies/outsourcing   **1**

Overall Rating   **3**

Figure 8-34. Response/standard comparison.
CooperComm Working Model

O'Connor, Mike **Sales Representative** *Competency Text*	Job Standard ▮	At Standard ▮	Below Standard ▮	Above Standard ▯	Variance	Comp. #
General Information						
Organizational Information					0	0101
Basic Industry Knowledge					(1)	0102
Policies and Procedures					0	0103
Legal Review and Approval					0	0104
Diversity					(1)	0105
Sexual Harassment					(1)	0106
Management/Leadership						
Planning					0	0201
Leadership					0	0202
Ethics					(1)	0203
Counseling					0	0209
Open Book Management					0	0210
Sales/Marketing						
Account Planning					1	0301
Complex Account Selling					1	0302
Product Strategies					(1)	0303
Sales Call					1	0304
Questioning					0	0305
Competitive Activities					(1)	0306
Negotiating					(1)	0307

O'Connor, Mike
Sales Representative
Competency Text

Response: Job Standard | At Standard | Below Standard | Above Standard

Competency Text	Values	Variance	Comp. #
Territory Administration	4 / 4	0	0308
Trade Shows	2 / 3	(1)	0309
Technical			
Product Knowledge	4 / 3	1	0401
Services Knowledge	4 / 3	1	0402
Contracting and Consulting	4 / 2	2	0403
Project Management	4 / 2	2	0404
Administration			
Expense Reporting	3 / 2	1	0503
Order Entry	2 / 2	0	0504
Financial Justification	1 / 2	(1)	0505
Personal Computing			
Operating System	4 / 3	1	0601
Word Processing	4 / 3	1	0602
Spreadsheets	4 / 2	2	0603
Presentation Software	3 / 3	0	0604
Database Management Software	2 / 1	1	0605
E-Mail	4 / 3	1	0606
LAN Access	3 / 3	0	0607
Mainframe Access	2 / 2	0	0608

(continues)

Figure 8-34. *(continued)*

O'Connor, Mike **Sales Representative** Competency Text	Job Standard ▉	Response At Standard ▉	Below Standard ▉	Above Standard ▢	Variance	Comp. #

Personal Development

Assertiveness	3 / 2	1	0701

Nonverbal Communications	3 / 4	(1)	0702

Conflict Management	3 / 3	0	0703

Creativity	3 / 2	1	0704

Change Management	2 / 2	0	0705

Humor	3 / 3	0	0708

Listening	4 / 4	0	0709

Memory	4 / 2	2	0710

Presentation Skills	4 / 3	1	0711

Personal Styles Analysis	2 / 5	(3)	0713

Time Management	3 / 4	(1)	0714

Writing	3 / 4	(1)	0715

Quality

TQM	3 / 2	1	0801

ISO 9000	1 / 2	(1)	0802

Customer Service	4 / 3	1	0803

Process Improvement	3 / 2	1	0806

Figure 8-35. Leader comparison.

Leader **Wilson**
Person **O'Connor, Mike**

Subordinate's current knowledge & skills were assessed by the supervisor using the following scale:

5—Consistently exceeds minimum requirements for the position.
4—Exceeds minimum requirements in some areas.
3—Meets minimum requirements for the position.
2—Does not meet minimum requirements in some areas.
1—Does not meet minimum requirements.

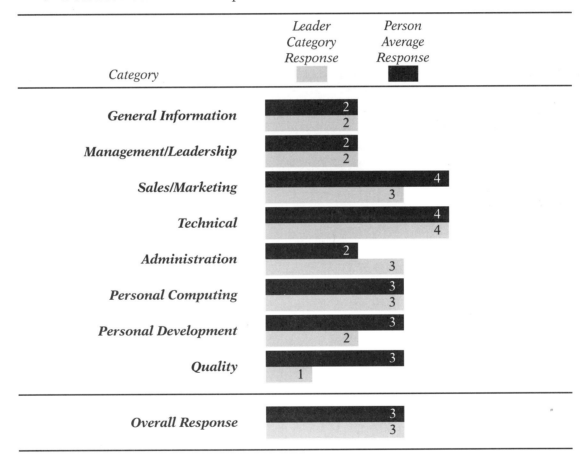

Figure 8-36. Priority development needs.

O'Connor, Mike Sales Representative Competency Text	Response				Gap	Comp. #
	Job Standard	At Standard	Below Standard	Above Standard		
Personal Styles Analysis		2 / 5			(3)	0713
Product Strategies		4 / 5			(1)	0303
Competitive Activities		4 / 5			(1)	0306
Basic Industry Knowledge		3 / 4			(1)	0102
Nonverbal Communications		3 / 4			(1)	0702
Time Management		3 / 4			(1)	0714
Writing		3 / 4			(1)	0715
Diversity		2 / 3			(1)	0105
Sexual Harassment		2 / 3			(1)	0106
Ethics		2 / 3			(1)	0203
Negotiating		2 / 3			(1)	0307
Trade Shows		2 / 3			(1)	0309
Financial Justification		1 / 2			(1)	0505
ISO 9000		1 / 2			(1)	0802

Figure 8-37. Priority development needs (with resources).

O'Connor, Mike **Sales Representative** *Competency Text*	Job Standard ▮	*Response* At Standard ▮	Below Standard ▮	Above Standard ▯	*Gap*	*Comp. #*
Personal Styles Analysis		2 / 5			**(3)**	0713

> ***Resources:*** Interviewing—seminar
> Multi-form Negotiating—seminar
> Team Building—seminar
> TIPC Personal Styles Analysis—seminar

Product Strategies		4 / 5			**(1)**	0303

> ***Resources:*** Consultive Selling—seminar
> Multi-form Sales Strategies—seminar
> Reengineering—seminar

Competitive Activities		4 / 5			**(1)**	0306

> ***Resources:*** Decision Making with Risk—seminar
> Multi-form Sales Skills—seminar

Basic Industry Knowledge		3 / 4			**(1)**	0102

> ***Resources:*** Open Book Management—seminar

Nonverbal Communications		3 / 4			**(1)**	0702

> ***Resources:*** Stop It Now—book
> Bodybusiness—audiotape
> Bodybusiness—book
> Bodybusiness—videotape
> Effective Presentations—Seminar

Time Management		3 / 4			**(1)**	0714

> ***Resources:*** Always Bear Left—book

Writing		3 / 4			**(1)**	0715

> ***Resources:*** Effective Writing Skills—seminar

(continues)

Figure 8-37. *(continued)*

O'Connor, Mike **Sales Representative** *Competency Text*	*Job* *Standard* ■	*At* *Standard* ■	— Response — *Below* *Standard* ■	*Above* *Standard* ■	*Gap*	*Comp. #*
Diversity		2 3			**(1)**	0105

> *Resources:* Effective Listening—seminar
> Interviewing—seminar
> Leadership Thru Excellence—seminar
> Questioning Skills—seminar
> Stop It Now—audiotape
> Stop It Now—book
> Stop It Now—seminar

Sexual Harassment		2 3			**(1)**	0106

> *Resources:* Stop It Now—audiotape
> Stop It Now—book
> Effective Listening—seminar
> Interviewing—seminar
> Leadership Thru Excellence—seminar
> Questioning Skills—seminar
> Stop It Now—seminar

Ethics		2 3			**(1)**	0203

> *Resources:* Leadership Thru Excellence—seminar
> Stop It Now—audiotape
> Stop It Now—book
> Stop It Now—seminar

Negotiating		2 3			**(1)**	0307

> *Resources:* Decision Making with Risk—seminar
> Effective Listening—seminar
> Multi-form Negotiating—seminar
> Questioning Skills—seminar
> TIPC Personal Styles Analysis—seminar

O'Connor, Mike **Sales Representative** *Competency Text*	Job Standard ■	At Standard ■	— Response — Below Standard ■	Above Standard ■	Gap	Comp. #
Trade Shows		2 / 3			**(1)**	0309

Resources: Consultive Selling—seminar
Effective Presentations—Seminar
Memory Fixing—audiotape
Memory Fixing—videotape
Multi-form Sales Skills—seminar
Questioning Skills—seminar
TIPC Personal Styles Analysis—seminar

Financial Justification	1 / 2				**(1)**	0505

Resources: Consultive Selling—seminar
Decision Making with Risk—seminar
Open Book Management—seminar
Process Improvement—seminar

ISO 9000	1 / 2				**(1)**	0802

Resources: ISO 9000—seminar

Figure 8-38. Individual development plan.

Name _____   Title _____   Supervisor _____

Business issue to be addressed	(Code) Competency Standard/Gap	Learning Resource	Priority	Course Date	Date Completed	Business result

Figure 8-39. Response/standard comparison (for new position).

O'Connor, Mike Manager (Future) Competency Text	Response				Gap	Comp. #
	Job Standard	At Standard	Below Standard	Above Standard		

ISO 9000

1 / 5 — **(4)** — 0802

Resources: ISO 9000—seminar

Legal Review and Approval

2 / 5 — **(3)** — 0104

Resources: Leadership Thru Excellence—seminar

Diversity

2 / 5 — **(3)** — 0105

Resources: Effective Listening—seminar
Interviewing—seminar
Leadership Thru Excellence—seminar
Questioning Skills—seminar
Stop It Now—audiotape
Stop It Now—book
Stop It Now—seminar

Sexual Harassment

2 / 5 — **(3)** — 0106

Resources: Stop It Now—audiotape
Stop It Now—book
Effective Listening—seminar
Interviewing—seminar
Leadership Thru Excellence—seminar
Questioning Skills—seminar
Stop It Now—seminar

Performance Planning

2 / 5 — **(3)** — 0205

Resources: Development Management—audiotape
Performance Planning—seminar
Reengineering—seminar
Situational Leadership—seminar
Strategic Planning—seminar

(continues)

Figure 8-39. *(continued)*

O'Connor, Mike		Job Standard	At Standard	Response ——— Below Standard	Above Standard		
Manager (Future)							
Competency Text						Gap	Comp. #

Performance Reviews   [2] ... [5]   **(3)**   0206

> *Resources:* Conflict Management—audiotape
> Conflict Management—videotape
> Development Management—audio tape
> Effective Listening—seminar
> Effective Writing Skills—seminar
> Interviewing—seminar
> Performance Reviews—seminar
> Questioning Skills—seminar
> Situational Leadership—seminar

Personal Styles Analysis   [2] ... [5]   **(3)**   0713

> *Resources:* Interviewing—seminar
> Multi-form Negotiating—seminar
> Team Building—seminar
> TIPC Personal Styles Analysis—seminar

Personnel Policies   [1] ... [4]   **(3)**   0501

> *Resources:* Interviewing—seminar

Leadership   [2] ... [4]   **(2)**   0202

> *Resources:* Decision Making—seminar
> Development Management—audio tape
> Effectance Motivation—seminar
> Effective Listening—seminar
> Effective Meetings—seminar
> Leadership Thru Excellence—seminar
> Open Book Management—seminar
> Questioning Skills—seminar

Ethics   [2] ... [4]   **(2)**   0203

> *Resources:* Leadership Thru Excellence—seminar
> Stop It Now—audiotape
> Stop It Now—book
> Stop It Now—seminar

O'Connor, Mike **Manager (Future)** *Competency Text*	Job Standard	At Standard	Response Below Standard	Above Standard	Gap	Comp. #

Salary Administration 2 / 4 **(2)** 0207

Change Management 2 / 4 **(2)** 0705

Resources: Change Management—seminar
Conflict Management—audiotape
Conflict Management—videotape
Process Improvement—seminar

Effective Meetings 2 / 4 **(2)** 0707

Resources: Conflict Management—audiotape
Decision Making—seminar
Effective Listening—seminar
Effective Meetings—seminar
Facilitation Skills—seminar
Team Building—seminar
TIPC Personal Styles Analysis—seminar
Time Management—seminar

Facilitation 2 / 4 **(2)** 0804

Resources: Conflict Management—audiotape
Conflict Management—videotape
Decision Making—seminar
Effective Listening—seminar
Effective Meetings—seminar
Facilitation Skills—seminar
Team Building—seminar
TIPC Personal Styles Analysis—seminar
Time Management—seminar

Team Building 2 / 4 **(2)** 0805

Resources: Conflict Management—audiotape
Effective Meetings—seminar
Facilitation Skills—seminar
Team Building—seminar
TIPC Personal Styles Analysis—seminar

(continues)

Figure 8-39. *(continued)*

O'Connor, Mike **Manager (Future)** *Competency Text*	*Job Standard* ▮	Response *At Standard* ▮	*Below Standard* ▮	*Above Standard* ▯	*Gap*	*Comp. #*
Organizational Information			3 4		**(1)**	0101
Budgeting	1 3				**(2)**	0502

Resources: Open Book Management—seminar

| Statistics | 1
3 | | | | **(2)** | 0506 |

Resources: Decision Making with Risk—seminar
Open Book Management—seminar
Process Improvement—seminar

| Policies and Procedures | 2
3 | | | | **(1)** | 0103 |

Resources: Effective Writing Skills—seminar
Process Improvement—seminar
Reengineering—seminar

| Interviewing | 2
3 | | | | **(1)** | 0204 |

Resources: Effective Listening—seminar
Interviewing—seminar
Questioning Skills—seminar
TIPC Personal Styles Analysis—seminar

| Counseling | 2
3 | | | | **(1)** | 0209 |

Resources: Coaching and Counseling—coaching
Coaching and Counseling—seminar
Conflict Management—audiotape
Conflict Management—videotape
Effectance Motivation—seminar
Effective Listening—seminar
Interviewing—seminar
Questioning Skills—seminar
Situational Leadership—seminar

O'Connor, Mike Manager (Future) Competency Text	Job Standard ■	Response At Standard ■	Below Standard ▨	Above Standard ▨	Gap	Comp. #
Negotiating		**2**			**(1)**	0307
		3				

Resources: Decision Making with Risk—seminar
Effective Listening—seminar
Multi-form Negotiating—seminar
Questioning Skills—seminar
TIPC Personal Styles Analysis—seminar

Substance Abuse		**2**			**(1)**	0712
		3				
Reengineering		**2**			**(1)**	0807
		3				

Resources: Change Management—seminar
ISO 9000—seminar
Open Book Management—seminar
Process Improvement—seminar
Reengineering—seminar
Total Quality Management—seminar

Training	**1**				**(1)**	0405
	2					

Resources: Effective Listening—seminar
Effective Meetings—seminar
Effective Presentations—Seminar
Facilitation Skills—seminar
Humor in the workplace—seminar
Memory Fixing—audiotape
Questioning Skills—seminar
Situational Leadership—seminar
TIPC Personal Styles Analysis—seminar

Core Competencies/ Outsourcing	**1**				**(1)**	0808
	2					

Resources: Customer Service—seminar
Process Improvement—seminar
Reengineering—seminar
Total Quality Management—seminar

Figure 8-40. Response distribution by competency (for sales representative).

Category Competency Code Competency Text	No. of Respondents	Ave. Response	Response Distribution 1.	2.	3.	4.	5.
General Information							
101 Organizational Information	9	4.22	0	0	2	3	4
102 Basic Industry Knowledge	9	4.33	0	0	2	2	5
103 Policies and Procedures	9	2.56	0	5	3	1	0
104 Legal Review and Approval	9	2.56	0	5	3	1	0
105 Diversity	9	2.33	0	6	3	0	0
106 Sexual Harassment	9	1.89	1	8	0	0	0
Totals for: General Information		2.98	1	24	13	7	9
Management/Leadership							
201 Planning	9	2.44	0	6	2	1	0
202 Leadership	9	2.44	0	6	2	1	0
203 Ethics	9	2.44	0	7	1	0	1
204 Interviewing	9	1.67	4	4	1	0	0
205 Performance Planning	9	1.56	4	5	0	0	0
206 Performance Reviews	9	1.44	5	4	0	0	0
207 Salary Administration	9	1.44	5	4	0	0	0
208 Coaching	9	2.00	3	4	1	1	0
209 Counseling	9	2.22	1	5	3	0	0
210 Open Book Management	9	2.78	0	2	7	0	0
Totals for: Management/Leadership		2.04	22	47	17	3	1
Sales/Marketing							
301 Account Planning	9	3.78	0	0	2	7	0
302 Complex Account Selling	9	3.78	0	0	2	7	0
303 Product Strategies	9	3.78	0	0	3	5	1
304 Sales Call	9	3.56	0	0	5	3	1
305 Questioning	9	3.78	0	0	3	5	1
306 Competitive Activities	9	3.56	0	0	5	3	1
307 Negotiating	9	3.00	0	4	1	4	0
308 Territory Administration	9	3.56	0	0	5	3	1
309 Trade Shows	9	2.89	0	4	2	3	0
Totals for: Sales/Marketing		3.51	0	8	28	40	5
Technical							
401 Product Knowledge	9	4.00	0	0	1	7	1
402 Services Knowledge	9	3.78	0	0	3	5	1
403 Contracting and Consulting	9	2.67	0	5	2	2	0
404 Project Management	9	3.00	0	2	5	2	0
405 Training	9	1.22	7	2	0	0	0
Totals for: Technical		2.93	7	9	11	16	2
Administration							
501 Personnel Policies	9	1.22	7	2	0	0	0
502 Budgeting	9	1.22	7	2	0	0	0
503 Expense Reporting	9	2.33	0	6	3	0	0

Category Competency		No. of Respondents	Ave. Response	Response Distribution				
Code	Competency Text			1.	2.	3.	4.	5.
504	Order Entry	9	1.89	2	6	1	0	0
505	Financial Justification	9	2.11	1	6	2	0	0
506	Statistics	9	1.33	6	3	0	0	0
	Totals for: Administration		1.68	23	25	6	0	0
Personal Computing								
601	Operating System	9	3.22	0	2	3	4	0
602	Word Processing	9	3.22	0	2	3	4	0
603	Spreadsheets	9	3.11	0	1	6	2	0
604	Presentation Software	9	3.22	0	0	8	0	1
605	Database Management Software	9	2.11	1	6	2	0	0
606	E-Mail	9	3.00	0	1	7	1	0
607	LAN Access	9	2.56	0	4	5	0	0
608	Mainframe Access	9	2.33	0	6	3	0	0
609	Internet Access	9	3.22	0	2	3	4	0
	Totals for: Personal Computing		2.88	1	24	40	15	1
Personal Development								
701	Assertiveness	9	3.56	0	1	3	4	1
702	Nonverbal Communications	9	3.00	0	3	3	3	0
703	Conflict Management	9	2.78	0	5	1	3	0
704	Creativity	9	2.78	0	3	5	1	0
705	Change Management	9	2.22	0	7	2	0	0
706	Decision Making	9	2.22	3	2	3	1	0
707	Effective Meetings	9	2.00	3	3	3	0	0
708	Humor	9	3.44	0	0	5	4	0
709	Listening	9	3.33	0	1	4	4	0
710	Memory	9	3.22	0	1	5	3	0
711	Presentation Skills	9	3.33	1	0	4	3	1
712	Substance Abuse	9	1.78	4	3	2	0	0
713	Personal Styles Analysis	9	2.67	0	3	6	0	0
714	Time Management	9	3.33	0	0	6	3	0
715	Writing	9	3.22	0	0	7	2	0
	Totals for: Personal Development		2.85	11	32	59	31	2
Quality								
801	TQM	9	2.89	0	2	6	1	0
802	ISO 9000	9	2.22	2	4	2	1	0
803	Customer Service	9	3.33	1	0	3	5	0
804	Facilitation	9	1.56	5	3	1	0	0
805	Team Building	9	1.56	4	5	0	0	0
806	Process Improvement	9	2.22	1	5	3	0	0
807	Reengineering	8	1.50	4	4	0	0	0
808	Core Competencies/Outsourcing	8	1.13	7	1	0	0	0
	Totals for: Quality		2.05	24	24	15	7	0
	Totals for: Sales Representative	610	2.64	89	1	189	119	20

Figure 8-41. Resource summary (by resource).

Selected Work Groups:	Selected Titles:	Selected Resources:
Region—01, Region—02	Manager, Sales Representative	Always Bear Left—book, Assertive Training—seminar, Bodybusiness—audiotape, Bodybusiness—book, Bodybusiness—videotape, Change Management—seminar, Coaching and Counseling—coaching, Coaching and Counseling—seminar, Conflict Management—audiotape, Conflict Management—videotape, Consultive Selling—seminar, . . . and MORE.

Resource Type

Resource Code	Resource Name

Audio Tape

Non **Bodybusiness—audiotape** _____
Total respondents below level for—Bodybusiness—audiotape   5

CM **Conflict Management—audiotape** _____
Total respondents below level for—Conflict Management—   6

Dev. **Development Management—audio tape** _____
Total respondents below level for—Development Management   2

Mem **Memory Fixing—audiotape** _____
Total respondents below level for—Memory Fixing—audiotape   5

SH **Stop It Now—audiotape** _____
Total respondents below level for—Stop It Now—audiotape   8

Book **Always Bear Left—book** _____
Total respondents below level for—Always Bear Left—book   5

NVC **Bodybusiness—book** _____
Total respondents below level for—Bodybusiness—book   5

Sex **Stop It Now—book** _____
Total respondents below level for—Stop It Now—book   8

COAC **Coaching and Counseling—coaching** _____
Total respondents below level for—Coaching and Counseling—   2

ASSER **Assertive Training—seminar** _____
Total respondents below level for—Assertive Training—   5

Chg **Change Management—seminar** _____
Total respondents below level for—Change Management—   3

CC **Coaching and Counseling—seminar** _____
Total respondents below level for—Coaching and Counseling—   2

CS **Consultive Selling—seminar** _____
Total respondents below level for—Consultive Selling   6

Cust **Customer Service—seminar** _____
Total respondents below level for—Customer Service—   7

DEC **Decision Making—seminar** _____
Total respondents below level for—Decision Making—seminar   3

DMR **Decision Making with Risk—seminar** _____
Total respondents below level for—Decision Making with Risk   8

Selected Work Groups:	**Selected Titles:**	**Selected Resources:**
Region—01, Region—02	Manager, Sales Representative	Always Bear Left—book, Assertive Training—seminar, Bodybusiness—audiotape, Bodybusiness—book, Bodybusiness—videotape, Change Management—seminar, Coaching and Counseling—coaching, Coaching and Counseling—seminar, Conflict Management—audiotape, Conflict Management—videotape, Consultive Selling—seminar, . . . and MORE.

Resource Type

Resource Code	Resource Name	
EFFEC	**Effectance Motivation—seminar**	
	Total respondents below level for—Effectance Motivation	3
LISTE	**Effective Listening—seminar**	
	Total respondents below level for—Effective Listening—	8
EM	**Effective Meetings—seminar**	
	Total respondents below level for—Effective Meetings—	3
EP	**Effective Presentations—Seminar**	
	Total respondents below level for—Effective Presentations—	7
EW	**Effective Writing Skills—seminar**	
	Total respondents below level for—Effective Writing Skills—	6
FAC	**Facilitation Skills—seminar**	
	Total respondents below level for—Facilitation Skills—seminar	7
HUM	**Humor in the workplace—seminar**	
	Total respondents below level for—Humor in the workplace—	1
ISO	**ISO 9000—seminar**	
	Total respondents below level for—ISO 9000—seminar	5
INTER	**Interviewing—seminar**	
	Total respondents below level for—Interviewing—seminar	8
LEAD	**Leadership Thru Excellence—seminar**	
	Total respondents below level for—Leadership Thru	8
NEG	**Multi-form Negotiating—seminar**	
	Total respondents below level for—Multi-form Negotiating—	8
SALES	**Multi-form Sales Skills—seminar**	
	Total respondents below level for—Multi-form Sales Skills—	6
SELL	**Multi-form Sales Strategies—seminar**	
	Total respondents below level for—Multi-form Sales Strategies	6
OBM	**Open Book Management—seminar**	
	Total respondents below level for—Open Book Management—	7
PERPL	**Performance Planning—seminar**	
	Total respondents below level for—Performance Planning—	1
PERRE	**Performance Reviews—seminar**	
	Total respondents below level for—Performance Reviews—	0
PI	**Process Improvement—seminar**	

Figure 8-42. Resource summary (by workgroup).

Selected Work Groups:	**Selected Titles:**	**Selected Resources:**
Region—01, Region—02	Manager, Sales Representative	Always Bear Left—book, Assertive Training—seminar, Bodybusiness—audiotape, Bodybusiness—book, Bodybusiness—videotape, Change Management—seminar, Coaching and Counseling—coaching, Coaching and Counseling—seminar, Conflict Management—audiotape, Conflict Management—videotape, Consultive Selling—seminar, . . . and MORE.

Resource Type

Resource Resource
Code Name Wk. Grp.

Audiotape

Non **Bodybusiness—audiotape**

    Region—01

        Total respondents below level for—Region—01   3

    Region—02

        Total respondents below level for—Region—02   2

    Total respondents below level for—Bodybusiness—audiotape   5

CM **Conflict Management—audiotape**

    Region—01

        Total respondents below level for—Region—01   3

    Region—02

        Total respondents below level for—Region—02   3

    Total respondents below level for—Conflict Management—   6

Dev **Development Management—audiotape**

    Region—01

        Total respondents below level for—Region—01   1

    Region—02

        Total respondents below level for—Region—02   1

    Total respondents below level for—Development Management   2

Mem **Memory Fixing—audiotape**

    Region—01

        Total respondents below level for—Region—01   1

    Region—02

        Total respondents below level for—Region—02   4

    Total respondents below level for—Memory Fixing—audiotape   5

SH **Stop It Now—audiotape**

    Region—01

        Total respondents below level for—Region—01   4

    Region—02

        Total respondents below level for—Region—02   4

    Total respondents below level for—Stop It Now—audiotape   8

Selected Work Groups:	Selected Titles:	Selected Resources:
Region—01, Region—02	Manager, Sales Representative	Always Bear Left—book, Assertive Training—seminar, Bodybusiness—audiotape, Bodybusiness—book, Bodybusiness—videotape, Change Management—seminar, Coaching and Counseling—coaching, Coaching and Counseling—seminar, Conflict Management—audiotape, Conflict Management—videotape, Consultive Selling—seminar, . . . and MORE.

Resource Type

Resource Code	Resource Name	Wk. Grp.		
Book	**Always Bear Left—book**			
		Region—01		
			Total respondents below level for—Region—01	3
		Region—02		
			Total respondents below level for—Region—02	2
			Total respondents below level for—Always Bear Left—book	5
NVC	**Bodybusiness—book**			
		Region—01		
			Total respondents below level for—Region—01	3
		Region—02		
			Total respondents below level for—Region—02	2
			Total respondents below level for—Bodybusiness—book	5
Sex	**Stop It Now—book**			
		Region—01		
			Total respondents below level for—Region—01	4
		Region—02		
			Total respondents below level for—Region—02	4
			Total respondents below level for—Stop It Now—book	8
COAC	**Coaching and Counseling—coaching**			
		Region—01		
			Total respondents below level for—Region—01	2
			Total respondents below level for—Coaching and Counseling—	2
ASSER	**Assertive Training—seminar**			
		Region—01		
			Total respondents below level for—Region—01	3
		Region—02		
			Total respondents below level for—Region—02	2
			Total respondents below level for—Assertive Training—	5

(continues)

Figure 8-42. *(continued)*

Selected Work Groups:	Selected Titles:	Selected Resources:
Region—01, Region—02	Manager, Sales Representative	Always Bear Left—book, Assertive Training—seminar, Bodybusiness—audiotape, Bodybusiness—book, Bodybusiness—videotape, Change Management—seminar, Coaching and Counseling—coaching, Coaching and Counseling—seminar, Conflict Management—audiotape, Conflict Management—videotape, Consultive Selling—seminar, . . . and MORE.

Resource Type

Resource Code	Resource Name	Wk. Grp.		
Chg	**Change Management—seminar**			
	Region—01			
		Total respondents below level for—Region—01		1
	Region—02			
		Total respondents below level for—Region—02		2
		Total respondents below level for—Change Management—		3
CC	**Coaching and Counseling—seminar**			
	Region—01			
		Total respondents below level for—Region—01		2
		Total respondents below level for—Coaching and Counseling—		2
CS	**Consultive Selling—seminar**			
	Region—01			
		Total respondents below level for—Region—01		3

Figure 8-43. Resource summary (by title).

Selected Work Groups:	Selected Titles:	Selected Resources:
Region—01, Region—02	Manager, Sales Representative	Always Bear Left—book, Assertive Training—seminar, Bodybusiness—audiotape, Bodybusiness—book, Bodybusiness—videotape, Change Management—seminar, Coaching and Counseling—coaching, Coaching and Counseling—seminar, Conflict Management—audiotape, Conflict Management—videotape, Consultive Selling—seminar, . . . and MORE.

Resource Type

Resource Code *Resource Name Wk. Grp.* *Title Code/Description*

Audiotape

Non   **Bodybusiness—audiotape**

    Region—01

      MGR Manager

                    Total respondents below level for—Manager   1

      SR   Sales Representative

                    Total respondents below level for—Sales Representative   2

                    Total respondents below level for—Region—01   3

    Region—02

      SR   Sales Representative

                    Total respondents below level for—Sales Representative   2

                    Total respondents below level for—Region—02   2

            Total respondents below level for—Bodybusiness—audiotape   5

CM   **Conflict Management—audiotape**

    Region—01

      MGR Manager

                    Total respondents below level for—Manager   1

      SR   Sales Representative

                    Total respondents below level for—Sales Representative   2

                    Total respondents below level for—Region—01   3

    Region—02

      MGR Manager

                    Total respondents below level for—Manager   1

      SR   Sales Representative

                    Total respondents below level for—Sales Representative   2

                    Total respondents below level for—Region—02   3

            Total respondents below level for—Conflict Management   6

Dev   **Development Management—audiotape**

    Region—01

      MGR Manager

                    Total respondents below level for—Manager   1

                    Total respondents below level for—Region—01   1

(continues)

Figure 8-43. *(continued)*

Selected Work Groups:	Selected Titles:	Selected Resources:
Region—01, Region—02	Manager, Sales Representative	Always Bear Left—book, Assertive Training—seminar, Bodybusiness—audiotape, Bodybusiness—book, Bodybusiness—videotape, Change Management—seminar, Coaching and Counseling—coaching, Coaching and Counseling—seminar, Conflict Management—audiotape, Conflict Management—videotape, Consultive Selling—seminar, . . . and MORE.

Resource Type

Resource Code	Resource Name	Title Code/Description Wk. Grp.	

Region—02

MGR   Manager

Total respondents below level for—Manager	1

Total respondents below level for—Region—02	1

Total respondents below level for—Development Management	2

Mem   Memory Fixing—audiotape

Region—01

SR   Sales Representative

Total respondents below level for—Sales Representative	1

Total respondents below level for—Region—01	1

Region—02

MGR   Manager

Total respondents below level for—Manager	1

SR   Sales Representative

Total respondents below level for—Sales Representative	3

Total respondents below level for—Region—02	4

Total respondents below level for—Memory Fixing—audiotape	5

SH   Stop It Now—audiotape

Region—01

MGR   Manager

Total respondents below level for—Manager	1

SR   Sales Representative

Total respondents below level for—Sales Representative	3

Total respondents below level for—Region—01	4

Region—02

MGR   Manager

Total respondents below level for—Manager	1

SR   Sales Representative

Total respondents below level for—Sales Representative	3

Total respondents below level for—Region—02	4

Total respondents below level for—Stop It Now—audiotape	8

Selected Work Groups:	**Selected Titles:**	**Selected Resources:**
Region—01, Region—02	Manager, Sales Representative	Always Bear Left—book, Assertive Training—seminar, Bodybusiness—audiotape, Bodybusiness—book, Bodybusiness—videotape, Change Management—seminar, Coaching and Counseling—coaching, Coaching and Counseling—seminar, Conflict Management—audiotape, Conflict Management—videotape, Consultive Selling—seminar, . . . and MORE.

Resource Type

Resource Code	Resource Name	Wk. Grp.	Title Code/Description	

Book   **Always Bear Left—book**

       Region—01

         SR   Sales Representative   ———

Total respondents below level for—Sales Representative   3

Total respondents below level for—Region—01   3

       Region—02

         SR   Sales Representative   ———

Total respondents below level for—Sales Representative   2

Total respondents below level for—Region—02   2

Total respondents below level for—Always Bear Left—book   5

NVC   **Bodybusiness—book**

       Region—01

         MGR   Manager   ———

Total respondents below level for—Manager   1

Figure 8-44. Resource summary (by person).

Selected Work Groups:	Selected Titles:	Selected Resources:
Region—01, Region—02	Manager, Sales Representative	Always Bear Left—book, Assertive Training—seminar, Bodybusiness—audiotape, Bodybusiness—book, Bodybusiness—videotape, Change Management—seminar, Coaching and Counseling—coaching, Coaching and Counseling—seminar, Conflict Management—audiotape, Conflict Management—videotape, Consultive Selling—seminar, . . . and MORE.

Resource Type

Resource Code	Resource Name	Wk. Grp.	Title Code/Description

Audiotape

Non   **Bodybusiness—audiotape**

    Region—01

      MGR Manager

          Chen, Bob   _____

                    Total respondents below level for—Manager   1

      SR   Sales Representative

          Sanchez, Lou

          Stratton, Lindsay   _____

               Total respondents below level for—Sales Representative   2

                  Total respondents below level for—Region—01   3

    Region—02

      SR   Sales Representative

          O'Connor, Mike

          Sakura, Lin   _____

               Total respondents below level for—Sales Representative   2

                  Total respondents below level for—Region—02   2

    Total respondents below level for—Bodybusiness—audiotape   5

CM   **Conflict Management—audiotape**

    Region—01

      MGR Manager

          Chen, Bob   _____

                    Total respondents below level for—Manager   1

      SR   Sales Representative

          Sanchez, Lou

          Stratton, Lindsay   _____

               Total respondents below level for—Sales Representative   2

                  Total respondents below level for—Region—01   3

    Region—02

      MGR Manager

          McDonnell, John   _____

                    Total respondents below level for—Manager   1

Selected Work Groups:	Selected Titles:	Selected Resources:
Region—01, Region—02	Manager, Sales Representative	Always Bear Left—book, Assertive Training—seminar, Bodybusiness—audiotape, Bodybusiness—book, Bodybusiness—videotape, Change Management—seminar, Coaching and Counseling—coaching, Coaching and Counseling—seminar, Conflict Management—audiotape, Conflict Management—videotape, Consultive Selling—seminar, . . . and MORE.

Resource Type

Resource Code	Resource Name	Wk. Grp.	Title Code/Description	
	SR		**Sales Representative**	
			Meyerhoff, Jim	
			Sakura, Lin	
			Total respondents below level for—Sales Representative	2
			Total respondents below level for—Region—02	3
			Total respondents below level for—Conflict Management—	6
Dev			**Development Management—audiotape**	
		Region—01		
	MGR		**Manager**	
			Chen, Bob	
			Total respondents below level for—Manager	1
			Total respondents below level for—Region—01	1
		Region—02		
	MGR		**Manager**	
			McDonnell, John	
			Total respondents below level for—Manager	1
			Total respondents below level for—Region—02	1
			Total respondents below level for—Development Management	2
Mem			**Memory Fixing—audiotape**	
		Region—01		
	SR		**Sales Representative**	
			Stratton, Lindsay	
			Total respondents below level for—Sales Representative	1
			Total respondents below level for—Region—01	1
		Region—02		
	MGR		**Manager**	
			McDonnell, John	
			Total respondents below level for—Manager	1
	SR		**Sales Representative**	
			Meyerhoff, Jim	
			O'Connor, Mike	
			Sakura, Lin	
			Total respondents below level for—Sales Representative	3
			Total respondents below level for—Region—02	4
			Total respondents below level for—Memory Fixing—audiotape	5

(continues)

Figure 8-44. *(continued)*

Selected Work Groups:	Selected Titles:	Selected Resources:
Region—01, Region—02	Manager, Sales Representative	Always Bear Left—book, Assertive Training—seminar, Bodybusiness—audiotape, Bodybusiness—book, Bodybusiness—videotape, Change Management—seminar, Coaching and Counseling—coaching, Coaching and Counseling—seminar, Conflict Management—audiotape, Conflict Management—videotape, Consultive Selling—seminar, . . . and MORE.

Resource Type

Resource Code	*Resource Name Wk. Grp.*	*Title Code/Description*	
SH		**Stop It Now—audiotape**	
	Region—01		
	MGR	**Manager**	
		Chen, Bob	_____
		Total respondents below level for—Manager	**1**
	SR	**Sales Representative**	
		Deaver, Stan	
		Sanchez, Lou	
		Stratton, Lindsay	_____
		Total respondents below level for—Sales Representative	**3**
		Total respondents below level for—Region—01	**4**

Figure 8-45. Resource summary (by competency).

Selected Work Groups:	**Selected Titles:**	**Selected Resources:**
Region—01, Region—02	Manager, Sales Representative	Always Bear Left—book, Assertive Training—seminar, Bodybusiness—audiotape, Bodybusiness—book, Bodybusiness—videotape, Change Management—seminar, Coaching and Counseling—coaching, Coaching and Counseling—seminar, Conflict Management—audiotape, Conflict Management—videotape, Consultive Selling—seminar, . . . and MORE.

Resource Type

Resource Code	Resource Name	Wk. Grp.	Title Code/Description Comp. #/Text	Title Stand.	Resp.	Var.

Audiotape

Non **Bodybusiness—audiotape**

Region—01

MGR **Manager**

Chen, Bob

| | | | 0702 Nonverbal Communications | 3 | 2 | (1) |

Total respondents below level for—Manager 1

SR **Sales Representative**

Sanchez, Lou

| | | | 0702 Nonverbal Communications | 4 | 3 | (1) |

Stratton, Lindsay

| | | | 0702 Nonverbal Communications | 4 | 2 | (2) |

Total respondents below level for—Sales Representative 2

Total respondents below level for—Region—01 3

Region—02

SR **Sales Representative**

O'Connor, Mike

| | | | 0702 Nonverbal Communications | 4 | 3 | (1) |

Sakura, Lin

| | | | 0702 Nonverbal Communications | 4 | 2 | (2) |

Total respondents below level for—Sales Representative 2

Total respondents below level for—Region—02 2

Total respondents below level for—Bodybusiness—audiotape 5

CM **Conflict Management—audiotape**

Region—01

MGR **Manager**

Chen, Bob

			0206 Performance Reviews	5	3	(2)
			0209 Counseling	3	2	(1)
			0703 Conflict Management	3	2	(1)
			0705 Change Management	4	3	(1)
			0707 Effective Meetings	4	3	(1)

(continues)

Figure 8-45. *(continued)*

Selected Work Groups:	Selected Titles:	Selected Resources:
Region—01, Region—02	Manager, Sales Representative	Always Bear Left—book, Assertive Training—seminar, Bodybusiness—audiotape, Bodybusiness—book, Bodybusiness—videotape, Change Management—seminar, Coaching and Counseling—coaching, Coaching and Counseling—seminar, Conflict Management—audiotape, Conflict Management—videotape, Consultive Selling—seminar, . . . and MORE.

Resource Type

Resource Code	Resource Name	Wk. Grp.	Title Code/Description Comp. #/Text		Title Stand.	Resp.	Var.
			0804	Facilitation	4	3	(1)
			0805	Team Building	4	3	(1)
			Total respondents below level for—Manager				**1**
	SR	**Sales Representative**					
		Sanchez, Lou					
			0703	Conflict Management	3	2	(1)
		Stratton, Lindsay					
			0209	Counseling	2	1	(1)
			0703	Conflict Management	3	2	(1)
		Total respondents below level for—Sales Representative					**2**
		Total respondents below level for—Region—01					**3**
	Region—02						
	MGR	**Manager**					
		McDonnell, John					
			0705	Change Management	4	3	(1)
			0707	Effective Meetings	4	3	(1)
			0804	Facilitation	4	3	(1)
			0805	Team Building	4	2	(2)
		Total respondents below level for—Manager					**1**
	SR	**Sales Representative**					
		Meyerhoff, Jim					
			0703	Conflict Management	3	2	(1)
		Sakura, Lin					
			0703	Conflict Management	3	2	(1)
		Total respondents below level for—Sales Representative					**2**
		Total respondents below level for—Region—02					**3**
		Total respondents below level for—Conflict Management					**6**
Dev	**Development Management—audiotape**						
	Region—01						
	MGR	**Manager**					
		Chen, Bob					
			0202	Leadership	4	3	(1)

Selected Work Groups:	Selected Titles:	Selected Resources:
Region—01, Region—02	Manager, Sales Representative	Always Bear Left—book, Assertive Training—seminar, Bodybusiness—audiotape, Bodybusiness—book, Bodybusiness—videotape, Change Management—seminar, Coaching and Counseling—coaching, Coaching and Counseling—seminar, Conflict Management—audiotape, Conflict Management—videotape, Consultive Selling—seminar, . . . and MORE.

Resource Type

Resource Code	Resource Name	Wk. Grp.	Title Code/Description Comp. #/Text	Title Stand.	Resp.	Var.	
			0205 Performance Planning	5	3	(2)	
			0206 Performance Reviews	5	3	(2)	
			Total respondents below level for—Manager			**1**	
			Total respondents below level for—Region—01				**1**
		Region—02					
	MGR	**Manager**					
		McDonnell, John					
			0202 Leadership	4	3	(1)	
			Total respondents below level for—Manager			**1**	
			Total respondents below level for—Region—02				**1**
			Total respondents below level for—Development Management				**2**
Mem	**Memory Fixing—audiotape**						
		Region—01					
	SR	**Sales Representative**					
		Stratton, Lindsay					
			0309 Trade Shows	3	2	(1)	
			Total respondents below level for—Sales Representative			**1**	
			Total respondents below level for—Region—01				**1**

Figure 8-46. Requirements by competency (by competency).

Selected Work Groups:	**Selected Titles:**	
Region—01, Region—02	Manager, Sales Representative	

Category	*Detail Level—1 (Competency)*		
Competency		*Ave.*	*Count*
Code Text	Work Group	*Below*	*Below*
General Information			
0101 Organizational Information			
		3.00	1
0102 Basic Industry Knowledge			
		3.00	2
0104 Legal Review and Approval			
		3.50	2
0105 Diversity			
		2.60	5
0106 Sexual Harassment			
		2.12	8
General Information		**2.55**	**18**
Management/Leadership			
0202 Leadership			
		3.00	2
0203 Ethics			
		2.16	6
0204 Interviewing			
		2.00	1
0205 Performance Planning			
		3.00	1
0206 Performance Reviews			
		3.00	1
0207 Salary Administration			
		3.00	2
0208 Coaching			
		2.00	1
0209 Counseling			
		1.50	2
0210 Open Book Management			
		2.00	3
Management/Leadership		**2.31**	**19**
Sales/Marketing			
0303 Product Strategies			
		3.50	6
0305 Questioning			
		3.00	2
0306 Competitive Activities			
		3.40	5
0307 Negotiating			

Selected Work Groups:
Region—01, Region—02

Selected Titles:
Manager, Sales Representative

Category   *Detail Level—1 (Competency)*

Competency Code	Text	Work Group	Ave. Below	Count Below
			2.00	6
0308	Territory Administration			
			2.66	6
0309	Trade Shows			
			2.00	4
		Sales/Marketing	2.75	29

Technical

Competency Code	Text	Work Group	Ave. Below	Count Below
0405	Training			
			1.00	1
		Technical	1.00	1

Administration

Competency Code	Text	Work Group	Ave. Below	Count Below
0501	Personnel Policies			
			2.00	1
0504	Order Entry			
			1.00	1
0505	Financial Justification			
			1.00	1
0506	Statistics			
			2.00	2
		Administration	1.60	5

Personal Computing

Competency Code	Text	Work Group	Ave. Below	Count Below
0601	Operating System			
			2.00	2
0602	Word Processing			
			2.00	3
0606	E-Mail			
			2.00	3

Figure 8-47. Requirements by competency (by workgroup).

Selected Work Groups:		**Selected Titles:**
Region—01, Region—02		Manager, Sales Representative

Category   *Detail Level—2 (Department)*

Competency			Ave.	Count
Code Text	Work Group		Below	Below

General Information

0101   Organizational Information
      Region—01

	3.00	1
Question #0101.	3.00	1

0102   Basic Industry Knowledge
      Region—01

      Region—02

	3.00	1
	3.00	1
Question #0102.	3.00	2

0104   Legal Review and Approval
      Region—01

      Region—02

	4.00	1
	3.00	1
Question #0104.	3.50	2

0105   Diversity
      Region—01

      Region—02

	3.00	2
	2.33	3
Question #0105.	2.60	5

0106   Sexual Harassment
      Region—01

      Region—02

	2.00	4
	2.25	4
Question #0106.	2.12	8
General Information	2.55	18

Management/Leadership

0202   Leadership
      Region—01

      Region—02

	3.00	1
	3.00	1
Question #0202.	3.00	2

		Selected Work Groups: Region—01, Region—02		Selected Titles: Manager, Sales Representative	

Category *Competency* Code Text	*Detail Level—2 (Department)* Work Group	*Ave.* *Below*	*Count* *Below*
0203 Ethics			
	Region—01	2.25	4
	Region—02	2.00	2
	Question #0203.	2.16	6
0204 Interviewing			
	Region—01	2.00	1
	Question #0204.	2.00	1
0205 Performance Planning			
	Region—01	3.00	1
	Question #0205.	3.00	1
0206 Performance Reviews			
	Region—01	3.00	1
	Question #0206.	3.00	1
0207 Salary Administration			
	Region—01	3.00	1
	Region—02	3.00	1
	Question #0207.	3.00	2
0208 Coaching			
	Region—01	2.00	1
	Question #0208.	2.00	1
0209 Counseling			
	Region—01	1.50	2
	Question #0209.	1.50	2
0210 Open Book Management			
	Region—01	2.00	2
	Region—02	2.00	1
	Question #0210.	2.00	3
	Management/Leadership	2.31	19

Figure 8-48. Requirements by competency (by title).

Selected Work Groups:	**Selected Titles:**
Region—01, Region—02	Manager, Sales Representative

Category   *Detail Level—3 (Title)*

Competency Code	Text	Work Group	Title—Standard	Resp.	Ave. Below	Count Below
General Information						
0101	Organizational Information					
		Region—01				
			Manager—4			
			Manager	3.00	1	
			Region—01	3.00	1	
			Question #0101.	3.00	1	
0102	Basic Industry Knowledge					
		Region—01				
			Sales Representative—4			
			Sales Representative	3.00	1	
			Region—01	3.00	1	
		Region—02				
			Sales Representative—4			
			Sales Representative	3.00	1	
			Region—02	3.00	1	
			Question #0102.	3.00	2	
0104	Legal Review and Approval					
		Region—01				
			Manager—5			
			Manager	4.00	1	
			Region—01	4.00	1	
		Region—02				
			Manager—5			
			Manager	3.00	1	
			Region—02	3.00	1	
			Question #0104.	3.50	2	
0105	Diversity					
		Region—01				
			Manager—5			
			Manager	4.00	1	
			Sales Representative—3			
			Sales Representative	2.00	1	
			Region—01	3.00	2	
		Region—02				
			Manager—5			
			Manager	3.00	1	
			Sales Representative—3			
			Sales Representative	2.00	2	
			Region—02	2.33	3	
			Question #0105.	2.60	5	

	Selected Work Groups: Region—01, Region—02		Selected Titles: Manager, Sales Representative			

Category *Competency* *Code*	*Text*	*Work Group*	*Detail Level—3 (Title)* *Title—Standard*	*Resp.*	*Ave.* *Below*	*Count* *Below*
0106	Sexual Harassment					
		Region—01				
			Manager—5			
				Manager	3.00	1
			Sales Representative—3			
				Sales Representative	1.66	3
				Region—01	2.00	4
		Region—02				
			Manager—5			
				Manager	3.00	1
			Sales Representative—3			
				Sales Representative	2.00	3
				Region—02	2.25	4
				Question #0106.	2.12	8
				General Information	2.55	18
Management/Leadership						
0202	Leadership					
		Region—01				
			Manager—4			
				Manager	3.00	1
				Region—01	3.00	1
		Region—02				
			Manager—4			
				Manager	3.00	1
				Region—02	3.00	1
				Question #0202.	3.00	2
0203	Ethics					
		Region—01				
			Manager—4			
				Manager	3.00	1
			Sales Representative—3			
				Sales Representative	2.00	3
				Region—01	2.25	4
		Region—02				
			Sales Representative—3			
				Sales Representative	2.00	2
				Region—02	2.00	2
				Question #0203.	2.16	6

Figure 8-49. Requirements by competency (by person).

	Selected Work Groups: Region—01, Region—02	**Selected Titles:** Manager, Sales Representative

Category			*Detail Level—4 (Person)*				
Competency						*Ave.*	*Count*
Code	*Text*	*Work Group*	*Title—Standard*	*Name*	*Resp.*	*Below*	*Below*

General Information

0101　Organizational Information
　　　　Region—01

Manager—4				
Chen, Bob	3			
Manager		3.00		1
Region—01		3.00		1
Question #0101.		3.00		1

0102　Basic Industry Knowledge
　　　　Region—01

Sales Representative—4			
Deaver, Stan	3		
Sales Representative	3.00		1
Region—01	3.00		1

　　　　Region—02

Sales Representative—4			
O'Connor, Mike	3		
Sales Representative	3.00		1
Region—02	3.00		1
Question #0102.	3.00		2

0104　Legal Review and Approval
　　　　Region—01

Manager—5			
Chen, Bob	4		
Manager	4.00		1
Region—01	4.00		1

　　　　Region—02

Manager—5			
McDonnell, John	3		
Manager	3.00		1
Region—02	3.00		1
Question #0104.	3.50		2

0105　Diversity
　　　　Region—01

Manager—5			
Chen, Bob	4		
Manager	4.00		1
Sales Representative—3			
Stratton, Lindsay	2		
Sales Representative	2.00		1
Region—01	3.00		2

	Selected Work Groups: Region—01, Region—02		**Selected Titles:** Manager, Sales Representative				

Category

Competency			Detail Level—4 (Person)			Ave.	Count
Code	Text	Work Group	Title—Standard	Name	Resp.	Below	Below
		Region—02					
			Manager—5				
				McDonnell, John	3		
				Manager		3.00	1
			Sales Representative—3				
				Meyerhoff, Jim	2		
				O'Connor, Mike	2		
				Sales Representative		2.00	2
				Region—02		2.33	3
				Question #0105.		2.60	5
0106	Sexual Harassment						
		Region—01					
			Manager—5				
				Chen, Bob	3		
				Manager		3.00	1
			Sales Representative—3				
				Deaver, Stan	2		
				Sanchez, Lou	1		
				Stratton, Lindsay	2		
				Sales Representative		1.66	3
				Region—01		2.00	4
		Region—02					
			Manager—5				
				McDonnell, John	3		
				Manager		3.00	1
			Sales Representative—3				
				Meyerhoff, Jim	2		
				O'Connor, Mike	2		
				Sakura, Lin	2		
				Sales Representative		2.00	3
				Region—02		2.25	4
				Question #0106.		2.12	8
				General Information		2.55	18

Management/Leadership

0202	Leadership						
		Region—01					
			Manager—4				
				Chen, Bob	3		
				Manager		3.00	1
				Region—01		3.00	1

Figure 8-50. Excel data extraction spreadsheet file.

	A	B	C	D	E	F	G	
1	cl_bname	name	tl_descrip	q_newm	qc_descrip	pq_answ	qt_desir	q_shorttxt
2	Region - 01	Chen , Bob	Manager	0101	General Inform	3	4	Organizational Inforr
3	Region - 02	Branigan , Beth	Administrator	0101	General Inform	2	3	Organizational Inforr
4	Region - 03	Encino , Joe	Manager	0101	General Inform	3	4	Organizational Inforr
5	Region - 03	Clemson , Mitchell	Team Leader	0101	General Inform	3	4	Organizational Inforr
6	Region - 01	Deaver , Stan	Sales Representative	0102	General Inform	3	4	Basic Industry Know
7	Region - 02	O'Connor , Mike	Sales Representative	0102	General Inform	3	4	Basic Industry Know
8	Region - 03	Clemson , Mitchell	Team Leader	0102	General Inform	3	5	Basic Industry Know
9	Region - 02	Branigan , Beth	Administrator	0103	General Inform	1	5	Policies and Procedu
10	Region - 01	Chen , Bob	Manager	0104	General Inform	4	5	Legal Review and Ap
11	Region - 01	Melton , Dan	Team Leader	0104	General Inform	2	3	Legal Review and Ap
12	Region - 02	Branigan , Beth	Administrator	0104	General Inform	1	4	Legal Review and Ap
13	Region - 02	McDonnell , John	Manager	0104	General Inform	3	5	Legal Review and Ap
14	Region - 02	Hanson , Skip	Technical Specialist	0104	General Inform	1	2	Legal Review and Ap
15	Region - 03	Encino , Joe	Manager	0104	General Inform	4	5	Legal Review and Ap
16	Region - 01	Chen , Bob	Manager	0105	General Inform	4	5	Diversity
17	Region - 01	Stratton , Lindsay	Sales Representative	0105	General Inform	2	3	Diversity
18	Region - 01	Grayson , Ben	Technical Specialist	0105	General Inform	2	3	Diversity
19	Region - 01	Melton , Dan	Team Leader	0105	General Inform	2	4	Diversity
20	Region - 02	McDonnell , John	Manager	0105	General Inform	3	5	Diversity
21	Region - 02	Meyerhoff , Jim	Sales Representative	0105	General Inform	2	3	Diversity
22	Region - 02	O'Connor , Mike	Sales Representative	0105	General Inform	2	3	Diversity

Learning Points

1. An automated CMAR tool should maximize applicability by being content independent. This also means that it is no substitute for an accurate model and valid assessment.
2. The design decisions of Chapter 2, such as individual or departmental competency models, will greatly impact programmed solutions.
3. The system is only as good as the accuracy of data entry. Proofing capabilities are essential.
4. Stand-alone systems require extensive administrative support for tracking status, updating personnel files, and distributing reports to employees, supervisors, and HR.
5. Management reporting is necessary to help organizations realize many of the cost-reduction and planning benefits. Individual reporting, coupled with effective counseling sessions and development planning, helps drive productivity improvements.

9

Delivering Competency-Based Applications Online

Internet technology enables the use of totally new approaches in the delivery of competency-based HR applications. Instead of the typical periodic method of one-time model creation followed by annual assessments, reporting, and development planning, online technology allows for continuous development and improvement of competency content and services. These competency applications can then be delivered over the Web by third-party providers or internally through an organization's Intranet.

The benefits of Internet technology are immediate. Existing documentation and development resources can quickly be repurposed for the Web by converting them to hypertext markup language (HTML) documents. HTML is a standard file output option for current office and graphics applications. All major computer-based training (CBT) applications provide a capability for creating HTML output. And there are an abundance of user-friendly Web page authoring applications that can be used by programmers and subject matter experts.

The HTML file format and Internet delivery technology also facilitates rapid development and updating of content. New documentation, courses, assessments, surveys, and administrative records can be instantly uploaded to the master server by anyone with password authorization. At that point, they are available to every authorized user within or outside the organization. Cycle times for online development and delivery are much shorter than for paper or batch methods.

Similarly, Internet/Intranet technology solves the administrative problems of delivery to end-users. Instead of requiring manual administrative systems as with Competency Coach, Web-based applications are immediately available to anyone having access to a browser-equipped PC with an Internet account. Internet/Intranet interactivity allows employees to access reference information, complete online learning courses, take knowledge tests, and fill out competency assessments and surveys—all done online using up-to-the-minute content.

Online competency-based HR applications are fully customizable. Additional programming can be added to provide more sophisticated database capabilities or specialized HR functionality. Organizations are not limited to the functionality of off-the-shelf packages. In addition, online applications are typically easier to program than stand-alone mainframe and server software.

Finally, online competency applications can integrate into existing back-end systems, such as training administration software or large-scale ERP packages. This helps reduce the duplication of effort by leveraging in-place technology and data files.

The current trend is for organizations to develop their new competency-based applications using the Internet. Large enterprises are acquiring specialized software, customizing it for specific needs, and integrating it into their legacy systems. Smaller organizations are utilizing outsourced service providers to fulfill competency services. Actual systems management is taking place either inside or outside the organization. With Internet technology, it does not matter where the master server is located as long as it is accessible through the Web.

The sample software described in this chapter comes from a leading-edge competency and learning applications developer. The software illustrates all the functionality described in this overview section. In addition, three live examples are included—two utilizing standard application functions and one showing a highly customized and integrated solution. This provides a development team with a thorough overview of the design considerations and capabilities of online competency systems.

An Online Example Using the LIBRIX
Open Learning System

Librix Learning, located in St. Louis, Missouri, is a provider of Web-based solutions for rapidly authoring, delivering, and tracking the assessment and development of potentially geographically dispersed employees (http://www. librix.com). Librix offers custom software development, application solutions, and turnkey net hosting services for providing complete implementation, monitoring, security, and backup.

The LIBRIX Open Learning System (LOLS) is an integrated, Web-based system that enables the enterprise-wide distribution and management of assessments, surveys, performance support, and training materials to a geographically dispersed workforce. In addition, with features such as online catalog and skills assessment, the LOLS helps organizations better track and manage the development process over all modes of delivery—classroom, videotape, audio tape, workbook, CD-ROM, as well as Web-based training—from anywhere in the world.

Content for LOLS can be created with any HTML-based authoring tool and can be used for online instruction and assessment, as well as for online assessment of off-line instruction. The LOLS Web-based interface is easy to customize, enabling integration into any organization's existing site's look and feel. In addition, the LOLS can be customized or extended with additional functionality to meet a client's unique training needs or to integrate with other back-end systems, such as SAP or PeopleSoft.

LIBRIX Open Learning System Components

LOLS consists of the functions shown in Figure 9-1. HTML input can be transferred from other Web-based sources, or can be created by applications such as FrontPage, Authorware, ToolBook, PowerPoint, and popular office or graphics applications. The Question Editor, a function of ActiveBuilder, allows the easy creation of any feedback instruments, such as assessments, surveys, questionnaires, or tests. ActiveBuilder bundles this content into a complete application and then uploads the appropriate files, along with any custom programming, to the OpenServer application running on a Web-hosting computer. OpenServer can then access the information it needs from existing or new SQL or Oracle databases.

Creating and Repurposing Content

The assembly of a feedback instrument or an online learning course begins in the ActiveBuilder module. Figure 9-2 shows the initial outline screen for an Internet-based course offered by the Department of Veteran's Affairs, "Medical Care for Persons with Spinal Cord Injuries." The three primary window icons represent the course outline, the course contents, and a student post-course survey. Interface icons at the top and on the left control the viewing, checking, manipulation, printing, and saving of the outline.

Figure 9-3 (on page 280) shows an exploded view of the course folder. Operations in this view follow typical outline conventions for reordering exist-

Figure 9-1. LIBRIX Open Learning System.

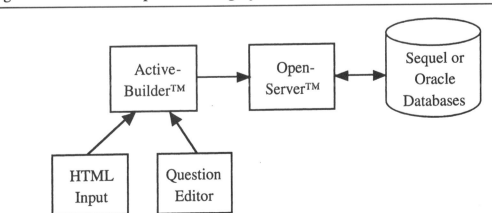

Figure 9-2. Initial outline screen.

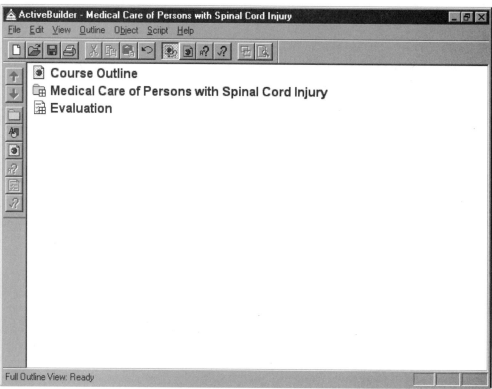

Figure 9-3. Course contents.

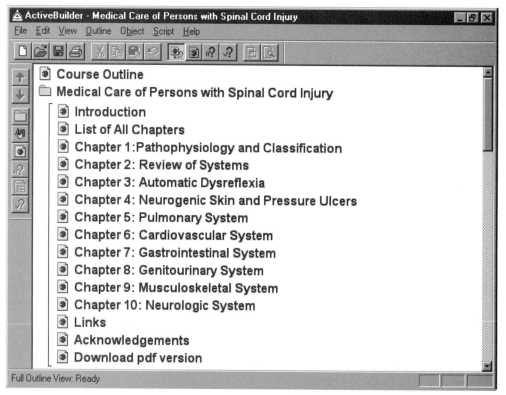

ing content and inserting new content. The outline function also facilitates building a hierarchy of chapters, sections, and pages for course contents. In this course, the icons show that each chapter is a single HTML document requiring the user to scroll down a continuous page. The software optionally allows for the automatic pagination of chapter contents so that users do not have to scroll.

HTML documents have many options for the inclusion of text, graphics, and multimedia content. Figure 9-4 shows a course page that contains text and detailed graphics information. If desired, users can save and print these pages using the standard file commands built into their Web browser. As stated earlier, content does not have to be specialized courseware created by a skilled CBT designer. A "course" can refer to any source material that needs to be accessed online. Therefore, ActiveBuilder can be used for creating online job descriptions, procedure manuals, performance support references, i.e., anything that can be placed into HTML format.

Adding HTML documentation is a simple matter of importing the appropriate data files created earlier. Figure 9-5 shows the dialog box sequence required to specify file names and locations for import. LOLS also has the capability to prompt the creation of new HTML information and will create an empty HTML file if the "Create a new HTML file" option is selected. Upon opening this icon in the outline, the user's default HTML editor is then launched by Windows. Files can also utilize a background graphic. This helps developers create content with a look and feel similar to the organization's existing Web pages. The background can be a standard graphics file used across an entire site.

This is the process used to import, create, and organize HTML content for Internet access by employees. Note that, unlike CBT software, LOLS does not help create the actual content. This requires specialized CBT applications such as Authorware or ToolBook, or office applications such as PowerPoint for presentations or Word for text. All LOLS requires is an HTML file. But unlike integrated training management systems that track only courses and feedback instruments created using their tools, LOLS is an open system providing these capabilities for any HTML content from any source.

Building Feedback Instruments

One of the most time-consuming aspects of many HR applications is writing the code to create interactive feedback instruments such as assessments, surveys, tests, and questionnaires. Programs such as Authorware and ToolBook

Figure 9-4. Course page.

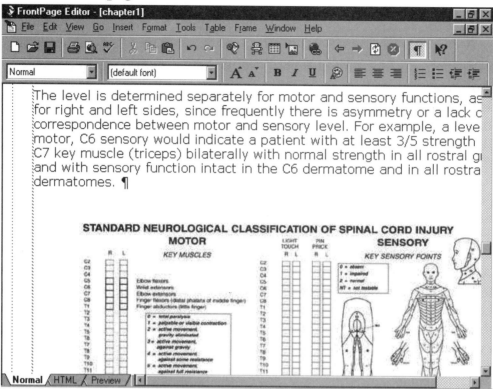

Figure 9-5. Importing HTML documents.

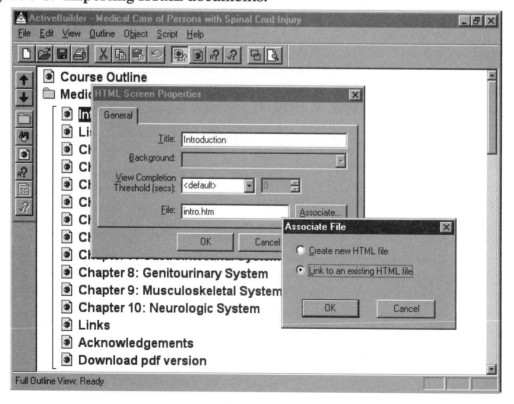

Assistant have extensive questioning, testing, and tabulation capabilities. A competency-based HR application must have the same functionality. Figure 9-6 shows an expansion of the Evaluation icon for the Spinal Cord Injury course. Each icon represents a single question. As with HTML content, questions can be created, managed, and reordered with simple outlining commands.

The question creation capabilities of ActiveBuilder are quite extensive. Figure 9-7 shows the main dialog box for creating nearly any type of query and feedback. The question is given a title and the text of the question is typed in. Depending upon the type of question, potential responses are listed and the correct answer is indicated by the corresponding checkbox. Pretests are an excellent way to help users mentally organize material and thereby increase learning, so both pre- and post-testing can also be specified. Additional answer explanations along with right-answer recognition feedback can be entered in fields at the bottom of the dialog box.

Figure 9-8 shows about a third of the built-in question formats that are accessible through a drop-down menu box. Note that both questions and answers can consist of text, graphics, or Net-based multimedia elements. Question and answer dialog boxes are linked so that the proper options are enabled based upon the question/answer format selected. Note at the bottom of the dialog box that there is an optional linkage back to the course materials. This lets the author immediately point users to supporting learning material when they miss a question or need to look up a hint.

Figure 9-9 shows the first tab of the question properties detail window. Formatting information can be input here. The author can also establish a screen Viewing Completion Threshold. Sometimes users will quickly click through screens, knowing that they may be tracked on whether or not they have accessed the screen. The threshold limit setting allows the designer to establish a minimum time that content must be on screen before being counted as "read." While this does not establish that the user actually studied the content, it does eliminate users easily fooling the system by merely bringing up each screen in turn before going on to the test section.

The pre- or post-test window as shown in Figure 9-10 (on page 286) allows designers to set a number of important performance levels. Users can be required to achieve a minimum score before being passed. Users may also have a limited number of opportunities to take the test before being locked out and referred to the administrator. The designer can also prevent the user from referencing any instructional material—in essence allowing for closed-or open-book testing. As before, standard background formatting can also be utilized for the testing screens.

Figure 9-6. Evaluation contents.

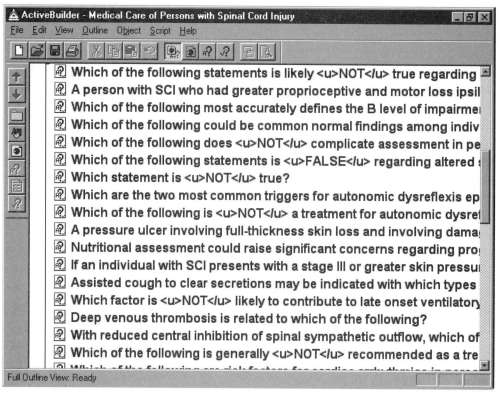

Figure 9-7. Creating feedback instruments with ActiveBuilder.

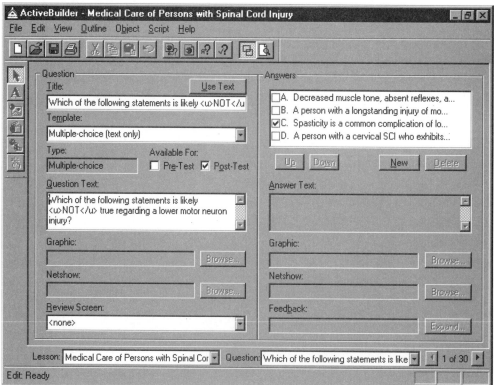

Figure 9-8. Built-in question formats.

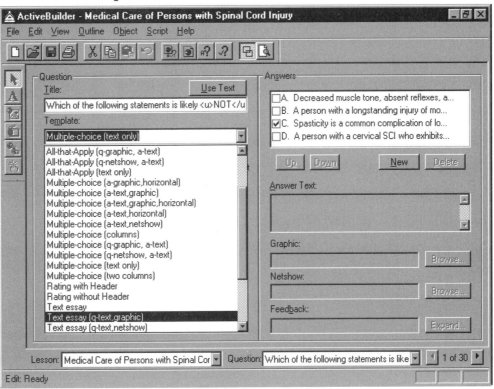

Figure 9-9. Course general properties.

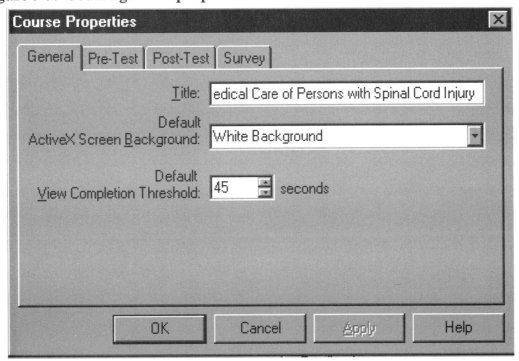

Figure 9-10. Course test.

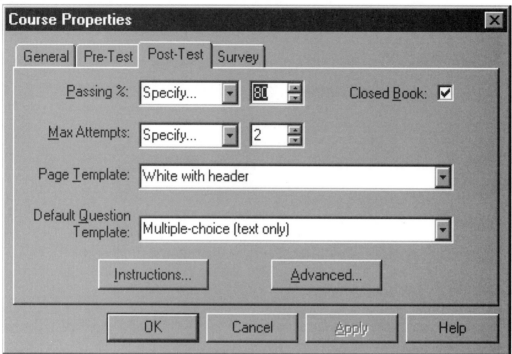

Additional testing details can be specified in the Advanced window as shown in Figure 9-11. Individual questions can be given different point values and weighting. The test can feature questions selected from a larger pool of possible questions so that each pass through the test is different. Questions and potential answers can be ordered sequentially or randomly. This makes it much more difficult to get a "cheat sheet" from coworkers and memorize the answers. Pass/fail grading can be done by the entire course or by sections. Finally, automatic pagination is specified here.

The remaining course properties are specified in the Survey tab, as shown in Figure 9-12. The author can select the conditions that make a survey available to the user. For example, users might not be able to complete an assessment without first reviewing the instructions "content." Or a test might not be enabled until the user has passed the course. This prevents users from studying up on the questions, then using the course search facilities to find just those answers. Passing the test and/or completing the survey can then be made a requirement for completion of the development activity.

Figure 9-13 shows an expanded view of the survey icon from the main menu. Similar to the process for content and testing icons, survey questions are managed and organized using the outliner interface. Each question is built

Figure 9-11. Course test (advanced).

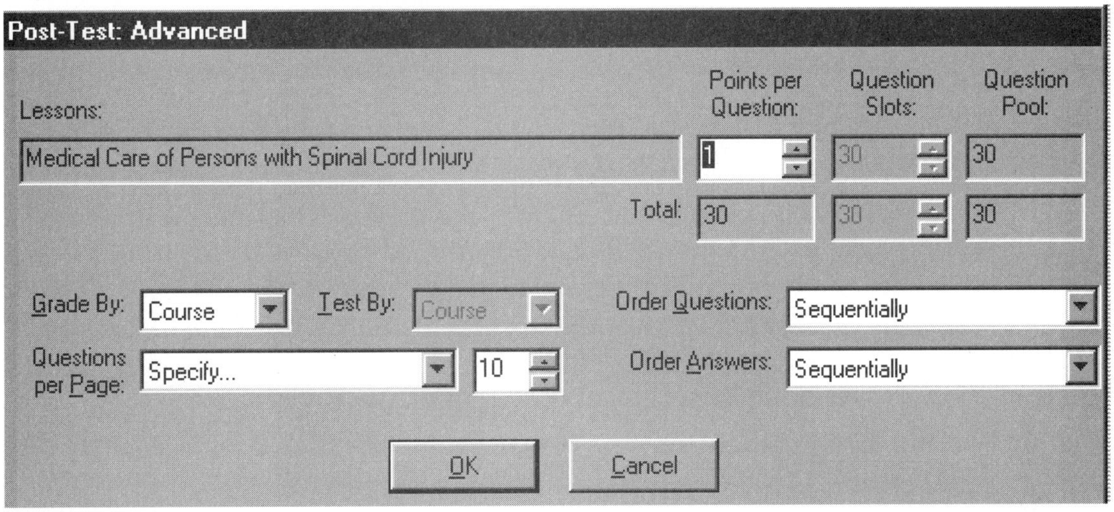

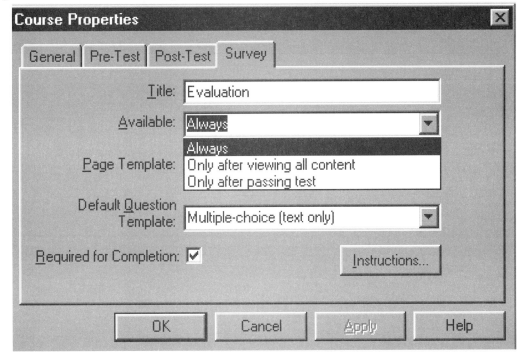

Figure 9-12. Course survey.

Figure 9-13. Survey contents.

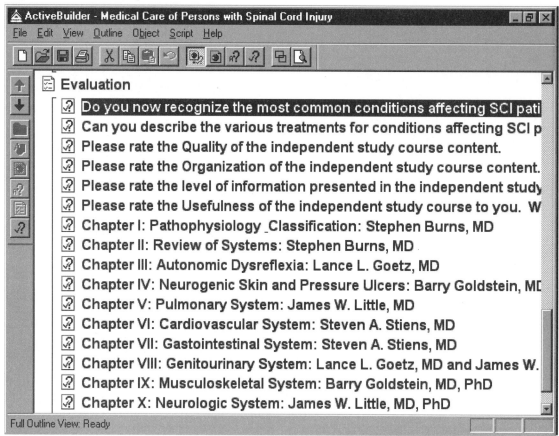

individually and can have the same characteristics of a test question, only there is no right/wrong scoring information maintained. Only responses are captured and tabulated.

Assessments, surveys, or feedback instruments are constructed using screens similar to those used for the creation of test questions. Figure 9-14 shows a screen used to construct the user feedback survey for the Spinal Cord Injury course. Note that the same question types as before are available and that potential answers are listed in pull-down menus when possible. Again, for easy reference, the survey information can be directly linked to the course content being evaluated. This lets users jump back to the course before filling out a response. The result should be a more accurate course evaluation, particularly if compared to evaluations in which the feedback is provided well after the course was completed.

Content and specifications developed in the Question Editor function within ActiveBuilder are assembled into an HTML document that is then combined with the other parts of the outline, and subsequently downloaded into OpenServer. Figure 9-15 shows a sample student feedback questionnaire that was built in the Question Editor and formatted for Internet delivery. Note that the evaluation can be tracked and linked to course completion requirements.

Figure 9-14. ActiveBuilder example.

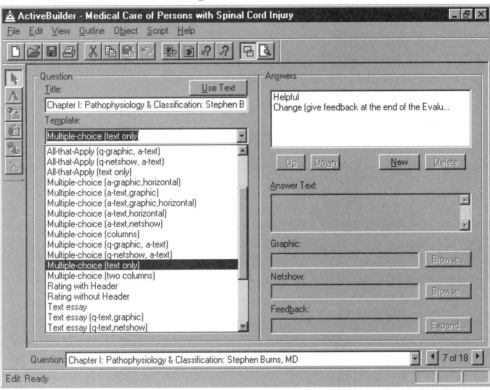

Figure 9-15. Evaluation example.

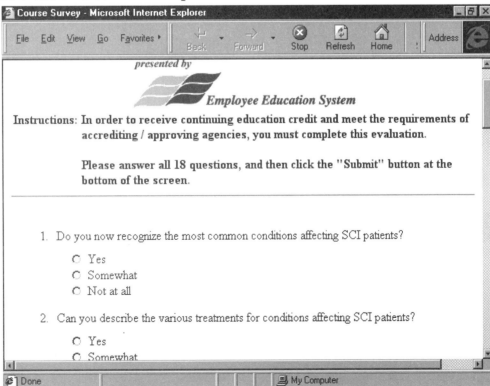

With this level of technology and feature set, regardless of the vendor, organizations do not need trained programmers to create online feedback instruments and content. Existing material can simply be output as HTML documents and inserted into an ActiveBuilder outline. Content experts with Web access can use its standardized procedures and fill-in-the-blanks operating environment to rapidly create highly customized, professionally designed interactive applications. With LOLS, changes are posted immediately to the OpenServer site so that required development and evaluation content can literally go from concept to implementation in hours without any IT assistance. This takes care of the content; the next step is to manage and use the results.

Online Application Administration

The next functional area of LOLS is administration. Figure 9-16 shows the initial administrator logon screen. There can be an extensive security system at work behind the logon process, because access rights design can get quite complicated. The overall goal of an online competency application is to push administration as far down the organization as possible, and to provide complete access flexibility.

LOLS allows the overall system administrator to set up local administrators with more restricted rights. For example, administrators might have access to all LOLS functions, but can apply those functions only to specific content or workgroups over which they have been granted control. A workgroup administrator might be able to modify privileges for some but not all users, or to delete some but not all content. Security needs to be controllable for all functional levels and for all types of data, depending upon the needs of the organization.

Figure 9-17 shows a portion of the data entry screen for setting up users. The menu list on the left of the window shows the controllable functions available to the system administrator in LOLS:

- Set up users and administrators.
- Establish workgroups.
- Set up course categories.
- Manage courses and development resources.
- Access and manage reports.
- Assign individual user privileges regarding users, groups, courses, and reports.

The administrator then performs the linkage process similar to that required within Competency Coach. In curriculum-based models, course requirements must be entered for workgroups and positions. Users must be placed in the system and have their authorizations designated. Figure 9-18 shows the process of linking users to workgroups. The drop down menu facilitates the completion of the form by providing a complete list of existing workgroups so that the administrator does not have to remember departmental

Figure 9-16. Administrator login screen.

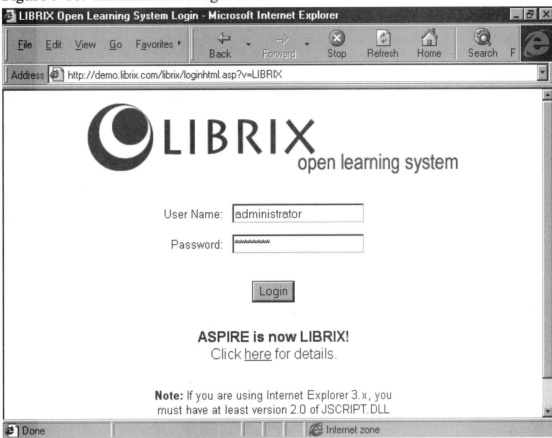

Figure 9-17. Entering user profiles.

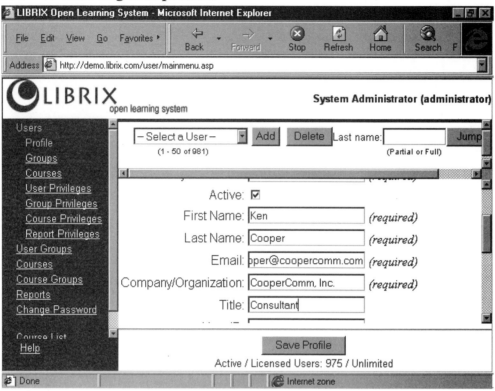

Figure 9-18. Linking users to workgroups.

codes or wording. This reduces data entry errors and avoids the accidental creation of different departments due to typos.

Once entered into the system, users can inherit properties of their position or workgroup. This saves additional data entry. Figure 9-19 shows the courses, entered earlier into the system, that are required for employees of the specified group.

When content and feedback instruments are completed, workgroups and users are defined, position requirements are entered, and user privileges established, the system is ready for live operations.

User Operations

Figure 9-20 shows an individual's status record and to-do development activities. This can typically be accessed by the individual and by any administrator with the authorization to view user records globally or by workgroup. This screen lists available development resources—in this case online training courses—and their completion status for this employee. It also lists any tests and evaluations that need to be completed by the user, along with their completion status.

Figure 9-19. Linking users to curriculum.

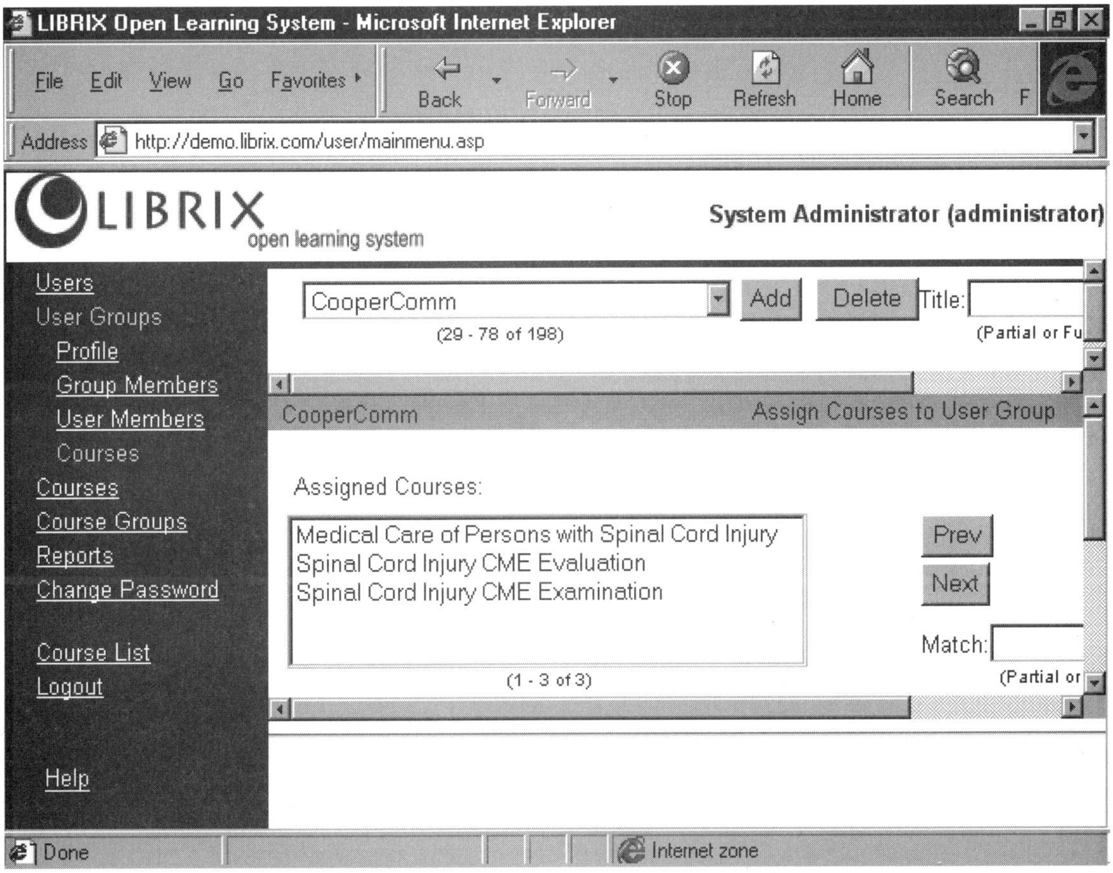

Figure 9-20. User development summary.

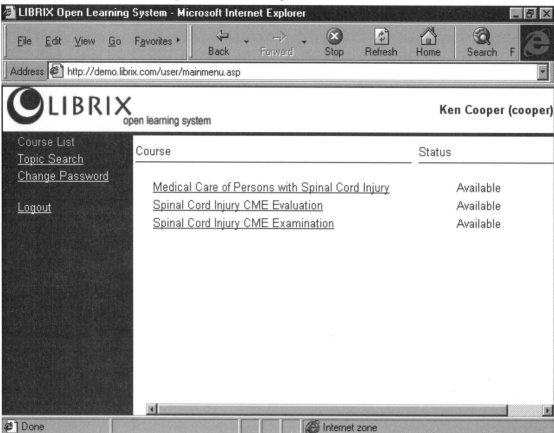

The Topic Search choice in the menu on the left allows the user to search through the available courses for any specific topic. For example, the user can find any pertinent medication information in the three listed courses by doing a "medication" word search. Every HTML course page that refers to the word will be listed and is accessible with the click of a button.

Figure 9-21 shows the results of clicking on the Spinal Cord Injury course. This is the user's view of the course created in Figure 9-3. Completion status for each chapter is tracked and reported as is the status of any tests taken or feedback forms completed. This is helpful for administrators in managing employee compliance with study assignments. It is also very convenient for end-users who work on courses sporadically and need to know what remains to be done when reconnecting.

Figure 9-22 shows the actual course screen resulting from the HTML content screen shown in Figure 9-4. Note the background graphics and page navigation elements that were not present in the HTML content file. Depending upon the settings entered into ActiveBuilder, these are automatically included, allowing content experts to create visually appealing interactive applications without being graphics or instructional design professionals.

Similarly, Figure 9-23 shows the associated test for the course from the

Figure 9-21. Course table of contents.

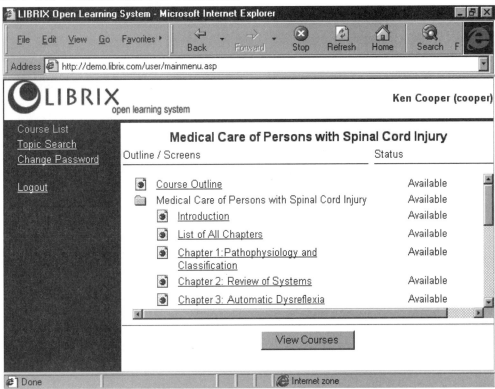

Figure 9-22. Course screen.

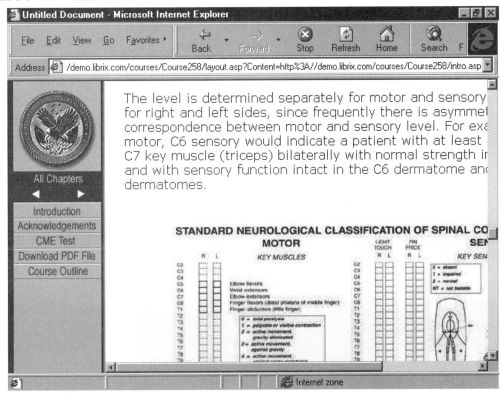

Figure 9-23. Course test.

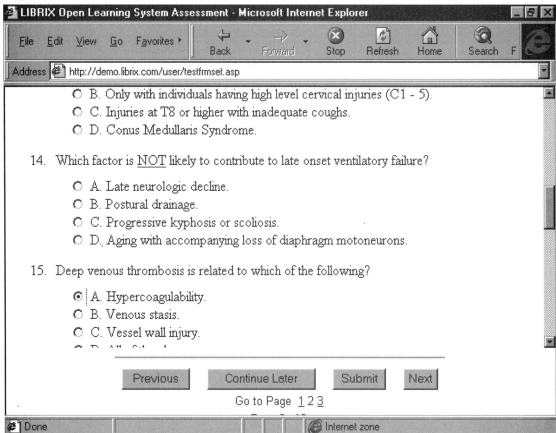

user's viewpoint. This is the result of questions created with the help of the Question Editor as shown in Figure 9-7. The buttons, bullets, text boxes, and other feedback graphics tools are created automatically by the Question Editor as part of the question type selection. Then when the question is completed, feedback or reference information is displayed as designated during development in the Question Editor. Note the page numbers at the bottom of the window. Here the designer has specified that LOLS automatically paginate the test to provide a screen-by-screen browsing experience through the questions rather than have a single long course document that must be scrolled. Again, this is done automatically for the author based upon a single checkbox entry.

Figure 9-24 shows a user test status screen that is viewable by the individual and any authorized workgroup or system administrators. LOLS automatically tracks each test attempt separately by date, keeping pass/fail records and success results by test question or section. This user is also kept informed about how many attempts are remaining. The button at the bottom of the screen makes it easy for the user to link back to the associated course.

Figure 9-25 shows a course evaluation screen that must be completed by the user in order to meet all requirements to pass the course. Note the different question types. Again, LOLS automatically formats the questions and creates

Figure 9-24. User test status summary.

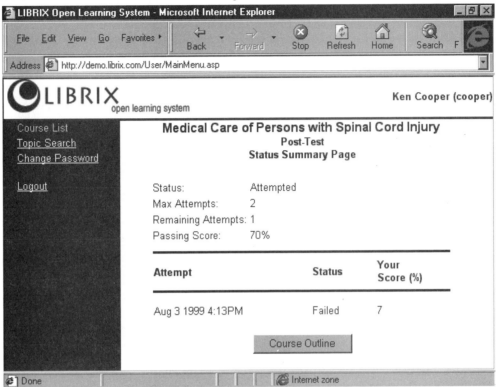

Figure 9-25. User course evaluation.

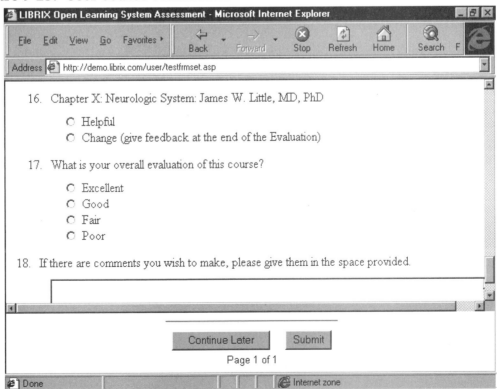

the buttons and boxes seen on this screen. Also, this author chose not to paginate the evaluation, leaving it as a long, continuous document. The buttons at the bottom of the screen allow the user to complete part of the evaluation, then come back and finish it later if necessary. This is a valuable feature in today's environment of constant interruptions.

This finishes the cycle of user interaction with the system. The workflow now shifts back to the system or workgroup administrator to track users' progress in completing all assigned development tasks.

Referencing Reports

The system administrator has control over all aspects of LOLS. As the person primarily responsible for the accuracy of competency information, the administrator has access to entry and proofing screens for users, workgroups, and courses. The menu on the left of the window in Figure 9-26 shows the overall categories of information available: administration, usage, progress, assessment, and survey. The drop down menu in Figure 9-26 shows the various administration content reports available.

The assessment drop down report menu is activated in Figure 9-27. It lists

Figure 9-26. Administrator summaries.

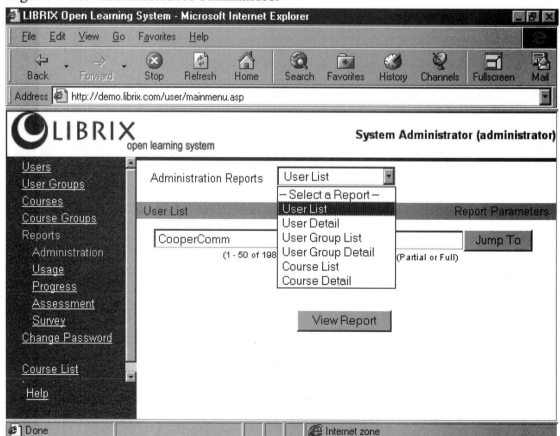

Figure 9-27. Assessment summaries.

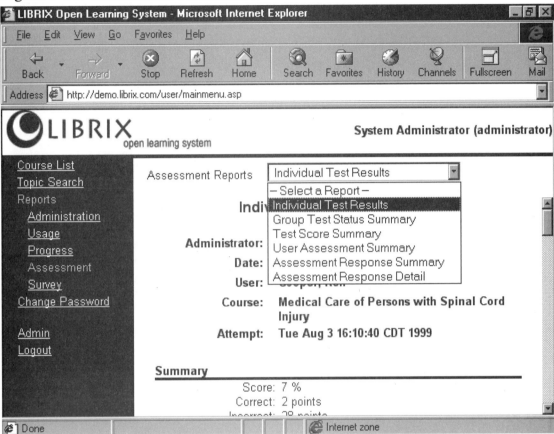

assessment reports that are available to the system administrator or to authorized workgroup administrators. Test and assessment results are available by date, and by individual or workgroup. Administrators can keep track of attempts, scores, and passing grades at any desired level of detail, all the way down to individual questions. This can be very helpful to authors in understanding what parts of courses are working or not working, and whether questions are effective in assessing actual competencies.

The final administrative screen shown in Figure 9-28 illustrates the process of creating workgroup administrators. Again, this is essential in moving responsibility for the competency application down into the workgroup, where the information resides and where it is of the most use operationally. Rights can be given for all user maintenance tasks, such as adding, deleting, and assigning systems rights to workgroup users. Administrators can also approve rights to change other system data, such as positions, courses, course content, assignments, evaluations, surveys, and assessments.

This group of samples from the LIBRIX Open Learning System is not a complete summary of its features, but it does give an overview of the level of functionality that is possible with Internet-based development and delivery technology. Web-based system capabilities, coupled with custom program-

Figure 9-28. Creating workgroup administrators.

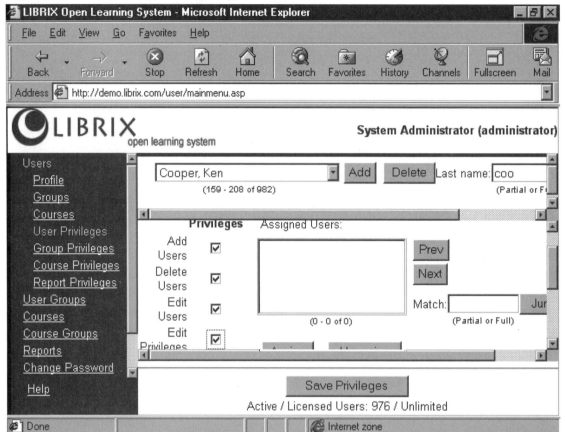

ming and the ability to access enterprise databases, are providing real-world solutions for many organizations.

Application: EmCare Performance Support System

EmCare employs approximately forty-five hundred emergency room physicians nationwide. EmCare needed to train its physicians on a number of administrative regulations and was having mixed success. An expensive training video had been created and distributed to a test group of four hundred physicians. A follow-up study found that only 30 percent had seen the video. Then new regulations changed the content and made the video obsolete before it could be formally released.

For the next round of development, EmCare decided to create the online solution shown in Figure 9-29. Web-based applications could potentially reach all its physicians, as opposed to EmCare shipping a package and then hoping the physicians will open it and use it. An online approach also made sense because the content could change at any time, with the regulatory bodies expecting immediate compliance.

Figure 9-29. EmCare performance support system.

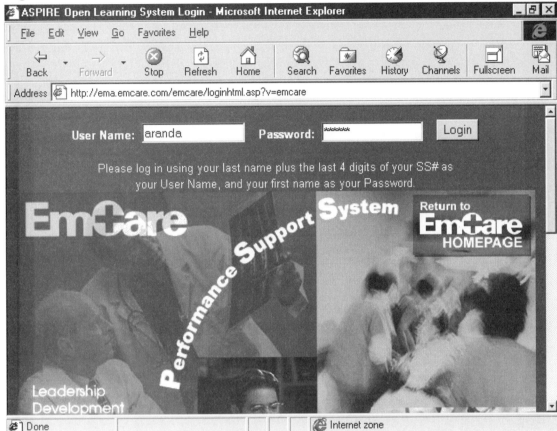

Once in the system, the physician can access an individual user screen that lists the current status of assignments. A physician's to-do list can include courses, assessments, and evaluations as shown in Figure 9-30. The menu on the left also lets users search for topic information and access reports.

The EmCare system shows a different course access method than the standard LOLS approach. The entire course outline, along with testing and an evaluation, is listed in the menu area on the left. Figure 9-31 also shows how streaming multimedia information can be included in online courses. The content window contains an animation that is accompanied by a voiceover explaining the bulleted items appearing on the screen.

Figure 9-32 shows a different type of element in a course. Here a learning interaction is embedded within the course content. The course automatically grades items with checks or Xs as the corresponding buttons are clicked. This is similar to what happens in an evaluation, except that no record is kept of the response.

The user or administrator can check up-to-date status on assignments using the progress report screen shown in Figure 9-33. This helps users, CMAR administrators, and managers who are authorized to access the progress screen's track and manage the timely completion of required development activities.

Figure 9-30. User assignments.

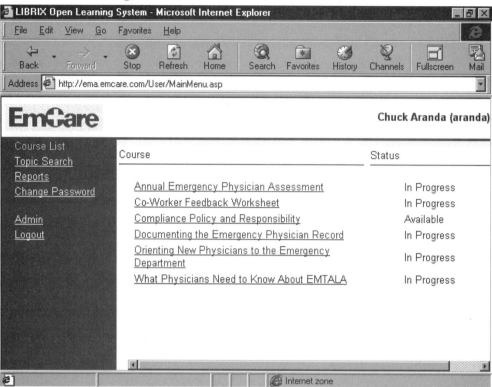

Figure 9-31. Multimedia course element.

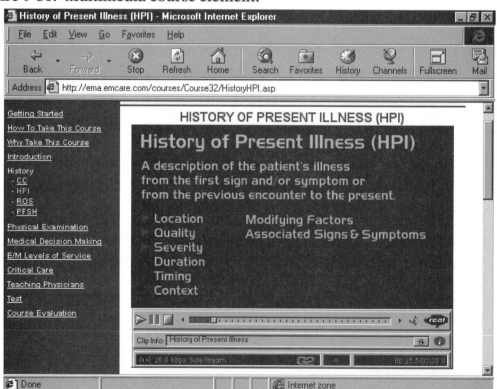

Figure 9-32. Interactive course element.

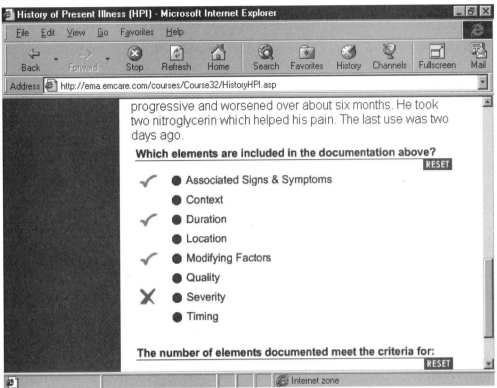

Figure 9-33. User progress summary.

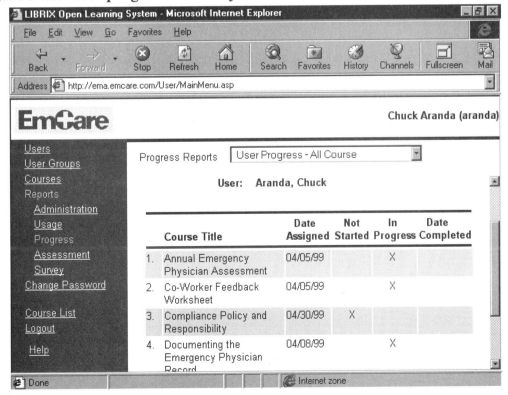

EmCare's online approach to competencies is helping it distribute essential information to its emergency room physicians. The online system also facilitates content creation and updating in an environment that can change rapidly, and where reporting mistakes can result in significant financial penalties.

Application: Mallinckrodt Sales University

The Critical Care division of Mallinckrodt, Inc. is a leading supplier of anesthesia and respiratory-care equipment to medical facilities throughout the world. A key feature to Mallinckrodt's Web site is its online Education Center that offers courses and assessments for respiratory care practitioners and nurses. The implementation features on-the-spot grading, review screens for questions that are answered inaccurately, and the automatic printout of a certificate of completion when the test for a course is passed.

Mallinckrodt is also providing a comprehensive online Sales Performance Support System, which features a unique online self-directed New Hire Orientation program that automates all aspects of bringing new employees up to speed on products, procedures, and administrative requirements. These are all examples of how competency-related services can extend into other HR applications, both inside and outside the company.

Figure 9-34 shows the opening screen to Mallinckrodt Sales University. Global functions of reference material, courses, reports, and administration are available to users.

Figure 9-35 shows the main library of resources offered by the system. Users can reference a course catalog and review developmental activities and resources that are assigned to them. The interface is different from the EmCare application, following the Windows tab convention that makes interaction more familiar. Listings use the outline method, with line items expandable by clicking on the icon or text description.

This user's current status is shown in the expanded outline view in Figure 9-36. All available assessments are listed along with the user's current status as available, in progress, or completed. More detail is available by clicking on any individual line item. The courses and assessments follow the format of LOLS screens shown in this chapter.

Mallinckrodt's system has received a positive reaction in the industry, generating an article in the summer 1998 issue of *FOCUS Journal for Respiratory*

Figure 9-34. Mallinckrodt Sales University.

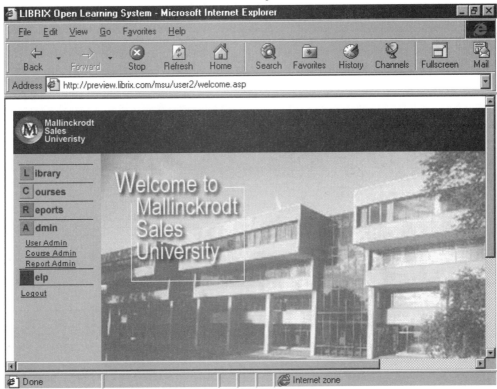

Figure 9-35. Resource library list.

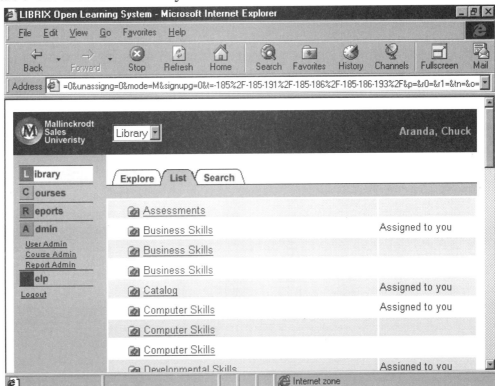

Figure 9-36. Resource library details.

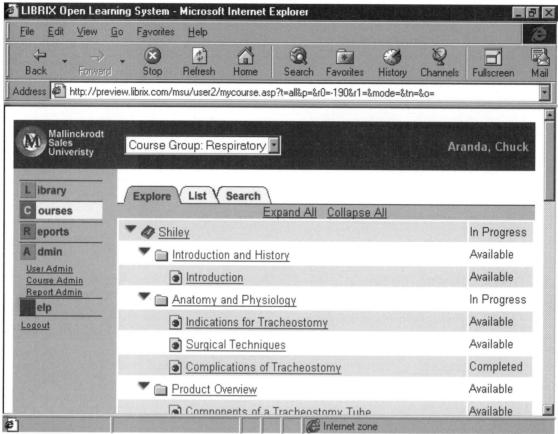

Care Managers and Educators. One of the Education Center's online courses, "Pediatric Tracheostomy," has been approved for continuing education credit by the American Association of Critical Care Nurses and the American Association of Respiratory Care. This is good publicity for Mallinckrodt, and it helps users meet their medical certification needs.

Application: Anheuser-Busch Wholesaler Integrated Learning System

Anheuser-Busch (A-B) is the world's largest beer manufacturer. The Busch Learning Center (BLC) needed an easy-to-use, cost-effective tool to enable employees and partners to acquire and maintain proficiencies in critical areas. The current implementation is an on-demand, any time, anywhere, Web-based solution providing skills assessments, performance support, and training materials. The approach is a customized application with many useful features that integrate functions.

The previous skills assessment and training planning had been done in a batch mode with Competency Coach as described in Chapter 8. The paper-based, stand-alone, batch-oriented process took three months to administer and analyze for approximately six hundred field sales managers. Turnaround time for the assessment and reporting was cut to two weeks with the Web-based solution and was completed for less than half the cost. Additional benefits included real-time management access to the individual skills assessment results and gap analyses for each employee and region.

The application has worked so well for the field sales force that A-B has developed a Wholesaler Integrated Learning (WIL) system that combines nearly every service of the BLC into an online delivery model. Figure 9-37 shows the sign-in screen for WIL. The system offers reference information, a complete learning activity catalog and schedule, and a wholesaler skills assessment that is linked into learning resources, schedules, and training administration for online enrollment and record keeping.

Upon accessing the WIL system, wholesaler personnel can complete a basic skills assessment that is customized to their specific needs. The competency model supporting the assessment was tested and used in field operations for five years and was adapted for wholesalers. The assessment, as shown in Figure 9-38, was developed and maintained with the Question Editor of LOLS.

Upon completion of the assessment, users can get immediate feedback on their developmental needs. Figure 9-39 shows an example report in the user data screen. The menu on the left allows the user to look up assignments generated from previous assessments, search for specific learning topics, and access personal reports. This screen displays a gap analysis of the assessment as compared to specific job standards, and is the online equivalent of Figure 8-34, the Competency Coach's Response/Standard Comparison. Associated developmental activities can be displayed by clicking on the appropriate "Resources . . ." text.

Users can see the gap analysis report in different ways. Figure 9-40 shows the gaps displayed by priority, which is determined by listing competencies with the largest gaps first. As was seen with the Priority Development Needs report in Figure 8-36, importance ranking data could also have been programmed in and used to sort competencies. Resources are available in this view by clicking on the appropriate text.

Figure 9-41 shows the screen generated by clicking on the "Results . . ." text for the Product Knowledge category, A-B Products Ingredients and Brewing competency. The relevant resources are automatically listed along with an icon indicating the type of learning offered: satellite, CBT, leader-led, on-the-job, or online.

Clicking on a course title sends the user into the A-B development resource catalog and training administration system. Complete scheduling, availability, enrollment, and record keeping functions are available in this module. As shown in Figure 9-42, course curriculums by topic and by position are also provided. Clicking on a title takes the user to scheduling and enrollment functions.

A-B has now expanded its online delivery of development services into

Figure 9-37. Anheuser-Busch Wholesaler Integrated Learning System.

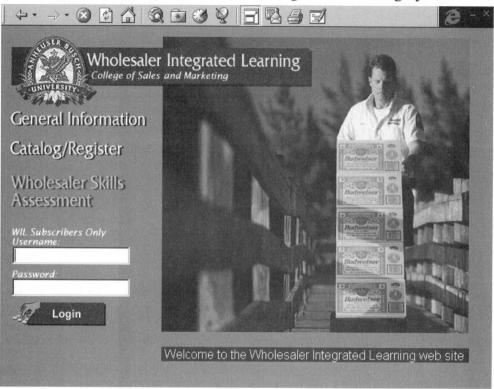

Figure 9-38. Wholesaler skills assessment.

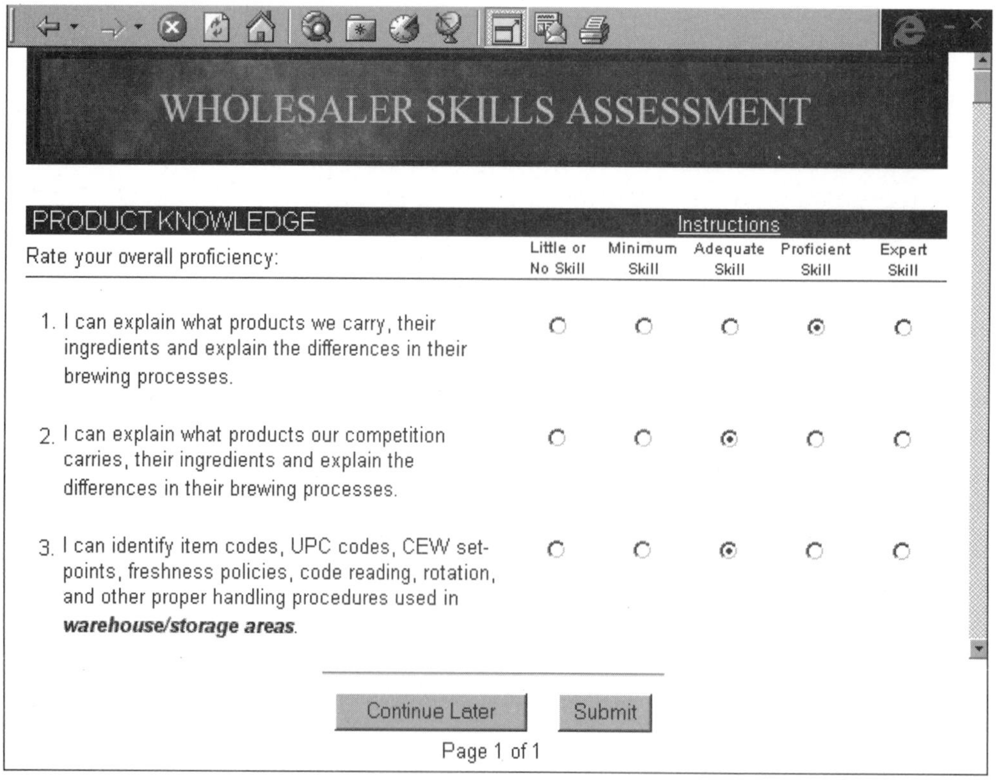

Figure 9-39. Competency gap report.

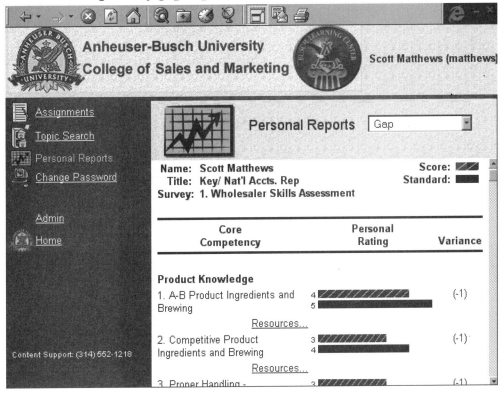

Figure 9-40. Priority gap report.

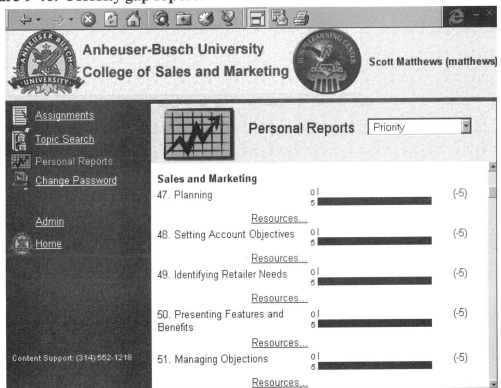

Figure 9-41. Applicable development resources.

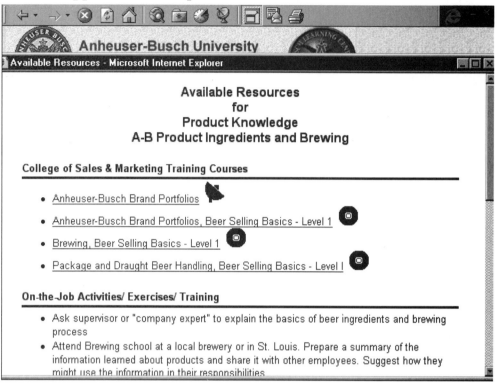

Figure 9-42. Development resource catalog.

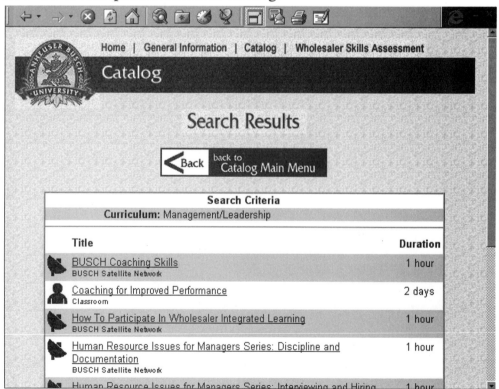

many other areas. One project involves using the system to test partners' understanding of key performance and contractual issues that were critical to the success of A-B. The online format received a 97 percent approval rating from field management personnel versus the previous paper method.

A-B has also begun using its online capabilities to provide services to its customers. One of the company's major retail partners, Applebee's, is taking advantage of A-B's online learning system to deliver modularized instruction to company-owned and franchised restaurants. An A-B product knowledge course, an introductory draft beer course, and a profit calculator are currently available on Applebee's University's Web site. The courses include assessment, testing, and course evaluation functions to ensure that the training maintains continuing effectiveness.

There are many advantages with this new approach. Productivity is increased. Employees not only can take the training in-store, but many are completing the courses at home using their own PC. Information is more accurate. Anheuser-Busch and Applebee's no longer have to print out and distribute voluminous product guides that are continually changing and soon out-of-date. Finally, record keeping is simplified and automated for centralized tracking of restaurant training status.

A-B is evaluating these services for a wide range of customers. Set-top boxes can be used for in-store or in-hotel training programs. In general, A-B is going to be delivering "outside the walls" development services to its customers.

The Future of Online Applications

Web technology lives on "Internet time," a clock rate faster than the real world. The one certainty in Internet development is that new tools, new technologies, and new capabilities are being developed. What is state-of-the-art today will be middle of the road in six months. Web development will continue to become simpler and more efficient. Tools such as the LIBRIX Open Learning System are continually evolving, with custom functions for specific clients being added to the general code base that is available to all customers.

Another major change for the Web will be increased communications speeds. The streaming character animation with voiceover in EmCare's application (Figure 9-31) is barely fast enough today for users with even the most capable dial-up modems. However, high-speed Internet connections will soon be widely available and priced well within the budgets of small businesses and individuals. The improvement in bandwidth will enable complete multimedia capabilities and more sophisticated interface functionality. This will result in more advanced applications and better competency development results for organizations of all sizes.

Learning Points

1. The technology is here today for online, any time, anywhere competency applications. Innovative organizations are already gaining significant competitive advantages and generating measurable business results with online competency-based HR applications.
2. Online competency applications facilitate continuous improvement efforts by allowing for immediate update and availability of new content, courses, and instruments.
3. The proper development environment should be able to repurpose existing content for the Web and should be easy enough to use by subject matter experts.
4. The proper development environment should have built-in, time-saving tools for performing repetitive functions such as screen formatting, navigation design, and building interactions.
5. An organization does not need to have in-house expertise. "Local" now means "accessible through the Internet." Outside vendors can create a virtual "inside feel" through Web-based development and Web-hosting services.
6. Get used to change. Today's functionality will not get organizations through tomorrow.

10

Competency Application Resources

This last chapter is a resource for HR professionals looking for tools and partners to assist in their organization's competency-based efforts. Previous chapters have shown that when it comes to CMAR, there is a lot to do and a lot that can be done. The challenge is what to do after sorting through the philosophical questions and design decisions. Useful information can be hard to obtain from the outside. Internet searches may return thousands of entries for performance improvement or none at all for competency modeling.

Following are lists of organizations that provide competency-related products and services. This is not a complete collection of vendors nor even a complete summary of all the services of the organizations listed. There are several organizations that did not make the list because while they provide useful HR offerings, they are not competency focused. In other cases, only a partial listing of the complete line of services and products appears below.

The best way to investigate these vendors is to browse their Web sites. You will see a wide range of navigational ease and information detail, but the sites of listed organizations are all helpful. The availability of online or downloadable demonstration systems is noted where applicable. Organizations that have libraries of competencies, existing models, and sample assessments are included whenever possible. This is typically the number one request from HR professionals beginning a competency modeling project.

Inclusion in this chapter is not necessarily a recommendation for the respective organizations. Although these vendors are all respected providers in the HR community, the suitability of specific products and services will vary according to an organization's custom competency-related needs.

Keep in mind the delay between when this chapter was written and when it is being read. This delay is magnified on the Internet, where one month is like six months in real time. Publications, software, and services have evolved since this list was assembled. Use this chapter to select organizations for further review, and then browse their Web sites for up-to-date details.

Associations/Providers

Associations offer the greatest range of services, from conferences to a variety of publications. Several have extensive model libraries or competency-related books and provide research services and survey information.

AAIM Management Association
8514 Eager Road
Saint Louis, Missouri 63144-1496
(314) 968-3600
http://www.aaimstl.org

AAIM is a nonprofit regional association of nearly 1,100 member organizations, representing all sectors of the economy and all sizes of companies. AAIM was founded in 1898 by employers needing a regional resource for networking and training. Competency-related AAIM members services include:

Current Business Information. Corporate members have unlimited, no-charge access to services such as a business research hotline, audiovisual library, regional and national compensation and benefits surveys, and the AAIM research library.

Peer Networking. AAIM hosts monthly member discussion groups for twenty-two different positions, from president to administrative assistants, and many specialties in between.

Human Resources Management. Consulting services include customer satisfaction and employee opinion surveys and compensation/incentive planning.

Part-Time Personnel Management. Outsourced personnel services include recruitment, search and placement, selection assessment, reference checking, drug testing, and setting up employment physicals.

Education and Process Improvement Services. AAIM provides an extensive list of scheduled seminars, general interest events, and custom training. It also sponsors the St. Louis Regional Quality Institute, and the Curriculum Based Centers of Learning described in Chapter 3. Of particular interest are the curriculum assessment and development services and the Intranet-based learning resource database.

American Compensation Association
14040 North Northsight Boulevard
Scottsdale, Arizona 85260
(480) 922-2020
http://www.acaon-line.org

American Compensation Association (ACA) is a nonprofit group of more than 25,000 human resource practitioners who design and manage employee compensation and benefit programs. ACA offers a variety of training, periodicals, reports, publications, services, and events to members and nonmembers.

Publications. The *ACA Journal* periodically presents articles focusing on competencies. Through its Compensation and Benefits Bookstore Plus, ACA offers a wide range of useful HR publications. Of particular interest is the Performance Management section of its catalog, which lists a number of competency-related books. The latest catalog features books on 360 feedback, competency-based performance improvement, competency case studies, McClelland/McBer job competence assessment (JCA) methodology, and generic job models. The Compensation Management section contains other related information, such as designing skill-based pay systems, pay for performance issues, and examples of performance appraisals.

Certification. ACA offers two certification tracks, the Certified Compensation Professional and the Certified Benefits Professional. ACA also offers certificate programs in the six HR areas. The certificates require passing three ACA examinations in the area of specialty. Requirements for the two certification programs were not available at the time of publication. ACA certification seminars are two and one-half days long and include testing at the completion of the course. They all are excellent examples of curriculum-based competency models.

American Management Association
1601 Broadway
New York, New York 10019-7420
(800) 262-9699
(212) 586-8100
http://www.amanet.org

The American Management Association (AMA) is a nonprofit, "membership-based educational organization that assists individuals and enterprises in the development of organizational effectiveness, the primary sustainable competitive advantage in a global economy." AMA has approximately 70,000 individual members and 10,000 corporate members worldwide, and it serves about two million customers annually.

Events. AMA sponsors the Annual Conference & Exposition, Human Resources Conference & Exposition, and various membership conferences.

Seminars and Workshops. AMA offers training in twenty-two major content areas, with fourteen courses listed in the Human Resources and Training area alone. Of particular interest are seminars on succession planning, workplace testing, instructional design, managing the training function, and performance management. A search engine is available on the AMA Web site to help find specific courses by topic.

On-Site Training. AMA offers consulting services, needs analysis, and off-the-shelf, customized, or specially developed training programs for specific clients. Self-paced learning courses are available in seventeen categories and five additional special series.

Publications. AMA publishes *Management Review*, research reports, and the Web-based TrendWatch information service. A sample research report summarizes AMA's annual survey of job skills testing practices.

Book Publishing. AMA's publishing division, AMACOM, publishes books in twenty-five categories, with thirty-two books listed in the Human Resources section of its latest catalog. Of particular interest are books on succession planning, job descriptions, hiring and orientation, and 360-degree feedback.

American Society of Training and Development
1640 King Street
Alexandria, Virginia 22313-2043
(800) 628-2783
(703) 683-8100
http://www.astd.org

The stated mission of the American Society of Training and Development (ASTD) is to provide leadership to individuals, organizations, and society to achieve work-related competence, performance, and fulfillment. Founded in 1944, ASTD represents more than 70,000 members from 150 countries. ASTD services include:

Events. ASTD sponsors a number of workplace and learning performance events, such as the annual International Conference & Exposition, ASTD Technical Training Conference & Exposition (TechKnowledge), Interactive Multimedia, and the National Leadership Conference.

Certificate Program. A six-course Human Performance Improvement certificate program is offered. Preparation courses are available in public enrollment seminars, internal organization seminars, and in partnership with local universities and ASTD chapters.

Publishing. ASTD publishes books, *Training & Development* magazine, *Technical Training* magazine, *Human Resource Management Quarterly*, Info-Line reports, and the ASTD Buyers' Guide for training-related products and services. Other products include audiotapes and videotapes, and software for training, training administration, survey management, CBT, and training strategy.

Special Interest Groups/Forums. ASTD currently sponsors forty-seven special interest groups. Competency-related groups include: career development, human performance technology, and performance and quality improvement.

Enterprise Solutions. The ASTD provides benchmarking services, a strategic training audit, and collaborative performance research in conjunction with large organizations.

Research Department. ASTD offers a research capability based upon its Industry Insights benchmarking database. It also publishes *State of the Industry, International Comparisons, Standardized Training Outcomes*, sector or regional trends, and customized reports.

International Society for Performance Improvement
1300 L Street N.W., Suite 1250
Washington, D.C. 20005
(202) 408-7969
http:/www.ispi.org

Founded in 1962, the International Society for Performance Improvement (ISPI) is an international association focusing on improving workplace productivity and performance. ISPI has more than 10,000 international and chapter members throughout the United States, Canada, and forty other countries.

ISPI's mission is to improve the performance of individuals and organizations through the application of Human Performance Technology (HPT). HPT is a systematic approach to improving productivity and competence. It is a combination of three fundamental processes: performance analysis, cause analysis, and intervention selection. It can also be applied to individuals, small groups, and large organizations.

Events. ISPI sponsors an Annual Conference and Expo and a large list of one-day preconference workshops. The other main event is the HPT Institute, a three-day program offered at locations around the United States. The Institute focuses on helping development professionals make the transition from a training department to a performance improvement organization.

Publications. ISPI publications include the *Performance Improvement Journal*, a magazine for practitioners, and the *Performance Improvement Quarterly*, a peer-review journal providing an outlet for the latest research. Other ISPI publications include monographs, the Information Kit collections of articles, and books.

Many of ISPI's publications are leading edge. For example, its book, *Criterion-Referenced Test Development: Technical and Legal Guidelines for Corporate Training* by Sharon Shrock and William Coscarelli, focuses on details of creating valid assessments and tests. It covers the basic philosophies of testing, legal issues, methods of test interpretation, test construction, test items and rating scales, test validation, and the organization and administration of tests.

Linkage, Inc.
One Forbes Road
Lexington, Massachusetts 02173
(781) 862-3157
http://www.linkageinc.com

Linkage is a privately held company that offers services similar to that of the nonprofit associations listed in this section. It is a leading provider of organizational development and corporate education programs, products, and services for HR professionals. Offerings include:

Events. Conferences have included titles such as 360° Assessment Conference, Best of Performance Management Conference, Competency-Based Tools and Applications Conference, International Competency Conference, and the Assessment, Measurement and Evaluation of Human Performance Conference.

Workshops. Linkage offers several competency-focused training seminars, such as Introduction to Competency-Based Systems; Building Competency-Based Selection, Performance and Learning Systems; Foundations of an Accelerated Competency System; Tools of an Accelerated Competency System; Introduction to Assessment, Measurement, and Evaluation; and Implementing Competency-Based 360° Assessments.

Library of Competencies. Linkage has a library of existing competencies that is available through its Accelerated Competency System services.

Publications. Linkage has an extensive list of competency-related books and handbooks that are accessible by subject through a product search engine.

Linkage also has a full range of other related services, such as consulting, research, implementation assistance, and Accelerated Competency System Certification.

National Occupational Competency Testing Institute
500 North Bronson Avenue
Big Rapids, Michigan 49307
(800) 334-6283
(616) 796-4695
http://www.nocti.org

The National Occupational Competency Testing Institute (NOCTI) is a non-profit organization specializing in assisting employers with hiring, training, and promoting employees. NOCTI's strength is its extensive inventory of over 150 standardized position assessments that have been nationally validated to reflect entry-level and experienced worker skills. The standardized assessments include both written and performance test modules. NOCTI has assessments for a number of production or plant-level categories that many organizations find difficult to model. NOCTI services include:

Job and Task Analysis. In this process, all steps and decisions that need to be done are documented. These tasks are then analyzed for frequency, difficulty, level, and relative importance. NOCTI delivers a two- to three-day Job and Task Analysis workshop that can identify eight to fifteen job categories and 100 to 300 associated tasks. The tasks are then linked to position requirements in seven major areas.

Test Development. Custom-written or performance tests can be created for specific positions, and NOCTI can provide the test scoring, database management, item analysis, bias review, and readability study for both custom and standardized tests.

Workshops. A variety of on-site workshops are available to help organizations establish and maintain a continuing assessment program. These cover complex issues, such as setting standards, establishing cut scores, creating skills certification programs, and developing pay-for-skills programs.

Society for Human Resource Management
1800 Duke Street
Alexandria, Virginia 22314
(703) 548-3440
http://www.shrm.org

The mission of the Society for Human Resource Management (SHRM) is to "represent, inform, guide, and lead the human resource profession into the 21st Century." SHRM offers an extensive set of HR-related services, a list requiring an extended visit to SHRM's Web site. Relevant competency-related services include:

Events. SHRM sponsors several conferences, including the SHRM Annual Conference & Exposition, Diversity Conference & Exposition, and the Employment Law & Legislative Conference.

Certification Programs. SHRM, through its Human Resource Certification Institute, administers the Professional in Human Resources and the Senior Professional in Human Resources programs. Applicants require two or more years of nonexempt HR experience and must pass an examination. Recertification is required in three years, either through successful retesting or through meeting minimum contact-hour requirements for developmental activities. Test preparation courses are available in seminar or online formats.

Information Center. SHRM maintains a library of white papers, model HR surveys, a job description data bank, and an *HR Magazine* subject index. Articles from two SHRM publications, *HR Magazine* and *HR News*, are available online for searching and reference.

SHRM Bookstore. This online bookstore features a wide selection of books from SHRM and other publishers. There is a helpful search engine that makes it easy to track down books on specific subjects. For example, a keyword search on the word "competency" found ten books addressing the topic, a search on "assess" generated twenty-six titles, and a search on "assessment" generated thirteen candidates.

Buyer's Guide. The online Buyer's Guide makes it possible to find vendors in many HR specialties. Categories that are competency related include Computer/HRIS/Software, Skills Testing, Surveys, and Training and Development. The Buyer's Guide page offers a search engine that makes it easy to locate firms specializing in the areas of interest. For example, "assessment" generated twenty-one potential vendors, while "competency modeling" generated only a single match.

Publishers

A number of publishers are familiar to HR professionals because of their extensive mail order marketing campaigns and catalog distribution. Others feature popular product lines and publication series that are helpful in CMAR efforts.

Crisp Publications, Inc.
1200 Hamilton Court
Menlo Park, California
(415) 323-6100
(800) 442-7477
http://www.crisp-pub.com

Crisp Publications is best known among HR professionals for its "50 Minute" series of reasonably priced, easy-to-use books. Crisp has expanded its book lines into other areas, including the Quick Read, Professional, Small Business/Entrepreneur, Management Library, and Retailing Smarts Series. In addition, Crisp publishes print, audio, video, CD-ROM, and online self-study learning products.

As a producer, Crisp will customize its products for specific clients, developing new content, printing unique versions, creating custom videos, writing leader guides, and creating pre- and post-assessments. This is supported by needs assessment, course design, train-the-trainer, facilitation, and competency-matching consulting services. The competency matrix shown in Chapter 4 is an example of how Crisp links competencies to its products.

Human Resources Development Press
22 Amherst Road
Amherst, Massachusetts 01002-9709
(800) 822-2801
(413) 253-3488
http://www.hrdpress.com

Human Resources Development Press publishes HR-related materials in twenty different subject categories, including instruments, organizational assessments, performance, and technology and training. The Instruments category in its catalog, for example, contains over twenty listings, with selected individual publications containing samples of twenty or more individual assessments. The Performance category lists a number of titles that specifically address competency issues.

Jossey-Bass/Pfeiffer
350 Sansome Street, 5th Floor
San Francisco, California 94104
(800) 274-4434
(415) 433-1740
http://www.josseybass.com
http://www.pfeiffer.com

Jossey-Bass is a publisher of development books and over twenty journals, including *Human Resource Development Quarterly*. Pfeiffer, an imprint of Jossey-

Bass, is a publisher of HR, business, management, adult education, and self-help materials. Pfeiffer has an extensive product list and a library of inventories, questionnaires, and surveys available in loose-leaf or CD-ROM format.

Both the Jossey-Bass and Pfeiffer sites have an online catalog, with either an alphabetical listing or a search by author, title, ISBN, or preset category. Without a keyword search capability, products can be hard to locate. For example, the Pfeiffer alphabetical listing consists of thirty-six pages of information. A CD-ROM-based library version is available on a purchase basis.

Lakewood Publications, Inc.
50 South Ninth Street
The Lakewood Building
Minneapolis, Minnesota 55402
(800) 328-4329
(612) 333-0471
http://www.trainingsupersite.com

Lakewood is the publisher of *TRAINING Magazine, Inside Technology Training, Technology for Learning, Creative Training Techniques, Training Media Review,* and *Potentials* among others. The Lakewood training Web site lists other resources, such as back articles from *Training,* a searchable publications archive, research information and reports, over 250 training site links, online surveys, and a free ask-the-experts site discussion area. Training Lit is a "catalog of catalogs" that contains information on a range of products covering topics such as self-assessment, 360-degree feedback, strategic competency assessment, leadership assessment, assessment instruments, career development, surveys, and testing software.

Teleometrics International
1755 Woodstead Court
The Woodlands, Texas 77390-0964
(800) 527-0406
(281) 367-0060
http://www.teleometrics.com

Teleometrics specializes in learning and assessment instruments and also offers seminars, videos, leader guides, and small-group exercises. Teleometrics' competency-related instruments are backed by academic behavioral theory and applied research and cover nine different organizational and personal topics.

Competency-Related Software

As Chapters 8 and 9 illustrated, there is a wide range in the capabilities of CMAR software systems. Comparing alternatives can be a daunting task, with lists of features each over one hundred items long. Some of the leading vendors include:

Librix Learning
12400 Olive Boulevard, Suite 505
Saint Louis, Missouri 63141
(314) 439-1100
http://www.librix.com

Librix is the developer of the LIBRIX Open Learning System (LOLS), profiled in Chapter 9. Librix software provides skills assessment, compliance and certification testing, training and performance support, and complete survey and feedback functions. Modules also exist for integrating LOLS into a development system containing a Web-based catalog, and training enrollment and completion administration. A leading-edge feature of LOLS is the live integration of online learning courses and content with assessments. As the name implies, the Open Learning System provides the capability to accept input from a variety of legacy sources.

Full customization is available for all LOLS modules, and Librix can provide outsourced services, such as Web hosting and site administration. A live demonstration system is available on the Librix Web site for a complete product capabilities review.

Nardoni Associates, Inc.
1465 Route 31 South
Annandale, New Jersey 08801
(800) 338-09701
(908) 730-9444
http://www.nardoni.com

Nardoni Associates, Inc., (NAI) is a developer of competency-based succession planning and management development systems. Competency-related software products include 360° Feedback, HR Pulse, and 360° on the Net. HR Pulse includes modules that can match an individual to multiple positions, find candidates for an open job, separate experience criteria from competence criteria, specify search tolerances for matching operations, automatically rank candidates to standards, and classify and examine suitable successors.

NAI can provide customized Internet/Intranet 360-degree assessment applications along with outsourced data processing and report production services. An online newsletter with current information is available on the NAI Web site.

Saba Software, Inc.
2400 Bridge Parkway
Redwood Shores, California 94065-1166

(877) 722-2101
(650) 696-3840
http://www.saba.com

Saba is a provider of large-scale Internet learning and competency management solutions. Its Education Management System enables businesses to rapidly assess, plan, deliver, measure, and improve the learning of users inside and outside the organization. Relevant individual products include Competency Manager, LearningOnline, and HR Connections. Saba also offers complete consulting, product training, educational, IT outsourcing, and Web hosting services.

SkillScape Skills Management Services, Ltd.
3318 Oak Street, Suite 19
Victoria, British Columbia V8X 1R1
Canada
(888) 262-6243
(250) 475-7525
http://skillscape.com

SkillScape is the developer of Competence Manager, an Internet-based competency and skill management program. Competence Manager integrates position competency models, team skill surveys, strategic skills surveys, personal profiles, and educational plan recommendations. An online demonstration can be arranged upon request.

SkillScape also offers the Starter Skills Database, consisting of over 6,500 bits of knowledge, skills, attributes, and achievements organized in a hierarchical structure from general competencies to detailed line items. The starter skills are contained in an Oracle database and can also be output in tab-delimited text format or interfaced with major ERP applications, such as SAP or PeopleSoft.

SkillScape can adapt Competence Manager for specific clients, and it also provides outsourced IT, programming, Web hosting, consulting, and fulfillment services.

SuccessFactors.com
425 Market Street, Suite 500
San Francisco, California 94105-2423
(415) 659-0300
http://successfactors.com

SuccessFactors is a provider of Web-enabled enterprise skills management software. Products include SkillManager, 360-Degree AssessmentManager, StaffingManager, DevelopmentManager, and the SuccessFactors.com People-

Soft Connection. Product training and implementation consulting services are available.

SuccessFactors provides three competency-related database products. The first is a database of over 1,200 competencies divided into twenty role families. The second database contains over 2,300 interview questions for use with the competency database. The third database is comprised of over 1,600 on-the-job developmental activities. All three databases support input to DevelopManager.

Training Administration Software

The first competency-based application for many organizations is training administration. These applications provide basic enrollment and completion record keeping, scheduling, and correspondence functions in a single integrated or stand-alone package.

Chris Collins, Inc.
P.O. Box 3404
Wichita, Kansas 67201-3404
(316) 942-4339
http://chriscollins.com

Collins has developed Training Register, a reasonably priced training software product addressing essential administration functions. Training Register provides for all enrollment, scheduling, training histories, curriculum and certification tracking, and correspondence. Users can optionally self-enroll and view their records over the Internet or network. A free evaluation version and supporting documentation are available for downloading.

Silton-Bookman Systems, Inc.
20230 Stevens Creek Boulevard, Suite D
Cupertino, California 95014-2210
(800) 932-6311
(408) 446-1170
http://www.sbinc.com

Silton-Bookman's Registrar, with over 5,000 installations in a fourteen-year span, is one of the leading training administration programs on the market. Registrar handles complete self-registration, registration management, correspondence, training histories, reporting, and CBT launching. The program manages employee training and development histories, and development plans. The programmable Requirements Tracking Option allows organizations to analyze individual and group development needs, track certifications, and prove compliance with industry or regulatory requirements.

Registrar, as a mature product, provides advanced features that are often not found in many competency-related products. For example, users who must be FDA compliant can take advantage of Registrar's Software Validation Kit that follows IEEE standards for software validation. There is also a training workshop to allow integrating Registrar data with Seagate Software's Crystal Reports tool.

Silton-Bookman provides on-site or remote consulting services and training. There are periodic user-group conferences covering a variety of related topics. A demonstration version of Registrar, containing a CD-ROM and the full product user Reference Guide, is available at no charge.

Syscom, Inc.
400 East Pratt Street
Baltimore, Maryland 21202
(800) 779-7266
(410) 539-3737
http://www.trainingserver.com

Syscom is the developer of TrainingServer and TrainingServer@Online, a family of training administration software. TrainingServer is a high-function, mature product with a features list six pages long. Many competency-related features are included such as linking skills to courses with proficiency levels delivered; linking requirements, competencies, and skills to jobs; monitoring OSHA, ISO 9000, or FDA requirements; certification tracking; managing competency profiles; and showing performance at module and task levels.

TrainingServer@Online gives any authorized user with a standard Web browser the ability to query and interact with the TrainingServer database. They can browse course catalogs, class schedules, job profiles, and individual transcripts. TrainingServer@Online lets users manage their own enrollments and reporting and provides administrators with access to rosters, attendance, and grades.

Syscom provides a user conference, training seminars, implementation assistance and consulting, and programming for custom reports. A free evaluation kit of TrainingServer software, an evaluation guide, and a tutorial are available, along with a free video overview.

Survey Software

A specialized HR application involves conducting, tabulating, and reporting on surveys. Unlike programs with built-in survey capabilities, such as LIBRIX Open Learning System or SkillScape Competence Manager, these applications focus solely on managing feedback processes.

Apian Software
400 North 34th Street, Suite 310
Seattle, Washington 98103
(800) 237-4565
(206) 547-5321
http://www.apian.com

Apian Software is the maker of Survey Pro for Windows, a full-function survey creation and analysis tool that has received strong reviews in the trade press.[1] The program was first released as a DOS version in 1991 and since then has gone through many iterations. Survey Pro appears to be especially strong in building reports and slides for the presentation phase. It also has the ability to handle surveys with different fields or questions, combining results for like questions and adding the unique questions to the overall analysis. Apian provides sample surveys and reports that can be downloaded for review.

An associated product is the Key.collect data-entry application. An extremely easy-to-use program, it lets CMAR administrators farm out the key entry of forms to temporary help, local departments, telephone interviewers, or tabulation houses. The resulting files are native to Survey Pro, so entries from multiple input sources can be imported to a survey with just a few clicks. Net.collect provides a survey entry and collection function for Web interactions. It requires HTML programming to create the survey form and some scripting to combine entries into an existing database.

Creative Research Systems
411 B Street
Petaluma, California 94952
(707) 765-1001
http://www.surveysystem.com

Creative Research Systems (CRS) is the developer of The Survey System, a complete software package for working with questionnaires. It includes capabilities to create questionnaires, capture interview data, import or enter data, and produce tables, graphics, and text reports. Optional modules include Enhanced Multiple Choice; Verbatim module for recording text answers and formatting reports; Voice Capture; E-mail Survey Software; Real Number module providing long number input and statistical capabilities; and the Statistics module for advanced functions, such as ANOVA, regression, and correlation.

The Survey System is fully compatible with Remark Office OMR. It accepts data and question labels created in Remark, and The Survey System can produce scannable questionnaires for Remark.

The CRS Web site currently has a very useful online sample-size calculator. Given the plus/minus confidence percentage desired, it can compute the sample size. Or it can compute the plus/minus confidence percentage for an existing sample. The site also contains articles explaining statistical significance, survey concepts, and design tips.

Perseus Development Corporation
222 Forbes Road, Suite 208
Braintree, Massachusetts 02184
(781) 848-8100
http://www.perseusdevelopment.com

Perseus Development is the creator of SurveySolutions for the Web, a development system for Internet-based surveys that touts ease of use and low cost. Features include survey design, Web-based or e-mail distribution, automatic collection of responses, survey analysis, and presentation creation. Perseus also offers SurveySolutions Express, a free downloadable version that is a simple survey tool for letting users add single-question surveys to Internet sites.

The Perseus Web site contains a set of sample surveys showing the product's capabilities, and it has useful white papers and reference information on successful surveying.

Raosoft, Inc.
6645 NE Windermere Road
Seattle, Washington 98115-7942
(206) 525-4025
http://www.raosoft.com

Raosoft, Inc., produces a family of database software for forms design, data collection, statistical analysis, and graphics creation. Products include EZSurvey for e-mail and Web-based surveys, SurveyWin for electronic forms and secure surveys, UAdmin for distributed data collection, Interform for sophisticated Web forms with large numbers of simultaneous users, and the EZReport data mining tool. Raosoft products are generally given good marks on their overall flexibility and functionality. On its site, Raosoft provides a downloadable demo version and sample surveys.

Other Raosoft services include public enrollment and on-site software training, three-day courses on how to design and administer surveys, technical design assistance, and general consulting.

Saja Software Inc.
6735 Snead Court
Longmont, Colorado 80503
(800) 945-0040
(303) 449-2969
http://www.surveyselect.com

Saja is the developer of Survey Select and Survey Select Expert, software tools for creating, designing, administering, tabulating, and reporting survey information. Surveys can be created in hard-copy form or for completion on PCs using a floppy disk or network, with e-mail, or online via the Web. Of particular interest are included bundles of over 800 existing questions organized by topic and prewritten introduction letters. Survey Select is also available for order on the American Society of Training and Development Web site, and a free demo version download is available at both Saja and ASTD Web sites.

Saja offers complete survey services on an outsourced basis. This includes survey design, administration, data entry (if hard copy), Web hosting (if online), analysis, and reporting. Clients can choose to buy Survey Select and work with Saja or, when third-party confidentiality is important, let Saja do the entire fulfillment.

Enterprise Resource Planning Software Contacts

Implementing ERP software is often a multiyear project costing millions of dollars. The HR department typically has little input into the software selection process and must adapt its systems to fit in with the new corporate-wide standard. HR application features of ERP systems are quite extensive, although few organizations have fully implemented competency-related HR module functions. Further information on the leading ERP vendors can be found on the following sites:

Baan Company	http://www.baan.com
J.D. Edwards World Solutions Company	http://www.jdedwards.com
Oracle Corporation	http://www.oracle.com
PeopleSoft, Inc.	http://www.peoplesoft.com
SAP AG	http://www.sap.com

This is just a partial list of vendors and is subject to change. CMAR applications, where they exist at all, are still in the beginning stages in many organizations. Competency products, especially Web-based solutions, are moving targets, with features and capabilities being continually enhanced. HR professionals can stay up-to-date by attending selected conferences and competency-related seminars, checking the sources in this chapter for new books and other publications, and regularly browsing the Web for updated products and new vendors.

Learning Points

1. The Web is a good place to start the search for information on CMAR products, but it is likely to be an overwhelming task because of the mass of data available.

2. There is a wealth of competency models, descriptions, and assessment questions from a variety of vendors. Although these can provide a starting point for the design team, organizations may find that it is just as easy to build custom models and assessments for their unique situations.

3. Live demonstrations are the best. If a vendor is truly Internet savvy, an application should be available on the vendor's Web site. Downloading or asking for interesting software samples or content is a viable second choice.

4. There is no reason to force an organization's special needs to fit into a standard application. Most vendors provide services for outsourced fulfillment, consulting, and customization of products.

Notes

1. Sheryl Canter, "PC Survey Says ," *PC Magazine*, 19 November 1996, 66.

Appendix

Competency Coach CD-ROM

Competency Coach is a stand-alone competency modeling and reporting relational database system that automates the preparation, tabulation, and printing of employee assessments and analysis reports. The sample included on the CD-ROM accompanying this book is a full-function, limited-save (maximum of ten people) version that contains the complete working-model data presented in Chapters 4 through 6. This allows readers to work with an example of a fully implemented CMAR application and to experiment with its operation and reporting.

The CD-ROM disk also contains files supporting Competency Coach. The files utilize convenient formats that can be conveniently read on many PC systems. Most text files are in a read-only PDF format that can be viewed and printed by the Adobe Acrobat Reader application. (A free download is available from Adobe's Web site (http://www.adobe.com). Other text files are in an RTF or DOC format that can be read and edited by word processing programs such as Microsoft Word. Spreadsheet files are in an SLK format that can be read and edited by many spreadsheet programs such as Microsoft Excel. Figure A-1 shows the folders that are included on the CD-ROM.

❖ *Getting Started*. This folder contains background information on Competency Coach and detailed instructions for installing the program and its associated working model data. Contents include a license agreement, descriptive program fact sheets, a CMAR white paper, and a quick-start guide.

❖ *Working Model Input*. This folder contains working-model source information, including the assessment text, competency standards, and resources. The assessment and standards spreadsheet are in editable formats.

❖ *Reports and Printouts*. This folder contains electronic versions of all the reports included in Chapter 8. They are organized into management, proofing, and user categories. Also provided are the blank assessment forms from Chapter 6 and an editable spreadsheet export file sample.

❖ *CC-Work*. This folder contains all program and data files for the working-model version of Competency Coach. General instructions for installing

Figure A-1. Competency Coach CD-ROM contents.

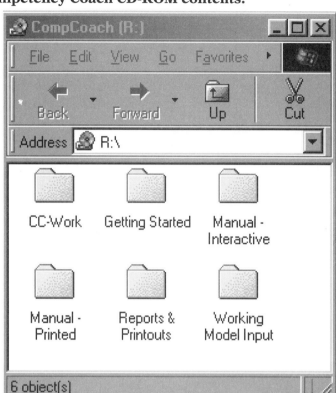

the program on a Microsoft Windows-based PC system are listed later in this Appendix.

♦ *Manual-Interactive*. This folder contains an electronic version of the program manual. Users can directly access Competency Coach information within the Windows help system format as shown in Figure A-2. This interactive reference allows users to quickly locate information using hypertext links and standard page navigation buttons. Figure A-3 shows a help window that lets users look up instructions based upon a topic index or a keyword search.

♦ *Manual-Printed*. This folder contains user reference manual files formatted for printing. The files duplicate what is in the interactive reference and are in modify-protected Microsoft Word 95 DOC format for easy printing.

The contents of the CD-ROM provide a complete package that allows CMAR developers to examine the design of an operational CMAR system and to utilize the CooperComm working-model competencies, standards, and assessment in their own efforts.

Installation of Competency Coach

Competency Coach has been designed to work with Windows 95/98 and Windows NT 4.0 operating systems. Installation is a simple series of operations.

Figure A-2. Interactive guide to Competency Coach.

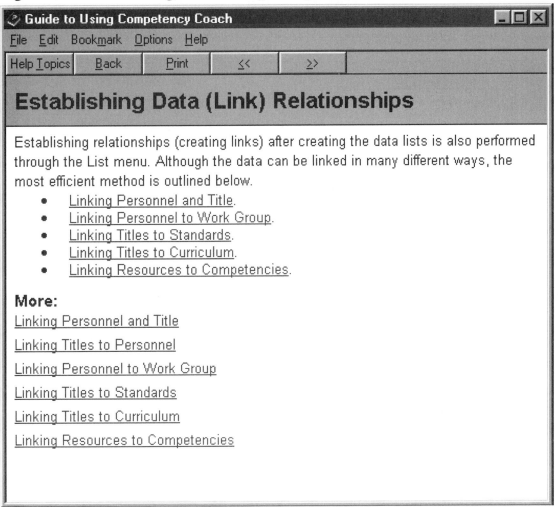

1. Insert the Competency Coach CD-ROM disk into the drive.
2. Open the CD-ROM's folder window from the Program Manager.
3. Open the "My Computer" folder window from the Program Manager.
4. Drag the "CC-Work" folder (and all its contents) from the CD-ROM window onto the C: hard disk in the "My Computer" window.
5. Drag the "Manual-Interactive" folder (and all its contents) from the CD-ROM window onto the C: startup hard disk in the "My Computer" window.

To run Competency Coach:

6. Double-click on the "skillmgr.exe" file in the "CC-Work" folder on the C: hard disk.
7. The first time the system is started, a "System Setup" screen will be

Figure A-3. Index and find capabilities in the interactive guide.

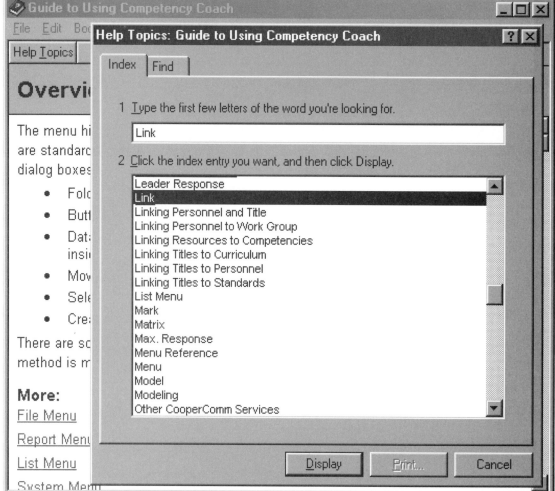

displayed. Click on the "Save" button to initialize the system. Competency Coach is now ready for operation.

8. To access the interactive help system, double-click on the "CC.HLP" file in the "Manual-Interactive" folder on the C: hard disk.

9. A printed manual can be created from Microsoft Word 95 or 97, or from any other program that can read files in these formats. Simply open the files in an appropriate word processor and print them out.

For convenience, users can optionally create shortcuts for "skillmgr.exe" and "CC.HLP" and place them in the "C:-WINDOWS-Start Menu-Programs" folder.

Important Note: Do not change the program directory name or folder location once you have first started and initialized the system. Leave it named "CC-Work" or else reinstall it from the CD-ROM into a different disk or folder name.

Competency Coach Facts Sheets

Figure A-4 presents a detailed description of Competency Coach, including an overview, functional description, technical specifications, and system requirements.

Figure A-4. Competency Coach facts sheets.

Competency Coach®

Are you spending your training and development dollars most effectively?

Competency Coach®
Consulting

- Customized to specific positions and your industry needs
- Can assist with all stages of competency modeling and measurement
- Utilizes "skill-based questioning" for verifiable skill assessment
- Complete scoring and reporting services available

Competency Coach®
for Windows

- Easy to use with minimal learning time
- Completely customizable to any job, any questionnaire, any resource
- Generates individual gap analysis
- Generates automated improvement plans with resource requirements
- Provides reports of who needs what resource
- Users can determine candidates for proposed training

The CEO's Challenge

- Raise the bar of each employee's competence
- Enable employees to deliver maximum value to our customers

The HR Challenge

- Model competencies required for improving business performance
- Measure every employee's current skill level
- Match current skill level to required standards
- Identify skill gaps
- Create individual employee development plans
- Prioritize and schedule development resources

Expected Results

- Development dollars targeted to identified learning needs
- Competencies raised to required levels … and beyond
- Career paths add value to your strategies
- Succession and promotion plans supported with data

Expected ROI

- Maximized value to internal and external customers from skilled, high-performance employees

CooperComm, Inc.

Multi-Form® solutions to:
Learning • Consulting • Research

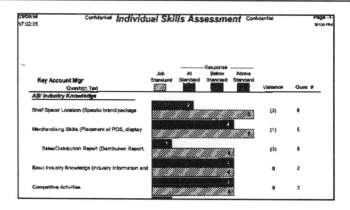

Reports Available

- Gap analysis by individual
  (color graphic or text)
- Priority Develop Needs
  of skill gaps by severity
- Managerial Overview Summary
  comparing respondent
  to manager's validation rating
  (color graphic or text)
- Resource Summary listing
  needs by resource available
  (by competency, department,
  title, name)
- Competency Response
  Analysis listing responses
  by competency
  (by department, title, name)
- Training Requirements
  by Competency
  (by department, title, name)
- Training Candidates
  by Resource
  (by department, title, name)
- Printouts of all data entry
  information for checking
- Creates Excel spreadsheet file
  for custom reports
- All reports available on-screen
  or printed out

- 486 PC 33MHz or faster recommended
- at least 8 MB RAM
- 5 MB of hard disk space free
- 640 x 480 VGA color monitor
- laser or ink-jet printer
  (color printing supported)
- Windows 3.xx, Windows 95/98
  or Windows NT

Cooper Comm, Inc.

16457 Wilson Farm
Chesterfield, MO 63005-4525
(636) 537-1100 (voice/fax)
http://www.coopercomm.com

Complete Customization

- Departments
- Job titles
- Individuals
- Competencies model
- Skills required
- Measurement questionnaire
- Resources (seminars, books,
  video, tapes, tutoring, work
  along, etc.)

Single Measurement Instrument

- Used for any number
  of job titles
- Stores multiple results per
  person for year-to-year
  tracking
- Can map an individual
  to standards for current job
  or job aspired to

Competency-Based Questionnaire

- Skill-based questions
- Level of competency required
  can vary by title

Validation

- Allows managerial validation
  by competency
- Can do "reliability audit"
  of random respondents
  to identify amount of self-
  rating bias (if present)

Competency Coach®

Facilitates Employee Development

- Identifies gaps between
  competencies required and
  competencies possessed
- Prioritizes gaps from most
  to least important
- Creates automated individual
  development plans
- Identifies resources required
  to raise competencies
  to desired levels
- Lets respondents map their
  competencies to a job
  aspired to

Facilitates Resource Planning

- Can start with individuals'
  needs and determine what
  development resources
  should be scheduled
- Can start with a specific
  development resource
  and determine who is
  the potential audience

Provides Training Effectiveness Measure

- Can link to the *CooperComm
  Training Registration System*
  (optional)
- Individuals with skill gaps can
  be cross referenced to
  seminar attendees to see if
  the seminar actually builds
  competencies

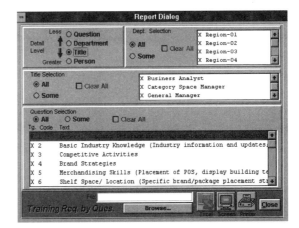

Selected Bibliography

Alvarez, Jose Luis and Rabade, Arturo, "The New Management Competencies and How They Are Learned," *Harvard Business Review*, (November 1977).

American Competency Association, *Raising the Bar: Using competencies to enhance employee performance*, (Scottsdale, Az.: ACA, 1996.)

Barborek, Susan and Brown, Jeff, "Using Competency Assessments to Support Changing Business Goals," *National Productivity Review*, 18:14, (Autumn 1999), 17–20.

Boyatzis, R. E. and Leonard, K. & Rhee, K. & Wheeler, J. V., *Competencies Can Be Developed, But Not in the Way We Thought*, (Capability, 1998).

Campbell, Andres and Sommers-Luch, Kathleen, *Core Competency Based Strategy*, (New York: VanNostrand Reinhold, 1988).

Cooper, Scott, Eton, Lawrence, Kierstead, James, Lynch, Brian and Luce, Sally, "Competencies: A brief overview of development and application to public and private sectors," *Research Directorate—Public Service Commission of Canada*, (April 1998.)

Cripe, Edward J., "Field Report: Competency systems add value that line executives can see," *Corporate University Review*, (May/June 1998.)

Cripe, Edward J., "Field Report: Competency systems add value that line executives can see," *Corporate University Review*, 6:3, (May/June 1998.)

Cripe, Edward J., and Mansfield, Richard S., *Value-Added Employee: 31 skills to make yourself irresistible to any company*, (Houston: Gulf Publishing Co., 1999.)

Dubois, David D., *Competency-Based Performance Improvement: A strategy for organizational change*, (Amherst: Human Resource Development Press, 1993.)

Dubois, David D., *The Competency Case Book*, (Amherst: Human Resource Development Press, 1998.)

Employee Relations Bulletin, "Competency Modeling: Matching employees to company needs," *Bureau of Business Practice*, (December 1996.)

Evers, Frederick, *The Basis of Competence Skills for Lifelong Learning and Employability*, (San Francisco: Jossey-Bass Higher & Adult Education Series, 1998.)

Fox, Donna, Kennedy, Jim, and Vitale, Susan, "A New Form of Competency Modeling for Lasting Business Results," *Consulting Journal*, (1997.)

Gorsline, K., "A Competency Profile for Human Resources: No more shoemakers children," *Human Resource Management Journal*, 35:1, (1996), 53–66.

Green, Paul C., *Building Robust Competencies: Linking human resource systems to organizational strategies*, (San Francisco: Jossey-Bass, 1999.)

Guggenheimer, Pat, and Szulc, Mary D., *Leadership Competencies*, (Menlo Park: Crisp Publishing, 1991.)

Kochanski, Jim, "Competency-Based Management," *Training and Development*, 51:10, (October 1997), 40–45.

Lucia, Antoinnette D., and Lepsinger, Richard, *The Art and Science of Competency Models: Pinpointing critical success factors in organizations*, (San Francisco: Jossey-Bass/Pfeiffer Publications, 1999.)

Lewis, Robert E., "Cockeyed Competencies (And How to Correct Them)," *Training*, (May 1997), 132.

McClelland, David C., "Testing for Competence Rather Than Intelligence," *American Psychologist*, (January 1973), 1–14.

McClelland, David C., *Human Motivation*, (Cambridge University Press, 1998.)

Parhalad, C. K., and Harnel, Gary, "The Core Competence of the Corporation," *Harvard Business Review*, (May 1990.)

Parry, Scott C., "Just What Is a Competency? (and why should you care?)" *Training Magazine*, (June 1998), 58–62.

Parry, Scott C., "The Quest for Competencies," *Training Magazine*, (July 1996), 48–56.

Quinn, Robert E., *Becoming a Master Manager—A Competency Framework*, (New York: John Wiley & Sons, 1995.)

Rothwell, William J., and Sredle, Henry J., *The ASTD Reference Guide to Professional Human Resource Development Roles and Competencies*, (Amherst: Human Resource Development Press, 1992.)

Schoonover, Stephen C., *Human Resource Competencies for the Year 2000: A professional's toolkit for performance development*, (Falmouth, Ma.: Schoonover Associates, Inc., 1998.)

Sibbett, David and the staff of *HBR*, "75 Years of Management Ideas and Practice 1922-1997," *Harvard Business Review Supplement*, (September-October 1997.)

Spencer, L., McLelland, D., and Kelner, S., "Competency Assessment Methods," in L. J. Bassi & Russ-Eft (Eds.), *What Works: Assessment, Development, and Measurement*, (Washington: American Society of Training and Development, 1997.)

Spencer Lyle M., and Spencer, Signe M. *Competence at Work: Models for superior performance*, (New York: John Wiley & Sons, 1993.)

Stone, Florence, "A New Definition of Corporate Competencies," *Management Review Supplement*, 84:6, (June 1995), SS1–SS2.

Stone, Florence M., and Sachs, Randi Toler, *The High-Value Manager: Developing the Core Competencies Your Organization Demands*, (New York: AMACOM, 1996.)

Strumpf, Lori, & Mains Kristine M. *Building Workplace Competencies*, (Lincolnwood, Ill.: NTC/Contemporary Publishing Group, 1993.)

Walton, R.E. and Lawrence, P.R., *HRM Trends and Challenges*, (Boston, Harvard Business School Press, 1985.)

Wood, Robert, Wood, Tim, and Payne, Tim, *Competency-Based Recruitment and Selection*, (New York: John Wiley & Son Ltd., 1998.)

Zemke, Ron and Zemke, Susan, "Putting Competencies to Work," *Training*, (January 1999), 70–76.

Index

About the Author

Kenneth Carlton Cooper, Ph.D., is the President of CooperComm, Inc., a St. Louis-based HR consulting firm founded in 1976. He has spoken to over 2,000 audiences on topics of personal and organizational productivity and competency development. Ken's consulting clients have included organizations such as Anheuser-Busch, Apple, Iomega, Business Training Library, American Institute of Banking, Civil Service Commission, LIBRIX Learning, and Monsanto. Ken is also the developer of "Competency Coach® for Windows," a relational database competency modeling and reporting application.

Ken has degrees in Industrial Engineering and Administration & Management, and has taught in the Management programs of University of Missouri and St. Louis University. He has written for publications such as *Administrative Management, Women in Business, IBM SPD Journal, Trainer's Workshop, Training, Life Insurance Selling,* and *Manage,* and his books have been published internationally. Ken is a Registered Professional Engineer, a Certified Administrative Manager, and a Certified Speaking Professional.

Ken can be contacted at:

> CooperComm, Inc.
> 16457 Wilson Farm
> Chesterfield, Missouri 63005-4525
> USA
> (636) 537-1100
> http://www.coopercomm.com
> http://www.competencymodeling.com